On Power

Also by Robert L. Dilenschneider

A Briefing for Leaders

Power and Influence

The Dartnell Public Relations Handbook

On Power

ROBERT L. DILENSCHNEIDER

HarperBusiness
A Division of HarperCollins*Publishers*

HarperCollins books may be purchased for educational, business, or sales promotional use. For information please write: Special Markets Department, HarperCollins Publishers, Inc., 10 East 53rd Street, New York, NY 10022.

FIRST EDITION

Designed by Irving Perkins Associates

Library of Congress Cataloging-in-Publication Data

Dilenschneider, Robert L.
On power / Robert L. Dilenschneider. — 1st ed.
p. cm.
Includes index.
ISBN 0-88730-652-7 (cloth)
1. Power (social sciences). I. Title.
HM136.D47 1994
303.3—dc20 93-5277

94 95 96 97 98 ❖/RRD 10 9 8 7 6 5 4 3 2 1

To my mother,
who understands the subtle sources of power
and who has long mastered its use,
with the finest of touches
and to the best of ends

CONTENTS

ACKNOWLEDGMENTS

Ron Beyma, who is a business strategist and communications counselor in Europe and the United States, helped to conceptualize this book. I want to thank him for his valued contribution.

At The Dilenschneider Group, my assistant, Joan Avagliano, for her tremendous support in coordinating all of the details and intricate processes that go into preparing a manuscript such as this for publication. This is the third major book in which her indispensability to me has been demonstrated. Scott Chesney for his persistent and extensive support work in the research and fact-checking of the manuscript. John Kasic was another valued contributor in his help on logistics, especially in the technical area.

At HarperCollins, Virginia Smith, my editor, for her dedication to creating a book that would really deal with power in its conceptual aspects, rather than its trivial ones; Frank Mount for his astute editorial guidance and exceptional skill in sharpening the message in the book; Laura Starrett for her keen eye in the final copy editing of the manuscript.

Mark Greenberg for his role in the development of the initial concept of the book.

Reid Boates, my agent, for his foresight in recognizing that the timing was right for such a book to be written and for his suggestion of the title.

No one institution may be able to help us advance the positive goals of power better than the leading-edge press, and I applaud their efforts. For the reader who scans the endnotes, they will find a rich supply of further reading. Some may also note that a rather large portion of those articles referenced come from the *Economist* and that is for one simple reason: that particular publication enjoys a distinct and enviable edge at this time in addressing breaking news in the context of power dynamics, especially at the global level. I appreciate the insights of all the authors and publications that I cite, but I feel compelled to single out that fine British publication as well.

To the hundreds of colleagues and executives around the world who encouraged me to continue writing.

And my special thanks to my wife, Jan, and my sons, Geoffrey and Peter, for their patience and support throughout the completion of this project.

INTRODUCTION

The vantage point of this book is the powerful person—the person practicing, defending, and enhancing power—not the individual serving the powerful or aspiring to attain power in a significant sense for the first time. However, *On Power* is as much intended to benefit others by showing how powerful people think and behave as it is intended to help the already powerful become even more so.

Many essays on power are too specialized. Once only generals, princes, and high church officials truly held power, and it's no surprise that the classic works on power were first published as textbooks in military strategy, diplomacy, and religion. But, today power is mostly economic or social. What should we call these people? Rather than talking about leaders or the empowered, I think it's easiest to call people with power simply the *powerful.* And, more accurate, too, because power today is eclectic. Before, for example, the rules of warfare were a distinct discipline from the laws of diplomacy and neither had anything to do with the principles of religion. Today, these and many other disciplines converge to create the modern lexicon of power.

Consider recent power legends: Ronald Reagan's acting ability *was* a cornerstone of his presidential power. Henry Kissinger's diplomacy was the basis of *his* power. Golda Meir's intellectual stamina encapsulated her power, just as a cryptic mystique defined the Ayatollah Khomeini's. Bill Cosby's enormous capacity to discuss and defuse racial issues—developing pride and creating humor at the same time—is his hallmark. Sam Walton's skill at engaging and motivating the common person was *his* power mainstay. Today, in boardrooms and warrooms, university faculty lounges and network control booths, conference centers of great charities and the back rooms of its greediest cartels—all players look sideways at one another for cues on what works in the world of power and what doesn't. They sift, adapt, and apply. Republicans use the same polling techniques as Democrats; the pin-striped pension actuarials who work for management are none other than those retained by union bargainers; and human-rights crusaders craft emotional appeals every bit as relentless as those of the hucksters of cosmetic surgery and reclinable beds. Applications differ, but it all adds up to power.

Power is only important because it enables people to get things done . . . for themselves or for others.[1] People pursue power because it promises rewards: These people could be after money, or they may want to feed the starving, or perhaps they want glory . . . or revenge . . . or appreciation. In any case, power is only sought after for the purpose of getting something done. Being "power-crazed" and "obsessed with power for its own sake" are deluding, senseless images. Power without an application or a goal is meaningless. Mother Teresa wants the rice bowls of Calcutta ladled full now, just as Madonna wants the rush of a titillated, adoring audience. Make no mistake, both want power. Both need it to achieve their ends.

If power is the ability to get things done, it must usually—though not exclusively—be done through others. This challenges the classical rendition of power as pained isolation. Icons of brooding solitude populate the world of power images from Caesar to Nixon. But power is mainly a social act. Some rare geniuses, like Leonardo da Vinci or Buckminster Fuller, had the self-assurance to spend

---

1. I'm sure that I'm not the first to define power as getting things done. The formulation, I am told, has been around a long time, and I lay no claim to originating it. Rather this book explores the implications of that definition for powerful people in the new world of the knowledge economy, lateral organizations, fragmented social values, and intense media scrutiny.

their days talking to future generations. Most power deals with *now* and is usually done through others.

Some people who exercise power as a social act may have such a genius for designing human relationships that their modeling survives long after they have ceased to be a player. In this sense, power or the true extent of power does not always make itself known immediately. Alfred Sloan's organizational strategy for General Motors existed long beyond Sloan's tenure with the company and may have even had a broader impact on industrial thinking generally than it did just on General Motors. But this is a dimension of power that the individual cannot control, and that can neither be taught nor learned. The powerful can attempt to lay a foundation for the future, but they cannot steer its outcome, as Neville Chamberlain learned when he attempted to appease Hitler with the Sudetenland and assure "peace for our time." Social power working fundamentally in the present is the range and scope of this book.

Some observers have reasoned that power is not as important in today's less hierarchical organizations as it was in the era of the "Great Pyramids"—when large, steep, and heavily layered organizations dominated industry and other social structures. In fact, the opposite is true. Power is more important in modern organizations *because* its use is far more subtle when it is unbundled from authority. In fact, less hierarchy and less of a command mode make the exercise of power vastly *more* important and tougher to do. Also, the practice of power for individuals is virtually the same as the practice of power for organizations. As Chapter 4 will develop in some detail, the powerful person is usually the center of a complex and extensive organizational structure. While this is evident for the president of the United States and corporate presidents, it is equally true for many researchers and creative artistic talents. In fact, nearly all powerful people surround themselves with a formal or informal network which enables them to exert power.

Since power in a democracy works on consent, power is upheld and advanced through what constituencies yield, not through what is taken from them. The first hierarchies to crumble were political ones during the great revolutions of the nineteenth and twentieth centuries. Only relatively recently has the democratic model been extended to companies, because the knowledge component of work has dramatically increased. This development forces the powerful to behave differently today. As orchestrators of often complex knowledge, the instant reaction of today's powerful is to confer, not to assert. And, the input the powerful seek is often emotional and intuitive as well as intellectual. For example, when Nebraska senator Bob Kerrey is confronted with a policy choice, he is reported to ask his advisers "How do you feel?" not "What do you think?"

Certainly, modern power is complex and filled with nuances, but why isolate power as a separate discipline today? Aren't standards about power in narrower spheres such as diplomacy still relevant? There are indeed great books about the specialized use of power such as Machiavelli's *The Prince*—long deemed the classic on the topic. While Machiavelli's book is a true classic and deserves the closest study, this masterpiece does not address power in the modern sense of the term. *The Prince* is a treatise about intrigue, oppression, and coercion written by an ambitious civil servant humiliated by foreign invasion of the Italian city states. Its *realpolitik* and guile might work today in throwback states like Libya, Iraq, or Cuba, but running a complex, modern country by Machiavelli's dictums would be like piloting the control panel of a 757 with the steering wheel of a bus. Sir Kenneth Clark, a cosmic thinker and historian, has pointed out, "The Emperor Charles V had only three books beside his bed: the Bible, Machiavelli's *Prince*, and Castiglione's *Cortegiano* [*The Courtier*]." While the Bible probably has immortal staying power, Machiavelli's advice on court politics is about as useful today as Castiglione's tips on manners and chivalry. Perhaps the most important personal point about Machiavelli is that he was not a particularly powerful person and spent his later years clearly out of favor and power.[2]

2. The distinction between being out of power and being out of position or platform is further developed in the Appendix of this book.

But Machiavelli had an eye for power, and he is typical in that most of the useful input on power doesn't come from people who are personally powerful. Often the powerful's own persona and ego cloud their ability to describe how they are using the mechanics of power; and, too, the mighty are constantly clawing for how they will be remembered on the stage of history, so their talk is often considerably more virtuous than their walk. Perhaps the four most cited power theorists—Aristotle (who tutored Alexander the Great), Machiavelli (who helped guide the Medicis), Hegel (a professorial philosopher and newspaper editor), and von Clausewitz (the cerebral soul of the Prussian General Staff)—were all fundamentally advisers and scholars.

Power is not a subcategory of sociology, politics, warfare, religion, public relations, or psychology. Power—like values—is a factor in every sphere of human activity. It is not just that power is eclectic. Power is a rich study, worthy of standing alone. Separate disciplines emerge only when there are enough theories and facts to justify their existence. Psychology, for example, didn't become a science until the first scientific treatment of human behavior was published by Wilhelm Wundt in Leipzig in 1879. Before that, psychology sat in a domain somewhere between philosophy and religion. Until 1950, to use another analogy, biology and physics were respectable and established studies while their fusion into biophysics would have been as unimaginable as alchemy. Biology and physics remain important subjects today, but much of the real action has shifted to such hybrids as biophysics and biogenetics. While Mary Shelley or Aldous Huxley might have envisioned biophysical images in their novels, it wasn't until the middle of this century that the practice of biophysics became feasible. Similarly, an integrated approach to power—transcending its various uses—is now within reach, and is chiefly the offspring of wedding sophisticated techniques for opinion and attitude research with now innumerable pieces of evidence about the intuitive grasp of power in modern settings. This convergence, which is discussed in detail in Chapter 3, truly makes power a separate discipline—a discipline that deserves, above all, respect and proper handling.

Like law or business, power is an empirical study. As with both, a daunting grasp of *shifting contexts* is essential to exercise power. Supreme among these are listening and research, anticipating trends, and sensing when to stop listening and start acting. For this reason, the study of power is a study of cases rather than abstract principles. But these cases can often be briefer in length than those found in business or law. One finds the most telling episodes or statements of power when situations shift as in a corporate reorganization, the discovery of a new manufacturing process, or a conceptual breakthrough in the way that a serious social problem is analyzed. Many power principles can only be intimated through specific examples. A number of the illustrations I have chosen are highly specific. The exercise of power is essentially transactional. This book seeks to train the intuition, while it points out those instances where research and thoughtful analysis are essential prerequisites to action. The reader will experience the flexible positioning of Lorenzo de Medici, the organizational flair of AMR CEO Bob Crandall, the intuitive sweep of Coco Chanel, and the legislative mastery of former House Speaker Sam Rayburn.

As with any other discipline built on social doctrine, the emerging study of power has also been shaped by other outside forces. These include: the proliferation of information, the enfranchisement of whole new subgroups within society (minorities, the handicapped, nontraditional families, etc.), the speed and transparency of modern communications, and crushing economic pressures. Perhaps, "information theory," "social enfranchisement," "communications immediacy," and "economic triage" will also one day be defined and widely taught as independent disciplines. Unavoidably and unfortunately, the relevant aspects of these forces must, for the present, be integrated as ad hoc factors in any exposition of modern power.

In many respects, modern power has evolved imperceptibly, as undetectably as old power concepts have evaporated. In a 1990 essay, Peter Drucker (whom I will cite often in the early stages of this book) pointed out: "The first scientific census, the British census of 1910, famously defined lower middle class as the family that could not afford more than three servants. . . . Servants antedate history by millennia, and in 1913 they were the largest single employee group in any developed country. Thirty percent of all wage earners were domestic servants. They are all gone."

Shortly before the failed coup against Mikhail Gorbachev in 1991, I sat in Nikita Khrushchev's private conference room in the Silver Lake dacha outside of Moscow and reflected on the wall facing me, a wallpapered panel overlooking a massive table. The wallpaper was about thirty years old, and the color was uniformly faded except for a rectangle nearly two feet high and a foot and a half wide. Surely, Khrushchev's own picture had once hung there, as certainly did those of Brezhnev, Chernenko, and Andropov. When the wallpaper is one day replaced, I doubt anyone will care about that patch. Nonetheless, it is a poignant statement about power and freedom in Russia. It is no longer necessary in the Russian Republic to have Big Brother's icon staring down. True power shifts are often as quiet as they are dramatic.

This book has its own power aspirations. It strives to document what advisers to the powerful tell their clients. As with most advice, what is to be found are chiefly reminders and extensions of and explanations for what the powerful already know or at least suspect. My goal has been to arrange that advice more systematically than most clients ever hear it or—given the pace of power transactions—ever have the opportunity to absorb it. The reader will learn about the management of expectations, effective merchandizing of power, fulfilling the Awe Factor and avoiding the Wizard Fallacy. The principles of contemporary "pork" and plunder will be spelled out. The reader will also learn how the power structure surrounding the individual becomes an atomic building block—creating a multihuman impression and making powerful people seem larger than life. The need for skillful superficiality in the communication of the powerful will be explained along with why the essence of power is a burden, not an advantage.

Structurally, *On Power's* eight chapters and its appendix are really essays that address several fundamental aspects of power in modern society: 1) where power resides; 2) how power works; 3) how it is mastered; 4) how it is organized; 5) how it is managed; 6) how it is communicated; 7) what its emotional fabric is; and 8) how power can hopefully be put to higher use. The Appendix treats the resurgence of power. While these essays build the basis for a unified theory of power, the reader must remember that power must be exerted and expressed in vastly different ways— ways that strictly depend upon the specific context. This is an insuperable fact about power that can hardly be stressed enough. Ignoring this fact can lead one to attempt the ridiculous, such as rallying entire companies through consensus, browbeating environmentalists through intimidation, or combating impregnable bureaucracies with rational arguments. And, while the *powerful* remain persons for all seasons, there must still be a core of authenticity and, increasingly—I am delighted to say—of values for the powerful to retain power. How and why that is true is also grist for this book.

1

The Foundation of Power

Building from Drucker

We now know that the source of wealth is something specifically human: knowledge.

—PETER DRUCKER

What is the basis of power? What relationship exists between power and values?

We are all powerful to a certain extent when compared to someone who is not—an infant, for example. Ironically, the powerful themselves are forever complaining (they may be powerful, but they are still human) that they often feel *powerless*. They are at the mercy of secretaries, waiters, retail clerks, limousine drivers, flight attendants, or customs inspectors. But that is mostly howling over annoyance at not being in control of a particular set of logistics. That kind of power is situational, trivial, and not the domain of this work. Also excluded are people who are merely wealthy or famous. While many powerful people are both wealthy and famous, money and fame can also be gotten through inheritance, a craftily arranged marriage, dribbling a basketball, tattling juicy gossip to the press, or winking into a movie camera. While this luck or these skills may pay handsomely, they are not power in a meaningful sense. These are specifically not power as a significant social skill, one that gets things done. Powerful people are special and different, and they are few in number when tallied against the world's headcount.

Just who are they? Powerful people are those in the leadership circles of the world's great institutions—its large corporations, universities, governments, religions, newspapers, charities, armies, cultural centers, unions, and other decisive bodies. These people are powerful, in the highest sense, because of the official roles that they fulfill and the responsibility that they have for human affairs. Today, that generally means that they had the skills and prowess to earn these roles, which is itself a type of power. Another kind of powerful person is the thinker, teacher, researcher, critic, scholar, writer, analyst, dissident, or opinion-leader whose power derives from the intellectual or emotionally mobilizing contribution that they make to human understanding and innovation.

It is hard to guess how many truly powerful people there are in the world—perhaps one in a hundred, maybe one in a thousand. Certainly there are more powerful people than those one counts among ubiquitous celebrities, people who indeed have power, who seem to be everywhere, and always appear ready to interpret the daily flow of events—such folks as Henry Kissinger, Jesse Jackson, Lester Thurow, Margaret Thatcher, and Lee Iacocca. These figures all share a media-intensified power, and they respond to a need that almost all of us sometimes feel: We want the reassurance that someone really *is* running the world, even though that premise is sheer myth. After this group come the less visible powerful persons who govern the world's most formidable institutions. All the members of the Trilateral Commission, the board of General Electric, the UN Security Council, the Federal Reserve Board, and the Mont Pelerin Society are surely powerful people. Umberto Bossi (head of the Lombard League in Milan and an eloquent advocate of Northern Italy's secession from

Italy) and Roman Vaskuj (one of the most prominent young Czech entrepreneurs) wield great power in their own country even though neither has real global recognition. Among the ranks of powerful people number New York gay-rights activist Tim McFeeley; Haruki Murakami, the most widely read novelist in Japan; drug kingpin Pablo Escobar; Lady Judith Wilcox, chair of England's National Consumer Council; and Superbarrio, a masked wrestler in Mexico City who champions the poor and has been a modern Zorro in the fight against corruption.

Down every walk of life, you will find powerful people. But, most of them don't know one another or even know *of* one another. In fact, despite all the enticing conspiracy theories cooked up by screenplay writers and political paranoids, the powerful don't really form a unique elite or generally see themselves as a group. Most of the truly powerful people are so preoccupied with their own goals that they often think very little about their standing in the community, and their real interest in other powerful people is not to stroll in the right circles but to enlist other strong resources in helping to get things done. Another inescapable fact is that while certain *managerial* and *communications* skills are transplantable from one environment to another—and even if one were to disregard language and national culture differences—the power that matters in an MIT laboratory is quite different from the power that flourishes in the Venezuelan Congress or runs a *chaebol* in Korea.

What criteria set the powerful apart from all the others? Besides their competence, it is their ability to generate ideas, their sense of mission, their self-confidence, and their need for achievement, that is, their desire to get something done. How can you spot a powerful person? Look at his or her results. Are these people directly or indirectly responsible for getting a lot done? And especially, are they somehow responsible for getting a lot done through others? When I say powerful people, I mean those people who are often engaged in power, wield it astutely, and get things done. For reasons briefly noted above that will be discussed more thoroughly later, powerful people tend to cluster in groups. Some societies have higher concentrations of powerful people than others, and those concentrations drive the society outward, making it globally competitive. Certainly the United States, the Pacific Rim, and Western Europe fall into that category. These places are home to the densest populations of powerful people, at least as far as the most important range of events is concerned.

What *is* it that these powerful people are trying to get done? It's nearly axiomatic that powerful individuals seek to exert influence outside themselves. But, this is also true for organizations. Power for the individual in an organization is the ability to influence the direction of an organization that has a real impact. The Red Cross doesn't exist to administer itself, but to raise money and to care for disaster victims. The opera company in Covent Garden raises its curtain to enrich the experiences of its audiences. Sears wants to sell socks, while its Dean Witter Reynolds subsidiary wants to sell stocks to the middle-American consumer. All these institutions want an impact outside themselves.

The world has known a growing and changing realm of power. The truest test of any theory is that it must explain events. How, then, is one to explain the evolution of modern power? If wielding power is a skill, the origins of power are in a variety of eclectic disciplines that today are fractionated and highly specialized. Where are the deepest roots for modern power concepts to be found? The contemporary practice of power in businesses and other large organizations may owe most to the scientific advances of the eighteenth century. Dr. Jacob Bronowski and other scholars point out that it was then that engineers and physicists sought to define the scientific essence of power. Power became, Bronowski writes, "a new preoccupation, in a sense a new idea, in science . . . [during the Industrial Revolution.] [That] Revolution was the great discoverer of power. Sources of energy were sought in nature: wind, sun, water, steam, coal. And a question suddenly became concrete: Why are they all one? What relation exists between them? That had never been asked before . . . [T]he modern conception of transforming nature in order to obtain power from her . . . had come up to the leading edge of science."

Transforming forces into power started with nature. But, it didn't stop there. The power of physics was to experience both political and industrial transformations. What started with steam engines and boiler kettles found its social interpretation in the French and American Revolutions. Since then, one ideology after another has had its run on the power stage—choreographed by one power ideologist after another—from Tom Paine to Tom Peters, from Joe McCarthy to Mao Tse-tung. Powerful people began to see a commonality in at least some manifestations of social power and started to study what makes other powerful people tick, just as President William Howard Taft did when he bemoaned the fact that Mary Pickford outdrew him at train station whistlestops. "'All the people love you,'" Taft said to Pickford, "'and I can't have even the love of half the people.'"

As social theory developed so did human understanding of power. If you go to the Lincoln Memorial, Daniel Chester French's monumental statue of Lincoln depicts a person of great loneliness and isolation. It's an unforgettable statue but a faulty image because Lincoln was a master of the use of power and understood well that power derives from relationships. Indeed, modern power is not found in isolation, consequently very independent people are often awkward in contemporary power contests. In the 1992 presidential campaign, Ross Perot presented a viewpoint and initiative for change that many welcomed, but he was absolutely lacking the relationships and formal structure that could get him elected—no surprise for a person columnist George Melloan once characterized as "a one-band man" and for the Perot who reportedly described his erstwhile fellow nonmanagement directors at General Motors as "pet rocks." Mere months later, the same pattern was repeated in Korea as Chung Ju Yung, the founder of Hyundai, was defeated in a similar maverick bid for the Korean presidency. In our age, independence and the ability to get things done are often mutually exclusive.

Social power was really only harnessed in man-made organizations in the past two centuries. Even then, fear and survival remained awesome factors up until perhaps the past three decades. Engineered power in human organizations reached its apex *militarily* in the nineteenth century with the Prussian General Staff and *economically* in the late nineteenth and the early twentieth centuries—first with Frederick Taylor and then with Alfred Sloan's elaborate hierarchy for General Motors. The period of the two World Wars was a test of superiority between differing national structures.

Such modern writers as Robert Townsend (*Up the Organization*) and Eric Hoffer (*The True Believer*) have made important contributions to the study of power, but their focus was on the evils of conformity. They agitated for rebellion against *established* power structures. It is far different to function in an organization that revolution has already overwhelmed than in one that is currently locked in revolt, as Peter Drucker has so articulately pointed out. The information revolution of the twentieth century has done to organizations what the industrial revolution did in the nineteenth century.

Sociologist C. Wright Mills, in *The Power Elite*, painted American power in the first half of this century as an oligarchy and urged its democratization. Michael Korda in his 1975 book *Power!* recognized that the opportunity to attain power actually had *become* more democratic and said further: "It is the desire for power that keeps most people working." (While probably true then, this point rings less true two decades later, with the far more intense public scrutiny and other burdens of accountability that are now imposed on power.) Korda contends "life is a game of power" that "usually involve[s] the manipulation of people and situations to your advantage." He advises that "the trick is to develop a style of power based on one's character and desires." While he describes David Mahoney as one example of an executive who "sees power as a means of getting things done," that is only one option. Korda himself advances Silvano Arieti's definition of power: "the ability to bring about our desires." Consequently, while Korda's entertaining and thoughtful book treats issues like the symbolism and rituals of power or the benefits of a powerful person remaining "slightly mysterious," I believe that it does so in a more opportunistic way than the present book does, which may account for Korda's diagram drawings of office layouts and physical positioning for office parties.

By the 1970s, rebels emerged to challenge what had now become the "traditional" power structure of organizations and of society itself. Individually, the challengers were a motley band with vastly different roots and grievances. California flower children assailed the military-industrial establishment. Harold Geneen and other financial pioneers conglomerated and liquidated organizations purely as financial assets. Entrepreneurial wizards like Ross Perot, Steve Jobs, and Sam Walton created vastly successful enterprises outside the industrial mainstream. Rather than overwhelm established institutions, new kinds of organizations based on new power principles thrived alongside of old established ones. The world saw all kinds of power formulations blossoming in a seemingly contradictory jungle of power principles—communes, matrix corporations, terrorist death brigades, Greenpeace, Scientology, and Mother Teresa.

Another scientific contribution to the study of power is our changing understanding of survival. Every culture's interpretation of power rests on its fundamental rules of survival. Because the bare essentials needed to get by were so scarce, the children of ancient Sparta were officially schooled in the art of theft. In Poland, after the end of communism in the 1990s, "entrepreneurs" set up seminars in hotels on how to steal automobiles in affluent Germany and charged the "students" $1,500 for a day-long crash course. After forty years of communism, during which time unemployment was rampant and people were compelled to resort to the black market to survive, Polish society could not easily adjust to the niceties of Western property rights. At the end of 1989, Bruce D. Henderson—clearly a pathfinder in the annals of strategic thinking—wrote a piece for the *Harvard Business Review* on the origins of strategy. In it, he explained that "Darwin is probably a better guide to business competition than economists are." The real message in Darwin is not that those endowed with sheer mass and size triumph, but that survival, and ultimately power, goes to the most adaptable.

Adaptation often causes power to emerge in unforeseen places. A labor organizer for a public-sector union, for example, can exercise unexpected power by adapting his behavior to the principles of modern business. According to *Forbes*, Sgt. Harold Flammia, a former head of the San Antonio police union, kept a copy of Sun Tzu's *The Art of War* in his office. Flammia helped make San Antonio's law enforcement unit the best paid big-city police force in the nation (averaging $35,000 for five years of experience). Dubbed "the .44-caliber mouthpiece," Flammia was a consummate strategist. The police union then became the largest single PAC spender in San Antonio's municipal elections, Flammia presided over a one-hundred-line union phone bank to rally support on positions, and he hired "a political consultant . . . bombarding opinion makers with a steady stream of slickly produced pamphlets." This is adaptive, learning behavior, just as Lee Iacocca's opening membership on the Chrysler board to the UAW to solidify a partnership with the workers necessary to achieve the Chrysler turnaround, or IBM and Microsoft's decision to collaborate rather than to compete in the development of several operating systems.

Just as power in the scientific world has common features despite coming from an array of sources, power expressed in the social world has certain common features in diverse settings. In our age, it is heavily influenced by information, and it puts a premium on the ability to adapt effectively.

Competence as the Root of Power

The founder of IBM, Thomas J. Watson, Sr., often said, "I'm no genius. I'm smart in spots—but I stay around these spots." Rather than being expansive, modern power rests on defining its range with precision and must be especially careful to declare when it is speaking as a specialist or as a generalist. A general, a surgeon, or an economist is answerable to a court of peer opinion today that is far more vast and faster to respond than his or her predecessors would have been subject to in the past. Only "insiders" really grasp the issue of specialized competence, and the truth is that it is very hard to be a truly competent specialist. We rail against educators, government, business, and other institutions that seem so preoccupied with "pettiness" that they get little done. Surely, one reason this appears to be true is that there is relatively little specialized ability available when measured against the monumental tasks that must be done. A celebrated figure in the financial community once told me that an outsider to a given profession tends to exaggerate the malice and to overrate the competence of the people within that profession. If competence is the root of power, it's equally true that incompetence is the mother of weakness.

Generalists, however, are not doomed to extinction. One can also be a powerful generalist, but it must be clear that one is operating or speaking as a lay person or generalist. Consider the public communications of a powerful figure. Contrary to popular wisdom, reasonably intelligent people *are* entitled to comment as generalists over a wide range of topics. A U.S. senator is not a doctor, but needs a thoughtful position on health care, and is not an accountant, but won't get reelected without sensible views on tax policy.

The point is that people will only acknowledge power and that power can only endure if it is seen to be anchored in competence. Competence can either be specialized or generalist, but it is clearly one or the other. Also, the day of the broad generalist, lacking any specialized technical training, is coming to an end, and for a very simple reason. The knowledge economy and exploding technology require that a powerful person know very precisely what he or she is talking about. A religious leader taking positions about euthanasia must grasp the physiology of death to be regarded as competent. A university president, even if she is a specialist in the classics, must be able to judge the wisdom of research projects in the genetics laboratory. Fundamental computer literacy is essential today in such various enterprises as running a chain of supermarkets or directing the editing of a Shakespearean film.

While it's essential that the powerful be competent, that does not mean that they are active by nature. It's a common fallacy that power likes to act; it doesn't. In 1991, when asked about how to get the Russian message to really penetrate the consciousness of Pennsylvania Avenue, I told Russia's industrial czar Arkady Volsky: "I've spent twenty years of watching countries try to go straight to the White House. The White House doesn't act if it doesn't have to." My counsel to Volsky was that he would be much better off finding enticing reasons why the White House might *want* to act as opposed to conjuring up threats as to why it would *have* to act.

One's core competence is not always immediately apparent but usually requires the mastery of at least one technical skill. In his autobiography, Thomas J. Watson, Jr., points out that he really didn't discover *his* leadership competence until he became a pilot in World War II. It is very difficult to exercise power without feeling essentially competent in one or more important skills. Peter Drucker stands far ahead of his counterparts in providing management advice because he is seriously steeped in economics while his colleagues are mostly nimble with the parlor games of psychological one-upmanship.

Because power is a consciousness rooted in competence, it is hard to imitate power. There are fewer and fewer tracks to power that are both fast and enduring—especially when the power rests on a measurable trait. This is evident in how the Japanese have converted quality into immense commercial power. The Japanese success with quality is a towering competitive advantage, because quality is power in product comparisons. In pursuit of quality, the world industrial community has sought to imitate Japan's success. Still, many companies all over the world are failing to emulate the Japanese pursuit of quality successfully. The reason for the failure is that the imitating firms have focused on the end result of a quality product rather than the process leading to that product. They count how many "good" pieces they made and how many they had to throw away. Six Sigma—running a production line with 99.99966-percent perfect offspring—has become the leading mantra of non-Japanese manufacturers today, while I find that the numerical target is hardly taken so seriously in Japan itself. The Japanese didn't get to quality by improving their error rate. Instead, they altered their consciousness of quality, and that consciousness is difficult to imitate.

A comparable syndrome is found in people who want to become powerful through imitating the characteristics of power as glamorized by myth, fiction, and gossip. They attempt to stride with power, write with power, dine in power restaurants, and wear power clothing. This is to be distinguished from the "superficial" side of power as I use the term *superficial* in a positive sense later. Indeed, it is truly unredeemably superficial behavior and has become both a laughable caricature of power and a sure way to either lose power or never become powerful in the first place.

Focal Power

Focus is the most important dimension of discipline for a powerful person, and a clear agenda is the powerful person's most reliable expression of focus. Elizabeth Dole, former Labor Secretary and now a leading figure in the nongovernment public sector, has a superb grasp of focus. "For a political appointee in the Cabinet," she says, "a key point is identifying an agenda. In each job, I've tried to identify one or two points where I could make a difference. It's a special challenge to see that your senior team also owns those goals. You must make additionally certain that your objectives are measurable and time-lined." From a leadership standpoint, there is no more sound advice in the pursuit of focus.

All powerful institutions and individuals have focus, but there are many ways to organize to achieve focus. Great ingenuity is required to identify the right organizing principles that underpin focus. The *Wall Street Journal* has described how the firm Bausch & Lomb found a new strategic center of gravity for its business.

Bausch & Lomb grew up as a business centered on the making of high quality lenses used in microscopes, industrial instruments, and, of course, eyewear. As industries became more specialized, it made less and less sense to organize around the different applications for lenses. Bausch & Lomb got out of the instruments sector and adopted what the *Journal* calls an "above-the-neck" strategy. Sticking with the eyeglass, contact lens, and Ray-Ban sunglass businesses, Bausch & Lomb decided that its real credibility was with "above-the-neck" consumer products. So it bought a firm that makes ophthalmic solutions. Recognizing the problems of gum disease and hearing loss in an aging population, Bausch & Lomb now owns a plaque-fighting electric toothbrush company and a majority stake in a hearing aid firm. Noting a customer trend toward wholesomeness, they introduced a highly successful alcohol-free mouthwash. Of course, the Bausch & Lomb strategy just doesn't *seem* to have focus, it actually does. As in the Japanese example of quality, you can't simulate the idea, you must really have it. As another example, one of the reasons that Wendy's is a commanding performer today is that its leading competitors in the convenience restaurant business have lost their focus and have strayed aimlessly into an array of unrelated and sometimes implausible categories, ethnic foods in particular.

Focus is not defined by some need burning inside an individual to force his or her will upon the world. It is shaped by listening to the needs people and markets have, especially because those needs often change. IBM lost its stature and positioning in the computer industry when it failed to adapt its strategy quickly enough to the exponential growth in personal computers. When you decentralize information, you decentralize power. The world had decentralized the way it processed information, and IBM was still selling mammoth central processing—a battleship strategy for a submarine- and mobile-launchpad world. Even Cray Research, the pinnacle of the advanced computer industry, has been forced to compete on price as its aristocratic, high-power, megaflop machines became easier and easier to copy. It is not that IBM and Cray failed to focus. Both firms focused clearly, but the problem was that neither firm adjusted or focused on the world of information in the way that their customers did.

Focus is an expression of competence and a hallmark of power. Through identifying and persisting toward a limited number of related goals, the odds that things will be done and that they will be done well are improved.

How Do Wealth and Power Relate?

What drives people to want to do things and to do them well? There are many motivations, but few are as powerful as wealth. With communism ideologically bankrupt and everyone pursuing market economies of one sort or other, isn't it safe to conclude that if ever money were synonymous with wealth and power, now is the time and the age? Money talks, goes the saying, but that is no answer to the question: Is money really power? In a very real sense, wealth is power, but it is a serious error to equate wealth with money. The problem, as Peter Drucker has pointed out, really rests in our definition of *wealth*. An effective understanding of power requires an accurate definition of wealth.[1] In a secular world, wealth in one form or another is the principal motivation of the powerful and of the people through whom the powerful must get things done.

What if one imagines for a moment that wealth is not money? That money is just a medium for appraising wealth and not wealth itself is not a revolutionary idea. Countless studies have shown that truly successful (read: *powerful*) people in all walks of life, including business, are not fundamentally motivated by money. The powerful distinguish between wealth and money, even

---

1. Alvin Toffler also discusses topics like "wealth creation" in the information age in his writings, such as in the book *Power Shift*, in which he obviously writes about the general subject of power, too, and in a provocative and insightful way. If I had to characterize the differences in my approach to power from Mr. Toffler's, I would say that my treatment is less economic and technological and more focused on developing a modern theory for the human dynamics of power. My choice in evolving a concept of power from Drucker is a preference for the philosophical approach that Drucker uses to devise his ideas on power and knowledge.

though the vast majority of the people through whom they must operate do not. And, even if money and what it can buy are the end goal, you neither get money, nor expand it, nor keep it unless you have something much more fundamental. As Drucker puts it: "We now know that the source of wealth is something specifically human: knowledge. If we apply knowledge to tasks we already know how to do, we call it 'productivity.' If we apply knowledge to tasks that are new and different, we call it 'innovation.' Our knowledge allows us to achieve those two goals."

Ideas are the heart of genuine wealth, and ideas are equally the foundation of power. Learning and knowledge differ from precious metals in many ways. Most important, gold and platinum are prized for the relative stability of their worth, while knowledge constantly changes. Modern knowledge is also collaborative, which makes power essentially collaborative. One of the cornerstones of power in the 1990s is that those who know how to use real power know how to share it effectively. The most fundamental power of all, something even more primary than the possession of knowledge, is the capacity to learn. Learning creates tomorrow's ideas, the power of the future. The power of real knowledge is seen in the pedigree assigned to experience within certain companies. General Electric is a superb training school for managers. Recruiters carefully monitor companies like GE, Johnson & Johnson, Ford, and Motorola at all levels. These companies carry an assurance that their people have handled big situations on a global dimension and have a distinctive approach to learning and problem solving. In Japan, one of the reasons top managers pay so much attention to loyalty is that Japanese companies are quite transparent about how they manage within their businesses and among their people. They are rightly fearful of that experiential knowledge moving to competitors.

The transformation of knowledge to wealth has also changed the definition of property. According to Drucker, "in human history, nothing has had greater impact than the redefinition of property rights." In the knowledge age, there are entirely different rules regarding the relationship between ownership and power.

The old saw of possession being nine-tenths of the law is hard to accept when knowledge is the most valuable matter. Cygnus, a leading software firm, has formed a radical but perhaps indicative solution to the problem. Cygnus no longer charges clients for its products, only for their application—a dramatic example of true power (and value) being learning and the capacity to adjust to it.

The fundamentals of ownership change and so do the basics of power. Just as the terms of survival influence the prevailing approaches to power so does the scarcity or surplus of mediums of survival. For the bulk of human history, the central economic problem has been the lack of personnel and equipment to realize economic goals. The chief economic characteristic of the world today is just the opposite—an excess of both untrained people and industrial capacity relative to goals. This reality favors nations with exceptionally fine educational systems and efficient industrial capacity, giving special advantages to Northern and Western Europe and to Japan. The trade wars between Japan, Europe, and the United States are really disputes about excess capacity and the extent to which a nation should be permitted to subsidize its own excess capacity. As much as knowledge constitutes power and wealth, ignorance portends to weakness and worse. Subsidies exist to keep workers, who for whatever reason are ill-suited to function in the knowledge economy, employed.

Countries with large economic sectors that are not far along the knowledge (or power) curve feel paradoxical pressure. Italy is as fearful of deindustrialization and France of abandoning its family-farm agriculture as they are afraid of being closed out of the leading ranks of the knowledge economies. For the Third World, it's much worse. It's disheartening but true that the only assets of the Third World valuable to the advanced world are cheap labor and natural resources.

What separates the Third World from the First World? It is simply the level of competence each is able to execute. In the First World that competence stresses adaptability. True competence requires a certain kind of knowledge and has more to do with learning in the face of changing circumstances than a technical ability to repeat a skill. Power is valued and expresses itself most usefully in managing change, and both productivity and innovation are types of positive change. Analogously, power can be measured for its "productivity"—how *much* is gotten done. The process of creating new knowledge is an important dimension of power. Knowledge and ideas are what enable powerful people to be competent and that competence is expressed through both being productive and innovative.

What Breeds Power?

How do the powerful hone their craft? Power is rarely an isolated phenomenon in the information age. It may not love company, but it certainly prospers in it. If ideas are wealth and the medium of power, very little modern knowledge is created in isolation. It is far more appropriate to speak of power *among* near peers than of a single power looming over all others. As Michael Porter has written: "Competitive advantage arises when several local rivals pressure each other to advance. This not only breeds successful global competitors but benefits the entire national industry by stimulating specialised educational and research institutions and attracting entry into related industries." Thus, the domestic U.S. automobile industry grew weak in part because it didn't command the concentration of industrial focus which the automotive industry in Japan did, whereas Italy is a powerful global force in footwear and handbags because it has a number of high-quality, advanced-fashion producers of these articles.[2] Similarly, the graduate schools and post-graduate research centers of the United States present the world with an inordinate number of all high-tech scientific discoveries. Our ways of measuring the world and the capacity within its zones have changed. A traditional economic atlas dissected the world in terms of its sea levels, mean tempera-

2. It is also true that the Italians exploited lower wage rates and their own regulatory ineffectiveness on the environment and other industrial issues to boost their shoe industry. It is possible for certain institutions to exploit weaknesses, at least for the short term, converting them into power.

ture, or population density. A modern power atlas would segment it based on research laboratories, the sophistication of communications infrastructure, and the number of residents who could ply differential calculus or distinguish Brunelleschi from Bruno Walter.

Power is a matter of relative adaptability and survival. Henderson's point about Darwin's economic relevance rings true once again. High quality dialogue allows power to grow and adapt because it refines knowledge, and knowledge is the foundation of competence and thus power, too. Porter's competitive principle in fostering superiority works as well in settings that are not totally or not at all economic—from Lyons as a center for gourmet restaurants to Japan as the hub for koto playing.

The peer group of power creates its own hierarchy, and striving for the very highest seat is not necessarily an advantage or the best use of one's time. Within a highly concentrated power setting, it can be enormously rewarding to choose the right secondary role and suicidal to succumb to the urge to be first. The reason is simple: Being the most powerful or *like* the most powerful is neither always attainable nor necessarily an advantage. Two years ago, for example, British Petroleum tried to imitate Royal Dutch Shell (arguably the world's best managed oil company) and harmed itself in the process. British Petroleum is now making progress styling itself for a different niche and against a less mammoth standard. Often, there are advantages to being a heartbeat away from dominance. When AT&T suffered a massive systems failure several years ago, other phone companies consciously positioned themselves as backup systems and pointed out the risk of relying on a single phone system. This is no casual strategy; one must be very good to be a spare tire to an entire phone company. The Spanish airline Iberia, with Miguel Aguiló at the helm, made a similar decision when it stopped trying to be a major competitor in North America and locked on to a Miami hub to build its network in Latin America. Among giants in the pharmaceutical industry, the dominant trend in recent years has been to devote enormous resources to a limited number of patented drug concepts and hope that they will prove to be world champions. The strategy can be a high-stakes circuit around the roulette wheel. The Swiss company Ciba-Geigy, on the other hand, has delivered excellent performance with drug products that are not protected by patents. A *Wall Street Journal Europe* article describes how Ciba-Geigy has carved out niches for medical problems as diverse as epilepsy and arthritis, antismoking therapies (where they are known as "the patch company") and antidepressants. Compared with the advanced research powerhouses of the industry, this may seem as glamorous as selling used cars. When one thinks of the peerage of power, instinctively we stare at the top, while the real opportunity may be just below it.

Power Is Derivative and Accountable

Not only does real power generally rely on a strong, nurturing, and competitive peer group—for decades, Etonians dominated British government and business—it must also know to whom it answers. We tend to think of power being ultimate, as if there were a throne at the top of the pyramid—the buck truly does stop somewhere. That picture is a mirage. The powerful really do work for others—if not officially, in a nonetheless important and undeniable reality. Increasingly and because the world now shares a unilateral devotion to the market economy, the persons that they work for are individuals with considerable financial authority. In the business world, of course, the CEOs of huge corporations are accountable to their largest shareholders. We tend to think of these as a jury of peers, but that too is deceptive. Those shareholders were often members of "The Club"—retired executives or members of founding families. Today they are pension fund managers for the unions of public employees and investment banking analysts. In short, financial technocrats.

In government is it any different? Do elected officials have their most strictly managed accountability to their electorate . . . or even to their partisan supporters? In truth, neither. Governors and big city mayors shake in their boots before rating agencies like

Moody's or Standard & Poor's. Political agendas, too, rely on the power of the purse. At one time, such purses might have been filled by the local monarch dunning feudal dukes. Today, credit ratings have a comparable effect. In a real way, bond buyers for the largest security houses actually call the tune for the president of the United States. The skittish bond market following Clinton's election warned him; now its rally is rewarding him. How the bond market feels about Clinton and any future president will determine in a very real way, by the cost of servicing the national debt, the amount of money available to get things done on the political agenda; just as the analyst who follows the stock of a particular firm sets values that in turn permit plants to be built or products to be developed. In politics and business, the chief executive—rather than being the ultimate power—is seen by financial and analytic judges as being little more than a well paid but accountable custodian.

Similarly, our cobra-stare fixation with the pinnacle of power blinds us to how often power is derivative. As an illustration, even school children of tender years know that the Queen of England is a figurehead. She may have wealth and standing, but she is certainly no match for the British Prime Minister. What would happen, however, should the Queen of England and the heritage of Windsor royalty vanish from the theater of British politics overnight? It's quite probable that the United Kingdom would be hurled into a massive constitutional crisis. Labour M.P. Tony Benn observes astutely: "The fact is that a Prime Minister's powers are derived from crown powers, and they are greater than a President's. A Prime Minister, on his or her own, can create judges, bishops, lords, send troops to the Falklands. Beside this, Di and Fergie are absolute froth." Froth they may be, but royalty's figurehead powers (and, through them, those of the prime minister executive branch) still are directly derivative from a centuries-old public mandate and almost conceal the legal basis for British political authority. Absent royalty, could the prime minister appoint judges or make war . . . or would those duties and others like them fall to Parliament? However the duties would be split, one could scarcely imagine that a new division of power would go uncontested.

Figureheads often factor more deeply in the methodology of power than one imagines. While here we are dealing with figureheads as a power source, later we will see how figureheads can spring to life like Shaw's Pygmalion and become uncooperative partners in a powerful person or organization's own structure. In the business community, outsiders on boards of directors used to be figureheads. Then came the rapacious wave of hostile takeovers and management buyouts of the 1980s. (It should be noted that businesses are not really privatized in the most important sense when governments sell them to the public or to private owners, but rather when businesses are delisted from public exchanges, because that act is tantamount to the withdrawal of power from public control and accountability.) The resulting businesses aren't compelled to deal with all the affected constituencies, but the media and public still hold the outside directors accountable for the sellouts—especially since so many resulted in reckless downsizing and threats to employee pension plans. That's why so many outside directors are stewing in shareholder lawsuits or paying a king's ransom for liability insurance these days.

Being a director of Exxon or Sears was once a trademark of power, but that is changing. Here we come to what it means on a personal level to be powerful in the 1990s. As never before, there is a yearning to understand the dynamics of power because people know that power is itself changing. Fiction and fantasy still govern how we like to think of power because it is easier to imagine enjoying the trappings of power than to imagine exercising power skillfully. We continue to mistake the metaphors of antique power—its ermine robes or fat cigars—with the sheer work and self-denial modern power demands. We may update the furs and Havanas to Chanel scarves and Rolexes, but we are still entrapped by the thinking that power is a perquisite. In truth, it is a duty.

Even Charles de Gaulle sought to be more the servant of an agenda (a "Europe of Fatherlands") than a charismatic leader, perhaps because, as de Gaulle once put it, "the future lasts a long time." The powerful are truly becoming subject to the agenda of their followers. From the viewpoint of the powerful, there's no way to dismiss it: Exercising power is demanding and exhausting work.

Power at the very top is also costly and intrusive to the psyche. It takes a particular commitment to goals and a rigorous attitude toward life to endure living one's days in a thirty-five-pound bullet-proof vest, constantly facing Sony microphones and Hasselblad lenses. Modern power makes the individual transparent and respects no privacy—especially in a democracy. The very powerful learn that everything about them will be examined sooner or later, from whom they dated in high school to the behavior of their adolescent grandchildren.

Truth, Values, Leadership, and Power

Are there no ground rules that give the powerful any relief from these pressures? Once there were, but they are disappearing and the reason why is that the broad public has a love-hate relationship with the powerful. The powerful are needed to get things done, but they are also seen as blemished and corrupt. Even societies with little or no heritage of political freedom learn this cynicism with astonishing speed, as could not be better demonstrated than by the Brazilian senate's compelling Fernando Collor, Brazil's first democratically elected president in three decades, to resign after being charged with corruption a mere two years after he had taken power. Brazil, a country where political corruption always had been a way of life, has quickly developed new standards and new expectations. What public opinion thought Collor had been attempting to get out of the presidency was not what the Brazilian people had in mind.

Power abides only when a clear understanding of the truth exists between the powerful and those affected by the powerful. Some purists believe that truth defines or should define power. They are convinced that there is an absolute truth that underpins the facts of the world. Some very sophisticated thinkers have advanced this view, including Walter Lippmann. That there is a fundamental truth is implicit with Lippmann—"a community that lacks the means to detect lies also lacks the means to preserve its own liberty." The issue of what constitutes truth becomes exceedingly important in dealing with news or reportage, because it is that kind of information that brings the powerful, from board chairmen to Supreme Court nominees, to their knees. Lippmann surely implies that there *is* a fundamental truth: "The function of news is to signalize an event, the function of truth is to bring to light the hidden facts, to set them into relation with each other, and make a picture of reality on which men can act." Lippmann's attitude toward truth is inspiringly democratic and idealistic, but I can hardly accept it as authentic. In my view, Hu Shih's version of truth is a much sounder starting point: "Only when we realize there is no eternal, unchanging truth or absolute truth can we arouse in ourselves a sense of intellectual responsibility." In any power transaction, I contend, truth is the mutual version of reality with which the engaged are willing to live in order to get something done. In any sustainable world, the truth is anchored in the facts, but its real operational force ensues from being cemented in trust. If getting things done is the goal, reliability is crucial, and reliability is just not possible without a common understanding of what constitutes the truth.

If the breech in understanding is big, as it appears to have been in the Collor case, all bets are off. If it is small, diplomats can easily sweep it under the table. This in turn sets a general standard for the values surrounding power. As they become less standardized, they become more negotiable. Just as the importance of "truth" to power is in the operational control it provides, values are fundamentally neutral to the exercise of power. If this were not true, there would not be so many evil powerful people in history. There would be no accounting for the Hitlers or the Stalins. One positive sign is that modern evil people tend to be in power for shorter tenures. Evil people tend to create more enemies than virtuous ones do, and it is harder to impose deceit in the information age than it was in earlier times. Values are coming to the world of power. (How this is taking place will be discussed in more detail in Chapter 8.)

Exercising power without values is irresponsible, probably all high-minded people would agree, but the intrinsic goodness of values has nothing to do with how power works or how well it works—certainly not in the short term. Values may be important as guidelines or as criteria for measuring if power is being used in a worthwhile way. Values may even frame an emotional appeal locked up in a power transaction. But values are not inherently a part of power. What matters most for the powerful is that their values are *consistent* not that their values are *correct*. And, the powerful should suspend their moral judgments for a moment to see if this technical test of consistency is being met, and for a very pragmatic reason: Personal opinions can obscure consistent values and interfere with the professional competence and policy integrity of a powerful person, especially when measured against the person's official role. Generally, powerful people are required to have consistent values, and they get into trouble when they unveil controversial emotional convictions that are at odds with either their principles or their job duties. When President George Bush said he would stand by a grandchild of his if, hypothetically, she had an abortion, many felt that Bush had finally become more realistic about his abortion views and that was widely considered as positive. But Bush's ambivalence had a more damaging downside: It left the nation wondering about Bush's sincerity generally.

Former French Prime Minister Edith Cresson's ten-month rule, which ended in 1992, was marked by emotionalism and an unwillingness to focus her remarks. She offended the Japanese (saying their "overwhelming desire is to conquer the world") and had, before assuming office, taunted British men as not being manly enough—a criticism she refused to distance herself from strongly enough after becoming Prime Minister. These were unnecessary provocations for a French prime minister considering that France was obliged to be a leading advocate for international and European trade harmony. Because the trophy is so exhilarating—bringing down a major political leader—the media often bait the powerful into these kinds of debacles.

It is also possible for the powerful to avert these problems. Prime Minister Hanna Suchocka in Poland has exhibited good counter-strategies that do so. In her case, it was not personal inconsistency that was the stake, but a chaotic, splintered, and inconsistent Polish government trying to rule in the aftermath of communism. Charged in 1992 with putting together the fourth post-Communist government in just three years, Suchocka placed all of her cabinet members (including a former prime minister) on probation upon taking office. Not only did this step control bickering, it restrained the cabinet from taking the kind of freewheeling public positions that so characterized Edith Cresson's rule. Further, Suchocka took her own advice and focused herself on economic reconstruction while the mercurial and imperious Lech Walesa remained the dominant political force. The two arrived at a highly effective power truce. Suchocka was careful to control the situations and dynamics that could lead to inconsistencies of values without undermining the essential commitment to democratic governance.

While the demand for consistency is imposing and the behavior of the powerful is examined microscopically, a trend toward greater tolerance makes a broader range of values acceptable. Power is also now possible for individuals who had been discriminated against in the past. The power of women is likely to grow because the unfair rules—such as penalties for births out of wedlock and social pressure to stay at home—are losing their hold. There's no doubt that power has operated against a double standard since prehistoric civilization. When public standards change, so do scandals. In 1992 it was learned that the British health minister had borne a son out of wedlock twenty-five years ago. That same year the French environment minister bore a child out of wedlock and made no effort to hide the fact. Neither had any intention of resigning, and no one expected them to. Other sorts of behavior that excited public attention before are nearly ignored today. Writes Nicholas Lemann in the New Republic, "Kitty

Dukakis's memoirs have failed to ignite a spark in part because she becomes indistinguishable from one's old roommate who's become a basket case."

Tolerance is making power available to more people and that is a very good thing. When values as a whole are considered, another question must emerge—one about leadership and its linkage with power. The relationship of leadership to power is complex. All leaders must understand the use of power and actually use power, although all do not necessarily enjoy its use and some may find the wielding of power to be abhorrent rather than intoxicating. It is also possible for a person to be powerful and not a true leader— witness tyrants like Hitler or foreign ambassadors who earn their jobs for political patronage and perform them for personal gain. In our age few such leaders withstand the test of time. They find that their countrymen demand an agenda more productive of public good. This book offers advice to both leaders and the powerful, but always in the context of power. Modern organizational literature is clogged with books on leadership that are chock-full of moral truisms, as well as books on power that are jammed with dirty tricks. In this context, the intent of this book is to provide a legitimate portrait of power by recognizing that power is in fact morally neutral, while its proper use may offer moral opportunity.

THE FUNDAMENTALS

> Power is the ability to get things done. Competency and knowledge are the basis of power, and there are standards for being a competent generalist as well as an effective specialist. Although the powerful are expected to have consistent values, power is itself morally neutral.

2

The Mechanism of Power

*The Wizard Fallacy,
the Awe Factor, and More . . .*

*Lorenzo de Medici was a politician of genius who could
distinguish between the reality of power and its outward trappings.*

—Sir Kenneth Clark

How does power work?

Power is transactional. It is achieved, executed, and defended one
interpersonal transaction at a time. Power defies systemization,
but there is a remarkable similarity to the managerial and communications apparatus needed to conduct power in different contexts. Like energy, power is hard to store and to sustain. Fortune
500 CEOs better be able to string together quarter-to-quarter
earnings improvements or the board's compensation committee
will be tidying up the top management severance packages. Power
demands continuous success, but it has no absolute norms.
George Bush's popularity roller coaster after the Gulf War and

loss of the subsequent presidential election is ample proof of that. What worked in war certainly didn't work in peace.

Similarly, consider a college philosophy professor. Dramatic existential skepticism may underpin her power in the seminar room while her street-smart pragmatism wins dollars for her department at budget reviews. Her contagious enthusiasm is the hallmark of her commencement talks, and her tough but affectionate manner keeps her renegade teenage daughter in line. Each situation brings out a different power gambit and posture.

Power has also become transactional because we are now so badly disoriented by the world's philosophical, technological, and operational changes. As Peter Drucker writes, "Most of what we assume axiomatically no longer fits our reality, lending a surreal air to our work and lives. The world seems to have dissolved into a series of media events that appear either bigger than reality or totally formless." We can recognize this in our simplest behaviors. A keen analyst of modern baseball once remarked that if you watch the fans in a contemporary ballpark closely, after a while their gaze will drift from the playing field to the gigantic electronic TV monitors suspended over the grandstands or to the miniature portable sets they have brought with them. Edited, organized reality is more compelling and natural to us than direct observation.

While driving dogma is gone in the world of power, except perhaps for Islamic fundamentalism, the powerful are not swimming in a fully random world. They usually succeed by having a style that matches the majority of transactions they must conduct. Jack Gould, former dean of the University of Chicago School of Business, has just the right leadership style that works for the head of a premier business-school faculty. For example, when evaluating a new business strategy for the school, Gould would listen intensely during discussions, praise the perceptiveness or ingenuity of a contributor's remarks, encourage the risk-taking in developing an idea not borne by thorough research, yet always steer the discussion along the fine but clear line of an actionable decision. He's an outstanding collegial leader. Within the world

of a high-powered business school, there is a microcosm of different transactional needs—from buying equipment to alumni fund-
raising. So, mastering the needed range of transactions is no simple matter. Gould is also accomplished at transacting in a myriad
of different environments too, but he's an absolute natural for
the one where he has earned his bread and butter. Most powerful
people preside over a particular niche as their mainstay too.

Today, power is paradoxically at odds with the instinct to control. Those driven by control want to hammer the world so that it
will come to them down the fewest, straightest, narrowest avenues
possible. Power seizes the moment while control freaks would
rather run the schedule of events. Control is an obsession that was
typified in powerful people of the past. A good number of powerful people revert to a control mentality and lose power because of
it. They will invest enormous time and energy in a quest for total
control. When circumstances change, as they must, these people
are thrown off balance. Frustrated, they permit the world around
them to grow smaller and smaller, or they choose another world.
(The fallen Lucifer in Milton's *Paradise Lost* is a fine example:
"Better to reign in hell than serve in heav'n.") In a world that
rewards adaptability, controlling persons demonstrate how their
own flexibility has become calcified. They become less relevant to
the flow of events. A degree of control helps people gain and use
power. (Focus and discipline are impossible without it.) However,
an obsession with control nearly guarantees that a person *won't*
be really powerful. Control hampers the ability to listen and
observe; power is best learned observing individual transactions.
One learns about power from religious leaders, sports marketers,
motion picture directors, senior executives, physicians, financial
analysts, management recruiters, and a host of others and absorbs
the most constructive information about power by watching these
individuals transact outside of their tightly defined disciplines.[1]

We are rightly far more interested in how the Pope transacts

---

1. Generally, what constitutes power *within* a discipline quickly degenerates into
"politics" in the worst sense of the word and has little to do with sophisticated power
tactics.

business with Boris Yeltsin, spokespersons for the poor, or Jewish leaders than in what John Paul does with the College of Cardinals—even though the transactions with the College may be crucial to keeping the Pope's religious agenda on track. Returning to the Jack Gould example, dealing with a faculty laden with Nobel Prize winners is *not* at all like handling an audience of insiders, sworn to the same military, religious, or commercial mission. They are semi-independent, if not highly independent, and behave that way, while life in a large company is fundamentally an *inside* world. Public controversy is unwelcome and punished if detected, often severely. Internal differences are shrouded in politics, not true contests of power. The interesting transactions to watch are those that pit the CEO with forces outside of his or her constituency. If a Fortune 500 CEO is a financier by background, we want to know how he or she manages the marketers inside the company—not how the CEO manages the finance department. More importantly, we want to understand the CEO's dealings with vendors, unions, regulators, financial analysts, environmentalists, and the press. The CEO's struggles within the officer group may require energy and cunning, but these are really the province of keeping what is ostensibly one's own team aligned, and that is politics, not power.[2] Again, each of the various relationships that brings the top team (the powerful) into meaningful contact with others is essentially a series of transactions.

To see the world transactionally is by no means easy. One must have a liberating sense of objectivity to address events in a transactional way. The powerful always have the capacity to appreciate an issue's full scope and then to climb above it no matter how good or bad it may seem. Fortunately, they always seem to find the staircase that leads upward—a survival skill itself since, as crisis management expert Heinz Goldmann warns, it's very important not to be hypnotized by an event or an issue.

---

2. As has already been pointed out, the once cozily "interior" relationship between the CEO and the board can today turn hotly adversarial in a flash. The board is no longer a dependable part of the CEO's power structure, while the management team *is*, by definition, the CEO's power structure.

Approaches to power are also now more specialized, and this too makes power's use more transactional. Scientific power and power in society remain very much alike in certain patterns. Both, for example, are now as fragmented as shattered stemware in their scope. What if someone asked, Who is the greatest living scientist? Four hundred years ago, one could have confidently answered Galileo—especially if one lived in Italy or resided in the major courts of Europe, these being the real repository of active scientific knowledge then. Even forty years ago, one figure towered above all others. Albert Einstein was nearly everybody's idea of a great scientist—he was *the* "global brand" in science. I recently asked a group of scholars over dinner at the Cosmos Club in Washington who the greatest scientist of the last decade is. I got answers like "Well, there was the late *Andrei Sakharov* in nuclear physics ... but, of course, there's *Arno Penzias* in astrophysics ... and, you can't forget *Stephen Hawking* in theoretical physics." Just as no one expert dominates the sciences, let alone physics, no single Nick or Nora Machiavelli is (or could be) the dean of power these days nor will there be one in the future.

An important distinction must be made between transactional power and the conclusion that transactional simply means situational. Situational implies a passive, reactive character that is not a property of power, while transactional suggests intent and planning. Although they can shift with dashing velocity, transactions can be prepared for in advance. In contrast, people are *thrown* into situations. At an annual meeting, CEOs of large companies will drill themselves exhaustively on how to deal with questions about severed employees, angered minorities, hair-splitting analysts, investigative journalists, and mischievous agitators. Peers will grade a CEO on how well the answer is fine-tuned to the questioner. Transactions facing the powerful can revolve around the most seemingly trivial things, but their importance should only be gauged as to how behavior in the transaction is likely to be interpreted. During the 1992 campaign, when George Bush walked into a supermarket demonstration and marveled at the technology of a checkout scanner as if it were today's news, he committed a major and avoidable tactical blunder. The seemingly innocent aside was taken by many as shocking proof that Bush had lost touch with the everyday lives of Americans; he had not had an experience as fundamental as going to the grocery store in a nation where 67 percent of the items are read by optical checkout scanners. If George Bush didn't know beans about the modern supermarket, his staff *should have* anticipated the potential public impact of the *shopping demonstration transaction* well enough to know what he didn't know about the experience and to have briefed him on it in advance. However, if a senior manager is sitting on the dais of a management conference and a reporter strides in, tells her and the audience that the company's biggest plant has just blown up and asks why it happened, all the manager on the hotseat can do is say that she is anguished to hear this, that she must excuse herself from the meeting to confirm exactly what has happened, and that the company will get back to the press with further information as soon as it becomes available. That is a situation, not a transaction, and such a response is the only possible one.

Still, transactions are not always so planned that they appear on the calendar. When the president goes out for his jog on any given morning, he had better be prepared to field any question on the national agenda from a demonstrator he may encounter on the gravel path. Nor is it always the business of one's own country or one's own business. The power lexicon can change dramatically depending on culture, audience, historical events, and countless other factors. Exercising power effectively relies on the ability to detect context and to shift smoothly among the demands of different contexts. Modern power is increasingly "cross-cultural," requiring leaders to exert power upon others in different subgroups or organizations and within other nations and societies.

Continuity Must Underpin Transactions

The transactional nature of modern power can easily chop a leader's identity into a schizophrenic hash. An individual must balance transactional skill with a continuous identity, that is, he or she must be both adaptable and constant at the same time. Because organizations are so fluid, they and the roles and positions that comprise them are much less effective in giving a powerful person (or any person) a continuous sense of identity. At one time, and for a span of decades, the president of a steel company division (and all his predecessors captured in the oil paintings along the boardroom gallery) just worried about raw materials, production costs, and the union. Today, a person in that same job will have all these basic concerns, but is also likely to be darting in and out of environmental issues, involved in revamping the inventory computer systems, serving on a task force on foreign competition, and drafting a policy on day-care centers. And, that just within her or his own organization! The individual must compensate and provide the continuity of power once endowed by the organization. That means defining a clear personal identity and standing for certain distinct values, even if those values end up limiting the powerful person's appeal to broader audiences.

A modern figure who mastered the transaction but didn't offer enough personal continuity was former Soviet leader Mikhail Gorbachev. In office, Gorbachev communicated brilliantly and persuasively. His very smoothness, however, may have worked against him and made his ouster easier. It's even questionable if what happened to Gorbachev, some experts contend, could be called a coup since the entire Communist establishment lined up against him. Gorbachev's possibilities, by his own definition, were confined to what could be done within the existing system, and he attempted to work without a popular mandate. People did not know where he stood. The nightly news broadcasts outside of the Soviet Union after *glasnost* and before the coup would constantly carry paradoxical reports of Western leaders singing Gorbachev's praises while the people on the street were railing against the misery of Gorbachev's economic reforms. There was no continuity. Worst of all, such a continuity was probably within his reach. His opting out of direct presidential elections in 1990 was a serious error in judgment. Gorbachev also seemed too opaque in his philosophy. He let his words and plans be subject to too many interpretations: "The optimists thought that Mr. Gorbachev secretly wanted to turn his country into a democracy with a mixed economy, a vast new Sweden." Instead, according to a review of Russian expert Marshall Goldman's analysis of the failure of *perestroika,* "here was a man who sought to make the Soviet system more efficient, not to change it fundamentally." Because he didn't want to change it, Gorbachev spent too much time avoiding confrontation with the system. Yeltsin's people were already planning what to do after a pitched battle with the system was joined.[3] Gorbachev sank in the enormous task of trying to communicate with the needs of all Soviets and neglected the significance of the domestic Russian power base.

Curiously, this same lack of continuity on the home front later plagued Gorbachev's American counterpart, George Bush. In 1992, George Bush tried every possible tactic to adjust to changing contexts, but one must be very careful not to become mesmerized by the transactional nature of power itself. Bush seems to have made that mistake and it proved to be his undoing. Paul Gigot in the *Wall Street Journal* pinpointed a flaw in George Bush's management style: "Because he sends out no clear signals, everyone believes everything with Mr. Bush is negotiable. He is paralyzed by his own pragmatism." And, indeed, in the end, that pragmatism overwhelmed him.

There is another important caution to bear in mind while working in this challenging transactional reality. While the style of address can change and the emphasis of the message can differ, one cannot bob in and out of power transactions, appearing more superficial in one forum than another. Even though the angles and the questions may differ, the same level of toughness in interrogation and careful interpretation of answers should be expected when confronting the press, special interests, the financial com-

---

3. In contrast to Gorbachev, Yeltsin is brash, as in showing up at the G-7 summit in Munich in July 1992, after being only semi-invited. Gorbachev reminds one of Metternich or Kissinger. Yeltsin brings to mind the late Chicago mayor Richard Daley, Sr.

munity, industry observers, and any other critical audience. The more visible you are, the harder it is to appear consistent. The greater the number of topics you speak on and the more different audiences to whom you speak, the more your enemies and the media challenge the consistency of your messages. No business leader in Denmark today can address security analysts in Buffalo, New York, about the virtues of low-cost production in the United States without those claims being heard as a threat to job security back in Ålborg Copenhagen early the next morning, if not sooner. The vicious circle can often end disastrously as the powerful, in trying to combat inconsistency, display a growing obsession to appear consistent rather than effective in their transactions with different publics. Or the opposite can occur: Dismissing the importance of consistency, one may seem so blatantly contradictory that one is dismissed as disingenuous or as a bald-faced liar.

What is the defense? A defined personal identity, constant and clear values, and the realistic application of vision can help give a powerful person the needed sense of continuity in a highly transactional world. While we will learn more about vision in a moment and values later on, the reader is warned again that power is no easy matter in a very competitive world that can topple experienced and formidable talents in the dimension of Mikhail Gorbachev and George Bush.

Putting Vision in Its Place

Focus is the intensity and clarity of your leadership stare, while vision is what you choose to stare at. If focus is a fundamental of power, vision is its mechanistic counterpart. Powerful leaders require a sense of vision, but virtual libraries of misinformation about vision have been penned in recent years. Writing visions is not the primary skill; visions are much easier to articulate than to apply. Vision statements have become the rap songs of organizational America, and that is perhaps why so many organizations suffer from an appalling sameness both in statements *and* in visions. The powerful must know how to work with vision as a sculptor must be able to mold clay or chisel stone. A vision is not an idea; it is an idea transformed into a work, a work that is also constantly evolving. While a good number of people in powerful positions can articulate a clear vision, far fewer can find and crystallize an organization's or a movement's purpose in events. The ones who *can* generally have the highest standings in the leagues of the powerful.

As our experience with vision in the business world widens, it seems that many can articulate the vision of where they want to take themselves or their organization while few can do the harder work of the actual *taking*. The tougher problem, by far, is application of vision. The valuable and unique skill required is a relentless ability to search for and select those few incidents or points in time that illustrate vision and to convert them into forceful behavioral guidelines. Christ's life—as documented in his acts and parables—captures an entire system of morality with symphonic intricacy through a procession of mostly mundane events sprinkled with a few miracles. That is vision at work. Campbell Soup CEO David Johnson mocks the little plasticized vision statements people tote in their pockets. People don't believe or follow through on many of these truisms. James C. Shaffer, a quality expert with Towers Perrin, has studied employee attitudes in auto plants plastered with signs dramatizing a dedication to quality: "They know how far 'Quality is Our First Commitment' is from reality. One worker in an auto plant commented that 'the only signs you can believe around here are 'Pardon Our Appearance' and 'Wet Paint.'" In any case, sharing visions on a simple literary level is not a prime job of the powerful. The powerful have vision and verify and use it to energize everyone else— the people who get things done—to act.

Sam Walton didn't create the nation's biggest retailer by preoccupying his people with vision. Instead, he demanded that each of them identify on a weekly basis a single best-selling item and place their full commitment behind it. Between the competing items, he created a contest for dominance and shaped the retailing mix of what is probably the most successful selling concept in history. The powerful should always ask themselves what the key mechanical linkages are that will convince their constituents that they have vision and that they know what to do with it. For Walton, it was Double Decker Moon Pies and Ol' Roy Dog Food. For A. C. Nielsen, the world's largest marketing information company, it is supplying a superior network of cross-border data and analysis that befits the global economy and that can be manipulated by client users through modern work stations. For the theologian Dietrich Bonhoeffer, it was sacrificing his own life in conspiring to overthrow Hitler. For customers, clients, and congregations, each statement reached out as a tangible declaration of vision realized.

The Illusion of Statesmanship

The actualization of vision demonstrates that power structures insofar as they are meaningful are outwardly oriented. But, the outward projection of vision is tricky. Very few power structures are finely tuned enough to allow power to flow in both directions, that is, not many power structures, especially in business, are capable of being reciprocal. Rather, they are focused on exerting power externally. Generally, they absorb information and input chiefly to exert power better for their own ends. While mediation is becoming an ever larger part of the powerful person's role, it is possible for even the powerful to be seduced and exploited by trying to act as emissaries for an outside force. This happens often with business and government leaders of one nation who, even as they possess considerable intelligence and personal power at home, try to make themselves significant as emissaries of powerful foreign governments and to represent them back to their native country.[4] Despite all the high-priced lobbyists and the exhiliration of dabbling in world affairs, there is very little percentage in being an agent of foreign powers.

---

4. For a further discussion of this topic in political terms, the reader is recommended to Angelo Codevilla's *Informing Statecraft*.

How is this risk connected to the external pursuit of vision? In this very simple way: When looking outward to advance an agenda, one can never assume that these entities are mere neutral audiences or, no matter how weak or limited they may appear, that they are necessarily smaller or more vulnerable. The Japanese MITI certainly peers at the United States in a coordinated way, while United States industry has flailed through the problem of Japanese competitiveness on a futile industry-by-industry basis. Well-focused vision acknowledges these kinds of risk and strives to keep the flow of power transactions within sensible parameters and turns chance into opportunity—striking with the alertness of a skilled warrior.

Is the Pursuit of Power Strategic?

The transactional nature of modern power must be guided by applied vision, but it must also be appraised and interpreted with a fresh perspective. Contrary to the strongest intellectual instincts of recent decades, modern power is becoming antistrategic. Shortly before the attempted coup against Gorbachev, an editor of *Izvetzia* explained modern Soviet politics to me better than anyone else ever had. He said that Soviet politics was more like billiards than chess. In chess, you can plan out strategy in a sequence of moves; in billiards, each cue stroke creates a completely new context. Power everywhere is becoming more like billiards. This is another way of saying that power is in fact more transactional and less strategic. The demise of the Soviet Union has actually contributed to this new power scenario because the world no longer finds itself arrayed into camps of fundamentally balanced and deadlocked military power. The East-West conflict made it easy to think of the world in chessboard terms. Now there are multiple conflicting interests, each played out with differing speed and strength. The Russian editor's comments are amazingly consonant with the Stalk, Evans, and Shulman redefinition of strategy in their article on competition, published in the *Harvard Business Review* in the spring of 1992, in which they say "competition is now a 'war of movement.'. . . Successful competitors move quickly in and out of products, markets, and sometimes even entire businesses—a process more akin to an interactive video game than to chess."

This conversion has changed the role certain global institutions perform. While the World Economic Forum in Davos, Switzerland, which is held each February, remains one of the key gathering sites for the world's powerful, much of the tension that had been caused by the Cold War has come out of the meetings. Davos was an informal summit that brought ideological opponents together to talk beyond the current landscape of the global chessboard. Now power is more split, and economic issues at such gatherings over-power political diplomacy and occupy the space once filled by bloc conflicts. Economic bargaining has replaced political deal-making and ideological diplomacy.

In a world propelled by billiard-ball and video-game dynamics, the locus of power also shifts, often quickly, to unexpected places. Hazarding a guess on the distribution of power in the new federal government in 1993 America, one can expect that the Supreme Court is going to play a far more politically active role. Most of the controversy surrounding the Court in the last fifteen years has centered on the appointments of justices. Of all the issues that one associates with the Supreme Court, in the last decade, abortion has been the most visible, and the Court's decisions have pleased neither side. As the third branch of government, the Court was not inclined to intervene as a force between the legislative and the executive branches. Instead, the Court exerted power in the contest between the states and the federal government, particularly over abortion. That was where controversies arose. With President Clinton now enjoying the power of a Congressional majority, it is likely that the Court will refocus its attention back on the federal government—playing Constitutional watchdog as it did during the early Franklin Roosevelt years. One would hope that the members of the Court will vote their conscience and knowledge. But, the Court has also been known to echo public opinion. No court justice sits in isolation writing opinions, and the new distribution of balls on the table will provoke the Court to a new role.

In this transactional world of power, skillfully reading the true position of balls on the billiard table requires insight. To trace the changing pattern of power, new attitudes toward old disputes are one revealing source. Public attitudes toward celebrations, to cite a less expected source, are another. North America's 1992 Columbus Day events really shed perspective on the matter. The outdated, primarily male and European model of the celebration of conquest and conquerors was repudiated by native North Americans. The association with Columbus even hurt the attendance at the Pope's mass in Santo Domingo. (For some, the Pope just became another European invader, even though he preached a mission of aiding the poor.) Gauging the array of forces and the present trend, I seriously doubt that a big bash will be slated in 1998 to celebrate the five-hundred-year anniversary of Portuguese navigator Vasco da Gama's landing on the coast of India.

Instead of thoughtful and somewhat predictable strategy, the powerful are required to have the agile, elastic, and meteoric tactics that suits the world of transactional power. On this glimmering, ever-changing battlefield of power, a new primacy is placed on perception and expectation, because whether your power is growing or waning is solely determined by the last scattering of the orbs on the felt.

The Wizard Fallacy and the Awe Factor

The transactional nature of power makes *how* one is perceived especially important. As I have written elsewhere, people whose power is perceived as growing attract followers, authority, and advancement. People perceived as losing power are avoided, ignored, and find their ideas dismissed. This spiral is predictable for a world working with relative and not absolute norms and sniffing for weakness constantly. The rule of thumb should be no surprise: *Having your power underestimated is generally an advantage, while it can be very dangerous to be credited with more power than you actually have.*

How does this danger of being overestimated reveal itself and why is it such a threat? It stems from the search for villains, because *the general public doesn't believe the powerful seek out a proper level of accountability for their actions and their charters.* And the investigative media, special interests, and natural adversaries methodically work their way down the list of potential villains until one is found with deep pockets or a big ego or both. Then the spears start to land. Even though the present feelings of value and importance are gratifying, one day the forces of public opinion will demand to know why you weren't using all the power you allowed people to believe you possessed. I call it the Wizard Fallacy recalling, of course, the *Wizard of Oz.*

It is not the weak who succumb to the Wizard Fallacy. Generally, it is the powerful who don't object to being seen as stronger than they really are. The problem can be combated— mostly through the realistic education of opinion leaders and rigorous humility, but this is tough medicine to administer to oneself. One professional group that has truly suffered from this kind of image problem is auditors and accountants. As a result, auditors today are dealing with an enormous loss of power. A decade ago, the only publicity accounting firms received came on Oscar night when they marched on stage with the sealed letters holding the names of the award winners. Today, members of accounting firms are out publishing articles and making speeches to develop new business. They take positions, and they become targets of controversy. While the auditors have increased their exposure, the "eyes" of the public have increased their penetration. Similarly, few business reporters could even read an annual report twenty years ago. Now, some are specialized in doing nothing but that. Combine a rash of bankruptcies and business failures with inexplicable losses, and, today, everyone asks "Where were the auditors?!" As a friend of mine in the profession puts it, there is now an enormous expectation gap between what auditors are thought to be able to do and what they actually do.

In many ways, public respect for and confidence in the profession's judgment has been lost. Today, auditors are the "fall guys" in every business scandal and bank failure that comes around the corner. Professional liability insurance for many of them has tripled in the past five years. Forensic accounting, trying to put a tail on the poor performers in the profession, is now a growth industry. Plaintiffs are digging into the pockets of once deep-pocketed audit mammoths. One auditing giant, Laventhol & Horwath, has collapsed. The Big Eight have consolidated rapidly to the Big Six. Much of this was a direct consequence of audit firms suggesting that they could be bigger than they were. For example, they sold consulting services to clients and then contended that "Chinese walls" between the audit and consulting practices could protect adequately against conflicts of interest. The unwillingness to align expectations with reality also resulted from a greed for huge fees in the era of major takeovers and of fear, as the takeovers shrunk the number of large audit clients available.

While most Wizards often end up with self-inflicted injuries, circumstances and foes can also be a factor. Adversaries can inflate the power of those they want to portray as massive and ruthless conspirators. Two years ago a Washington lobbying firm awoke one day to find itself credited for things they didn't cause to happen, including the demonstration of a million people on the Mall against a cause they had been hired to oppose. By creating a fantastic Loch Ness monster, *their* opposition was whipping up an aura of power that didn't exist, portraying what was a grassroots groundswell as an orchestrated, lavishly funded campaign. In fact, the link between the rally and the lobbying group was simply fabricated to galvanize and inspire the opposition, and to a discernible degree it worked. The powerful also use the Wizard Fallacy as a tactic to expose a rival who deliberately avoids issues. In the spirit of democracy, defending the right to be heard and appearing to support rather than undercut the foe, they will say: "Let's hear what my distinguished colleague has to say about this topic." Of course, this is the last thing in the world upon which the colleague wants to comment knowing that the position is doomed to be unpopular and his or her silence to date has appeared to put him or her above or at least beyond the range of the issue.

When the Wizard Fallacy is the illness, humility, as said earlier, is the only cure. Only time will tell, but a new leadership at IBM, Westinghouse, General Motors, and a dozen other organizations will be tested for its ability to come back. I contend that the answer for each of these companies lies in the findings, and not in some hocus-pocus theory that might be advanced as a silver bullet.

I call the diametric opposite of the Wizard Fallacy the Awe Factor. If, as Edward Bernays contended, public relations and promotion crafted "large pedestals for small statues," the Awe Factor, conversely, is a giant of a statue striding atop a small pedestal. The Awe Factor is an organizational and individual extension of what marketing guru Philip Kotler deems the Delight Factor, by which Kotler means products that significantly exceed customer expectations. For the general public the formulation is somewhat different in the realm of power. The Awe Factor is the ability to give surprisingly strong performance at the time one is severely tested, and to do so time and again, often demonstrating new reservoirs of strength or talent. Never exaggerating his ego, solemnly reciting his duty, and generally dismissing himself with self-effacing modesty and humor, Abraham Lincoln's behavior epitomized the Awe Factor. In business, Warren Buffett's healing of Salomon Brothers has been in a kindred style. But, one should not interpret the modesty of great leaders too solemnly. There is a theatrical element that comes into play in successfully evoking the Awe Factor, too: The Awe Factor, resulting when powerful persons prove themselves to be even stronger than suspected, surely must *seem* instinctive, even when it is not, to prove effective. It also creates a wonderful defensive shield making adversaries reluctant to attack—unsure of what new strength they might call out of reserve and have to confront. But, a tone of humility must be ever-present. Without Clark Kent, would the Superman fable be nearly as compelling?

The Delight and Awe Factors can converge in the power of products. In 1992, the TV news program "60 Minutes" did an exposé comparing safety systems in cars to the types of car accidents that resulted in the most serious personal injuries. For all the talk about air bags and the solidity of the passenger cabin, the key hazard that most automakers (and regulators) were ignoring was rear-end collisions, which force an occupant backward on impact as the seat collapses. In the story, Mercedes-Benz was the shining hero. Their cars held up remarkably under this kind of test. Mercedes did not go out of the way to publicize that performance, which is a classic case of power derived from competence. That is not all, however; Mercedes shares its safety technology principles with other manufacturers *without charge* in the spirit of getting things done about auto safety. For a hard-fisted corporate giant to have such a powerful competitive advantage and to be willing to give it away certainly epitomizes the Awe Factor.

Sometimes, when trying to turn around a sagging business, the Awe Factor can be stashed away as a hidden reserve and then utilized to boost the impact when the company's fortunes turn upward. When French carmaker Renault recently staged a seemingly dramatic comeback in its performance and advanced its market shares in other European countries, the turnaround was astutely explained by Crédit Suisse First Boston auto analyst Dagmar Bottenbruch: "The company was never as bad as some people suggested." Worse than a tactical ploy, the Awe Factor also can be pretense. There are business and political leaders and scholars who distribute their intellectual capital in such a measured and languid way that one can only believe they are acting in the spirit of hyper-understatement. That kind of manipulation, though, can turn awe into suspicion overnight.

The Wizard Fallacy and the Awe Factor, it should be remembered, only mark the extreme poles on a scale that measures the expectations of power. Some of the readings can be manipulated, to be sure, but the real advice worth remembering is to shun wizardry and to build awe.

Dialogue as Power's Factory

Anchoring transactions in an active, tangible vision gives power continuity. Recognizing that expectations determine how power is

accepted helps the powerful manage transactions with more even-
ness and realism. But, if ideas are the foundations of power, what
permits those ideas themselves to grow? What mechanism actually fosters the ideas that become power? No activity is more
important to that end than *dialogue*. The power of Michael
Porter's proximate companies, the conferences of the CEO
Roundtable, the concentration of high-tech businesses in Silicon
Valley, the meetings of the National Security Council, the annual
outings at Bohemian Grove, the breakout sessions of the World
AIDS Congresses, and General Electric's Work Out idea-
exchange brainstorms all operate through and exist to enable one
thing above all else: dialogue. Dialogue is essential to authentic
power and to the effectiveness with which things get done. The
dialogue need not even be official or direct. Sheer proximity can
make it inevitable, as it is with the colony of gene splicers on
Route 128 outside of Boston or the guild of ad agencies on
Madison Avenue, who are constantly sharing ideas and fertilizing
one anothers' minds despite entrenched rivalries and fierce competition.

Dialogue is wedded to power ... and to taking its measure.
Dialogue flourished on the *agora* of ancient Athens. It made
Florence both the intellectual and mercantile capital of the
Renaissance. In our time, dialogue distinguishes New York even
more than its status as a financial center. Not just national talk but
global talk has been anchored in New York City ever since the
United Nations graced First Avenue. More than any other place,
New York is where the most powerful CEOs meet the financial community; where ascending social reformers find their theories
debated; where peacemakers bargain the terms and boundaries of
truces worldwide; where new artistic ideas are exposed and probed;
and where *everybody* meets the press. Gotham's Temples of Talk—
the Algonquin, the Four Seasons, the Brook, and the Oak Room of
the Plaza—are still dominated by major-league raconteurs from the
cultural, business, and political elite. In an era of faxes and modems,
video conferences, and videophones, why do they continue to con-
gregate in centers such as New York? Because *direct dialogue*

extracts valuable, irreplaceable information, especially about trust.

New York, in this first aspect of dialogue, that of taking measure, is an ongoing gladiatorial arena testing the mettle of power. In the coffee shops and meeting rooms of the Waldorf Astoria, trade association leaders and financial advisers fathom the trustworthiness of power nearly daily. At 71 Broadway, at the home of the Security Analysts Society, or at the rating agencies on Broadway or Church Street, CEOs are being hammerlocked and pinioned by the toughest, most relentless, and most irreverent minds around. Here, trust is being tested. In the seminar rooms of Columbia, in the foyers of the Metropolitan Club, and in an expansive array of other places, dialogue is used just as much to create trust.

The media have recognized the power of such dialogue and attempted to capture it, but outside of programs like the "MacNeil-Lehrer NewsHour" and "Firing Line," the effort has rarely succeeded. Television—and, above all, the talk show—has been poison to dialogue and to the art of conversation. Seventy years ago, Somerset Maugham wrote: "Conversation wants leisure." And, leisure is something that television, especially commercial television, doesn't have. Too often, dialogue is hacked to seven cuecarded minutes: no wandering, no digressions, no exploration—just two simple points, a saucy anecdote, and a dash of human interest. Talk-show dialogue is not conversation, it is staged performance, and it often aborts more ideas than it feeds.

If a powerful person wants to hone his or her dialogue skills, it is best done on the playing field of direct contact. Words are only part of the exchange. Expressions and gestures also disclose trust or expose deceit. The nonverbal element is of vast importance in cross-cultural dialogue. I've seen recent encounters between European and American top executives where the Europeans carried the day because they had mastered the art of something so seemingly trivial as the gesture of the raised eyebrow. Rather than making us more homogeneous, a global world demands a broader repertory of communication. Direct encounter is the only way to broaden that skill base.

If the need for time and reflection is an element in the first aspect of dialogue, the gauging of trust (which is, after all, verifying ideas about people), it is equally essential to the second, the evolution of ideas about things. Perhaps the best laboratory to examine how the power of ideas evolves through dialogue is the world of fashion. First, perhaps, because it is so unexpected a source. Second, fashion, taste, and power have always been interlaced. When Raisa Gorbachev donned her first designer gown for a public event, it did as much to bring down communism as when her husband quit the Party. Fashion also exposes critical information about how a society views timing and risk—critical data for the powerful to have.

Changes in the process of fashion are particularly revealing. In the seventies and eighties, for example, the direction of fashion development reversed itself so that more ideas from the barrio and Cockney flea market influenced what happened on Rodeo Drive and Saville Street than vice versa. This corresponds directly to the growing political and economic influence of social subgroups versus establishment citadels. In the summer of 1992, the fashion house Chanel advanced its *pret-â-porter* fashion shows a month earlier both in the spring and the fall. This put the ready-to-wear fashion unveilings a month closer to the couture shows. Pierre Berge at Yves Saint Laurent lamented that such acceleration could cause designers to lose "their souls." Accelerating the tempo of business, some feared, would make designers churn their products out faster and less thoughtfully. They also felt that the manufacturing pace of just-in-time inventory was coming to the world of fashion ideas, and that the dialogue (innovation) was being abandoned to the logistical flow (productivity).

The principles of how fashion really works are remarkably sophisticated, and I never truly understood them until Stanley Marcus, cofounder of Neiman-Marcus, explained them to me. Marcus argues against the preconception that taste in fashion is the work of some willful designer imposing an arbitrary idea on an eager and obedient public, perhaps with the help of critic and media accomplices. Marcus explains that "customers are the underestimated force in the development of genuine fashion. The great designers were essentially listening to women with sophisticated tastes." Marcus carefully emphasized the word *listening*. Rather than a stream of inspiration and bravura, the power of taste has actually been a dialogue . . . and, today's instant communication can place that dialogue at risk. "Fashion is communicated so much faster these days," Marcus believes, "that it actually kills many new trends before they become full-born." Gestation was once a vital part of the process. "A smart customer in Rome may have conceived an idea," he recounts. "Several months later, her counterpart in Rio would devise a way to simplify it. That's how the enduring fashion historically matured."

Instead of a continuous dialogue, even eminent fashion designers try to accelerate the process of development while playing it safe. The fashion community is mirroring the behavior of other taste-makers. According to Marcus, "fashion designers today are taking fewer risks. It's a parallel to Broadway where producers are taking fewer chances, too, and relying on more revivals. Politicians, also, tend to govern by the polls. They reduce their risks of being wrong—as well as being right." And Marcus knows about encouraging risk. He, for example, was active in prodding the late Emilio Pucci to move from sportswear to an entire line of designer clothes, because he sensed the relevance of Pucci's message.

We think of high fashion and art as the trappings of power. In truth, it is far more important for a powerful person to understand how fashion works than to own it. Just as it is much more useful to fathom how contemporary art works than to possess it. Trappings were once an essential mechanism of power because they set expectations. Today, the transaction sets the expectations and the powerful must conform.

In preparing for transactions, dialogue is the idea factory of power. The powerful both value dialogue and build their ideas in stages. As Kenneth Clark said about the Renaissance mogul Lorenzo de Medici: "He was a politician of genius who could distinguish between the reality of power and its outward trappings."

Medici was a poet, too, but not a clotheshorse like Louis XIV. The frontispiece to his book of poems shows him "in the streets of Florence, dressed as a simple citizen." Lorenzo's image had nothing to do with his knowledge level: He was a tastemaker and lavish benefactor of the arts. But, Lorenzo's ability to peel away trappings from the essence of power not only enabled him to anticipate and manage expectations better, it also distinguishes him as an early and highly successful exponent of the Awe Factor.

THE MECHANISM

Power is transactional: It defies systemization, but there is a remarkable similarity to the management and communications apparatus needed to exercise power in different contexts. Also, successful power transactions must be anchored in an identity that is continuous and not simply a collection of random "feats." The power dynamics that function for groups are essentially those that work for individuals—anchoring transactions in an active vision, managing transactions versus expectations, and fostering trust and ideas through dialogue.

3

The Mastery of Power

Beyond Ever-Pending Disaster

The way you keep score determines how you play the game.

—JOHN C. BURTON,
FORMER SEC
CHIEF ACCOUNTANT

Is exerting power intuitive or scientific? Is power a function of intelligence, instinct, or a combination of these or other traits?

The French may be passionate and emotional about the bouquet of a bordeaux and many of the other fine things in life, but they are analytical in their regard for power. The power fraternity of French society, the alumni of the Inspection Générale de Finance, holds two things in common: 1) graduation from the *Ecole Nationale d'Administration* (the best school in France and the training ground for its foremost civil servants), and 2) a tour of duty roving around France as paladins, asking embarrassingly tough questions about how taxpayer money is spent and/or wasted. With so much of French industry still nationalized and with the fluid crossover between political and industrial careers commonplace, it is no surprise that the *inspecteurs* determine the power style of France and that this style is rigorously quantitative and cerebral.

The British are absolutely the opposite. With the Cambridge and Oxford traditions still flourishing, the British groom their future leaders from their earliest years in mastering the fine art of getting along with one another. Brash perhaps in Parliament (theatrical is a truer reading), gentility remains a British behavioral cornerstone, and keen intuition about how to exert power obliquely and how to read people are second nature to the English.

These are stereotypes, surely, but they also capture national strengths and national weaknesses. The powerful in both societies know these weaknesses. So, it is hardly amazing that, when faced with a referendum, an election, a new product introduction, or a fund-raising problem, it is the *British* and not the French who have really been standard setters in quantitative analysis techniques. The *French*, on the other hand, who already have such a refined, almost innate grasp of numbers, pose instead broad, conceptual inquiries to get at the emotional heart of an issue. Their skills may be Cartesian, but they know that the missing ingredient is motivationally emotional.

The contrast and comparison between these two approaches may sound like the image of right and left brain hemispheres projected on an international scale, but it also creates a paradigm for the modern mastery of power. That mastery demands a synergy of the intuitive and quantitative (or scientific) approaches to power. Perhaps the nation that is furthest ahead in realizing such synergy is Japan. The Japanese culture blends the most elusive strokes of silkscreen painting with the world's most rigorous approach to quality control. Not only do the Japanese understand two-hemisphere brain power well, they also have decentralized its working to the broad base of Japanese productive society. In an homage to the Japanese achievement, Ferdinand Piëch, the head of Volkswagen, said in *Die Welt* shortly before advancing to that company's top job, "I believe that the Germans and Japanese are not at odds over the concept of quality. They just have different habits [or customs]. In Germany, one [worker] does the work and a second comments on what he finds wrong with it. If we could bring together both these positions into a single person, we could catch up to the Japanese. Possibly, the Asians could be characterized as being more sensitive, while we're more technical." In Piëch's mind and in mine, too, *that* synthesis *is* the power differential: integrating intuitive competence and conscious, critical analysis. The brilliance of Piëch's dissection is that he suggests the macro problem of competition should be solved projected upward from the assembly line and not mandated downward from the boardroom.

In the foreseeable future, those wanting to exert power will have to operate in a turbulent, chaotic environment and this kind of environment favors the dual thrust of intuition and analysis. In fact, since the upheavals beginning in the sixties, the corpus of successful power advice in democratic societies has fallen into two categories: 1) highly *quantitative* power principles—research- and statistics-driven—which form the foundation of modern marketing, and 2) equally *subjective* power approaches—which seem to rely on personal intuition and innate flair. They coincide with major breakthroughs in political campaigning and marketing, and fresh approaches to governance and organizational design. In the exercise of power, the Reagan presidency married exhaustive research with Reagan's own exceptional natural knack for acting presidential. In the use of power, the Reagan presidency was a breakthrough, but certainly no endpoint. Power will evidence itself in the future differently than in the past, especially as it's shaped by technology, information, global changes, and new organization structures. And, this will put new weight on the numerically rigorous aspects of power. It will also motivate the powerful to try to balance against this quantitative bias with intuitive flashes (and, alas, some quick fixes, too).

Since the quantitative side is more the learned skill, many assume that it is straightforward and easily learned. My experience with the powerful is that they know the essentials of both analysis and intuition, but they don't always grasp the pitfalls and the risks, especially of analysis. Beginning with that analytical side, modern history seems to say that opinion determines power. The

challenge is how to determine opinion. That is much harder than
it may seem, despite all the data processing advances and sophisticated mathematical models of the last decades. From having the
right benchmark research to amassing enough information to
define a reliable context, it is going to become increasingly difficult to get the necessary information with which to exercise
power.

Dangers of Flawed Analysis

Public opinion is a crucial agent in exercising power because it
provides enabling support and overcomes disabling opposition.
We speak of opinion leaders, but how exactly is opinion led? Like
a snake chasing its tale, opinion more and more seems *to be led by
being followed.* Commentator Robert MacNeil says: "Generally
politicians have converted leadership into followership. Using
sophisticated opinion surveying, they anticipate public attitudes
and are not leading people. Through surveying they can select the
button more accurately and get the bell to ring more quickly. "
Elizabeth Dole, one active voice in Washington, seems to agree
that such a risk exists and must be answered: "In dealing with the
important issues, we must practice leadership and not followership, letting the public opinion polls dictate what we do." A concern for public opinion is fundamentally a concern about choice:
What will people choose to want, to like, to do? No thinker did a
better job of explaining power in terms of public opinion than
Walter Lippmann. But Lippmann saw the limitations in the pub-
lic-opinion model of power as much as he understood the force of
public opinion. (Lippmann didn't dispute the vast influence that
public opinion has. He *did* argue with its effectiveness in keeping
a democracy properly guided. Public opinion, as Lippmann
described it, is projected as a "mystical force" taking "up the
slack in public institutions" and becoming a court "open day and
night.") Public opinion can only be a component of power. No
matter how sophisticated public opinion measurement becomes,
mastering public opinion is essentially a reactive discipline, while

insightful intuition is a leading one. We are finding that it is much easier to misuse seemingly overpowering, irrefutable analytical information than even the best trained minds may think. One of the biggest handicaps of a purely research-driven approach to power is the possibility of misinterpreting the research itself.

Averages, for example, are an enormous analytical problem. We've all heard of the statistician who drowned in a lake with an average depth of three inches. A look at quantitative data on Indonesia may provide a useful model for the typical problem. Indonesia is a very diffuse and somewhat exotic nation in many people's minds—a remote archipelago strung out in the South Pacific. Outside of respect for its oil reserves, the prevailing attitude toward Indonesia among global commerce has been to ignore it. After all, per capita GNP in Indonesia is below six hundred dollars a year, which causes not a few consumer-products manufacturers to dismiss Indonesia as a nonstarter for mass-market products. However, the global giant Unilever, as *The Economist* points out, takes parts of Indonesia seriously. The average GNP for the 14 million residents of Jakarta (a city that alone has more than three times the population of Ireland) is two thousand dollars—which is quite respectable in world terms. Another way to look at Indonesia is defining *who* has the wealth. *The Economist* also points out that the majority of the twenty-five largest business organizations in Indonesia are controlled by the Chinese of Indonesia. A third way to examine Indonesia is to study its religious profile: Indonesia, many are surprised to learn, is the largest Moslem nation in the world. In many respects, Indonesian power is uninteresting. In other respects it is quite compelling. Here is a society of nearly 200 million people (making it bigger than the Russian Republic), 88 percent of whom are Moslem, whose wealth is substantially controlled by expatriate Chinese, and whose cultural and political hub is by no means poor. The raw numbers about Indonesia—especially the gross averages—unveil next to nothing. The closer look reveals the richest ethnic group, the one you would approach if you were to enter Indonesia looking for investment capital, the best market for targeting consumer products, and the dominant cultural norms to be respected if you did business throughout Indonesia. These specifics can themselves be more sharply defined again and again.

Seeing the important statistical distortions for a population group can represent enormous influence and commercial opportunities. In the sale of something so mundane as razor blades, cultures generally go through evolutionary stages of development: first carbon blades, then stainless blades, and finally double-edged cartridges. Not in all of India. Gillette CEO Alfred Zeien explained the reasoning to *Forbes*: "Within India . . . 10 percent of the population has an income level above the average income in France. Those [affluent] people do not have to go through the carbon or stainless [blades] stage, and we are selling them a twin cartridge in India." In metropolitan areas, Gillette has 17 percent of the market. In fact, bygone intuition may have once understood India better than modern statistical averaging. Winston Churchill once said that India was no more a unified country than the equator was. It is hard to project the mainstream from images of the middle. This is what caused us to overestimate Soviet potential for so long. The gap between the knowledge level of Russian science and medicine and the rest of its economy is vast. Its space program and nuclear submarines may be guided by plasma-generation computers, but in the shops and schools where computers are commonplace in the West, Russia remains a nation of abacuses.

Averages are a formidable data problem. Lost tribes are another. Along with Indonesia and India, China has its Eastern mysteries, too, and perhaps the most bewitching of them is the *China* outside of *China*. There are 34 million ethnic Chinese living overseas (excluding the 21 million in Hong Kong and Taiwan). These people are, as a group, an intellectual and economic elite compared to the population of Mainland China. These 34 million may seem like a tiny fragment compared to the 1.2 billion inhabitants of the Chinese mainland. However, in 1992, *The Economist* published these study findings: The Chinese in Indonesia, while only "4 percent of the population, controlled 17 of the 25 biggest business groups," and, in the Philippines, "fewer than 1 percent of the people . . . are pure Chinese, but Chinese-owned companies account for two-thirds of the sales of the 67 biggest commercial outfits." The article goes on to say that, if you include Taiwan and Hong Kong, the overseas Chinese control between 1.5 trillion and 2.0 trillion dollars in "liquid assets." (In comparison, Japanese "bank deposits" are about $3 trillion.) The overseas Chinese fortunes are dominated by family empires. For example, the *Far Eastern Economic Review* puts the size of the Pao Empire (World International Holdings) at $1.5 billion dollars. Seemingly run by repressive technocrats at home, the underestimated factor in the Chinese economic equation is the diaspora of economic power beyond the country's boundaries, and their reach back into mainland China can be vast because of the importance of the family culture in all things Chinese. One can turn on Super-Channel in the middle of the night in London and other cities in Europe and see broadcasts that last for hours including economic development and investment opportunities in the PRC. Marketing directed at the city or the continental bourses? If so, why is so much of the programming *in Chinese*? These are efforts to woo prodigal money back home.

A very simple but common kind of data problem, is data prepared for the wrong purposes or data that are simply out of date. Not all quantitative information has equal authority even when it's correctly calculated. A number of Western investors misjudged market opportunities in Russia and other former Soviet republics when those markets were first aggressively opened at the end of the last decade, and bad data caused the problem. Economic information was collected in the old Soviet Union as a matter of national security, not to facilitate economic decision-making. Some of the data was very good, but it was focused on calculating military risk or looking at output potential and a number of salient factors were missing. When the game turned from Cold War to market economy, the state data was so unreliably patchy that intelligent decisions could not be made. In this case, unintentional disinformation surely obstructed power. Another very simple, but pervasive analytical trap is old data. Without a sense for the current context in which their audience is viewing and understanding them, a person's power is bound to be diminished before the electronic media. The context changes monthly— sometimes daily. The public's span of attention and recollection continues to erode at a remarkable rate. The Gannett Foundation did a comprehensive study of media coverage following the Gulf War. With the war launched and over by February 1991, the study found that by mid-March people were following the homecoming of troops but that interest in other aspects of the conflict had fallen off decidedly. The Iraqi conflict mobilized national attention on a scale not known since Viet Nam, and look how quickly it subsided. There is just too much competition for storage space in everyone's recall. If George Bush had trouble leaning on his war laurels within weeks of victory, imagine how hard it is for even massive organizations to say, "Remember the good things we did last year." Old data breeds false security. With so much competition for attention coupled with the transactional nature of visibility as well as power, one has to be out on the hustings communicating positive results day after day to secure and sustain a favorable impression. And, skillful updating moves from statistics to psychographic images if you talk to smart editors like John Mack Carter at *Good Housekeeping* or Myrna Blythe at *Ladies' Home Journal*. As the age of their reader advances, they change the norms of the magazine. The powerful must always bear in mind that the target audience of publics they are addressing—and the focus of the media through which they are best reached—is changing all the time.

So far this book has covered problems stemming from incorrectness of data methods. Improving the precision of data management overcomes only one potential flaw in data analysis. Another trap to be reckoned with is imputing a false motive to people's actions. In a democratic society things happen because of assent. People say yes to one brand of oatmeal or another, or one fund-raising drive or another, one religion or another. In each case a transaction involving the surrender of power is taking place.

Tallying the votes is simple, but explaining the why behind them is not. Relatively recent breakthrough research by the Leo Burnett advertising agency has made this fact clear. Simply comparing those who buy versus those who don't (as most marketing research has historically done) is a dangerous simplification. The why behind buying—what exerts power in a particular purchasing situation (ideological as well as commercial)—varies by product category. Projected to the organizational realm, the why behind accepting a certain kind of leadership or authority relies on the situation or the need. Just as ketchup buyers differ from cat food buyers, the world expects (buys) a different use of power to resolve environmental issues from that which is used to handle boardroom disputes. In a sense, this truth was discovered in courtrooms well before it was learned on Madison Avenue. Astronomical litigation settlements and jury justice have led to some of the most exacting motivational probing in modern history. High-priced attorneys spend millions of dollars each year on jury research. In its simplest form, law firms hire researchers to assemble shadow juries that resemble as closely as possible the demographic and psychographic makeup of the actual jury that will hear a case. After selection, the simulated jurors hear different arguments that might be used to advance the case of the lawyer's client. The winning arguments are culled from the losing ones, and the motivations for choosing each are examined. These opinion simulations and the search for the motivations behind them can substantially improve the odds of victory and lead to power over the real jury. This is very simply a game of stimulus and response, where the desired response is "Acquitted!" It can also be the analytical use of power at its highest level, but only if the why behind the individual votes is inspected. These same techniques are also applied to car-selling appeals, fund-raising solicitations, and election campaigns. This tactic's sophistication and its impressive success in recent history are important reasons why polls seem to lead decision-making and power rather than being a faithful follower.

A third barrier in the analytical study of opinion choices is the

growing resistance of people to even *being* studied and certainly
to being manipulated, no matter how good the ends may be. In
the era of optical scanning, Alvin Toffler says consumers pay with
both money and with information because their purchases are
automatically recorded and analyzed by scanning registers when
they pay. Consumers who may not be able to stop the data collection, such as scanning, resent the tailored information campaigns
that are built around scanning. Antimarketing activism is on the
rise. It's not just in scandals surrounding the paid "sponsorship" of editorial endorsements. The *New York Times* reported
that 1.9 million people have pulled their names off the lists of the
Direct Marketing Association. So far 480,000 have asked that they
be taken off of the roles of the telephone solicitors. That number
will surely climb. Lifestyle advertising is losing sway to hard-core
informational advertising, a sure symptom that people are reacting
to perceived manipulation. One can learn great truths in strange
places, and my first inkling of how sophisticated public resistance
was becoming to tailored marketing came from a newsletter called
The Tightwad Gazette, described in *Adweek's Marketing Week*.
In one issue of the newsletter, publisher Amy Dacyczyn asserts:
"It's all a matter of disregarding external information about
what the culture says we should be doing. . . ." For example,
don't put "generic maple syrup into a Mrs. Butterworth bottle.
This will teach your kids to grow up thinking brands mean something. . . ." A revolutionary thought. If brands don't mean something, the fact is that the entire world of commercial choice is
stood on its head. The implications echo out far beyond the supermarket aisles. It's easy to pour generic political candidates into a
John F. Kennedy bottle or generic charities into a United Way
bottle, and people are on to those scams. If one listened with
mature "statistical ears" to the tallies of the 1992 New
Hampshire primary, political experts were commenting on how
"research-driven candidates" (those who shaped their campaign
around the image and viewpoints the polls appeared to favor)
weren't doing as well as expected. That primary, I'm convinced,
was a watershed in the campaign if not also a watershed in politi-

cal campaigning. George Bush—served so well by poll-based political strategy in the 1980, 1984, and 1988 campaigns—went on to conduct what was essentially a poll-driven campaign. Ross Perot, relying on the Kentucky windage of his own instincts more than anything else, would let himself be poured into nobody's bottle. And Bill Clinton, coupling polls with instinctive saxophone playing and bus touring, became his own bottle, and saved his candidacy from early controversies in his campaign.

That the public is increasingly resistant to being manipulated in their choices is one reality that power analysts will have to deal with. That the public may actually be growing weary of choosing at all is another and perhaps even more important factor. In exerting power, one very important statistical measure to gauge and appreciate is the number and complexity of choices people face. In the historical world of power, tyranny was tyranny and tyranny preempted choice. Now we are finding that the apparent opposite is valid too. As Steven Waldman puts it, choice also invokes a tyranny and often a paralyzing one, especially in the four hours and nine minutes most Americans spend each day watching television and its marketing bombardment.

Choice is more than picking the right hairspray. It is the heart of life and the basis of power. Pursuing a vision constitutes the enactment of choices—those roads taken and those not. Democracy as a principle offers theoretically unlimited choice. Getting things done requires explicit choices, and people turn to the powerful to help them make the right ones. In this sense, an agenda is nothing more than a checked ballot of choices; people vote for the strongest agenda and then sit back to see if the leaders they have chosen have the skill and cunning to get the job done within the bounds of good conduct. Shareholders do this with management each year at the annual meeting: "Make a handsome profit; but also promote minorities, don't dump environmental garbage into our streams, and stay out of Libya when you do business." As the clock ticks toward the annual meeting, the board assesses if management is generally achieving the agenda. If it isn't, the board will recommend changing the

choices (how it does business or what business is done), or changing the management.

If you want to understand how crippling choice can be politically, the place to look is at societies that have not had it. Choice is
as enormous a problem as it is a blessing for any society that has
not had it and now does, and the powerful involved in helping to
make such a society successful must meet that challenge squarely.
Political commentators always berate the industrialized nations
for not giving newly democratized countries more financial support. That may be, but an equal or even greater problem is
preparing societies that have not had choice to exercise choice
well once they get it. (As we will see later, this is also a major problem in businesses that seek to "empower" employees only to see
their empowerment programs fail because employees are inade-
quately trained in how to exercise choice.) Saying that excessive
choice could be bad may sound positively undemocratic. After all,
in the political sphere, if the right to choose has been the cause for
which so many revolutions have been fought, and are being fought
even to the present day, why should regulating choices be such an
issue? Because there are easily *too many* choices, and people—
becoming paralyzed by choice—flee from having to make decisions, especially complicated ones, and willingly surrender that
right to some protector instead. In moderation, choice works. En
masse, it is overwhelming. This may be one important reason why
the Lithuanians, after staging a highly inspirational campaign for
both democracy and a national identity in liberating themselves
from the old Soviet Union, voted the successor party to the
Communists back into office barely a year after their first free
elections. Many democracies struggle with the cradle death of too
much choice in their infancy. At the end of the eighties, Poland
went from one-party rule to perhaps twenty parties in the *Sejm*
(the Polish parliament), even including a Beer Party. Poland was
transformed from a choiceless to a choice-crazed society. *Why?* It
is after all relatively easy to reject communism, especially if there
are no consumer goods and the secret police are peeking through
your curtains. But when communism is gone, the choices among

social democracy, full market economy, or any of a dozen alternatives between loom large.

For the industrialized nations, the problems are hardly simpler, although the domain is more one of consumption not politics. In eight years, the number of products stocked has nearly tripled while the number of new products introduced has about doubled, reports A. C. Nielsen. Is brand loyalty (meaning continuous brand power) possible in such an avalanche of clutter? "Choice erodes commitment," is how Waldman summed it up in an article called "The Tyranny of Choice," and he says further that: "The compulsion to take inventory of one's wants and continually upgrade to a better deal can help explain everything from the rise of the pathological channel switcher who can never watch one TV show straight through to staggering divorce rates and employer-employee disloyalty." The latter point may be worthwhile news for the in-basket of those at the helm. People shop for the right choice among the powerful for whom they work or vote. But, choice in the end is exhausting, and this is also a safeguard for those powerful who are wise guides. "Spend the optimum amount of time on each decision," Waldman says, "and pretty soon you run out of life." A powerful person will study hard to learn which particular choices are beleaguering their constituency most. In the 1992 presidential campaign, Bush's "family values" were as important as Perot's drumbeat of "controlling the deficit," but the need for economic renewal was the issue that Clinton championed and it was clearly the greatest concern for voters.

Even commercial marketers are now finding a virtue in simplifying choice. Marketers have traditionally been tempting people with decision after decision; and, surely for the last decade, the development of highly specialized niche marketing went hand-in-hand with trade-up strategies to enrich margins. Marketers have believed (and, with reasonable grounds, until recently) that more choice will mean more profits. In a typical household, if you can sell one product tailored for children, another for mothers, and another for fathers, you have the potential to sell three products where only one sale was made before. And because the products are tailored, you can try to charge a premium because the product supposedly has the added value of being designed for a special market. The public is beginning to understand and resent the tactic and the additional expense this means to the family budget. A new marketing concept is taking shape to restore brand power and overcome the "tyranny of choice" as well. In 1991, Lever Bros.' soap unit unseated P&G as the largest dollar-volume soap seller in the U.S. market. Lever had 31.5 share versus Procter's 30.5 says the *Wall Street Journal*. A major factor in Lever's success was the popularity of "Lever 2000"—an "all-in-one" family toilet soap. Lever 2000 is not "mass merchandising." It is a very carefully constructed product engineered to alleviate choice and also thereby to reduce consumer expenditure. A major move General Motors is sure to take under its new CEO Jack Smith is to "'de-proliferate' GM's vast and confusing array of cars"—a move talked about inside the company for years, says *The Economist*. This would eliminate "some of the virtually identical models sold under several different names. . . . Though GM bosses hotly deny it," the article says, "there is much talk of Mr. Smith merging the Oldsmobile division with Buick, or even shutting it down." There seems to be ample evidence that broad appeal, large-scale niches are once again coming into vogue because they represent both value and simplification.

The powerful have the toughest time in dealing with choice concerning projections over the future. "What future shall we believe in and plan for?" Most of those projections today are made using sophisticated quantitative analysis. No matter how rigorous, they are usually colored by some fundamental assumption on the part of the forecaster. Because the powerful are so anxious to "get it right" all of the time, many live in a world of *ever-pending disaster* that generally makes a poor distinction between possibility and real historical outcomes. Powerful people have historically kept advisers around them who would provide advance warnings against bad news. Even though they didn't listen, King Priam and the Trojans had Cassandra. Macbeth relied on the witches on the heath. Perhaps, because they are fictitious, Cassandra and the witches were pretty reliable. In modern times, despite the billions invested in them, the CIA and other contemporary services charged with detecting future crises have had a horrendous track record. The Shah was ousted from Iran and the Berlin Wall collapsed, and neither of these events was anticipated by Western intelligence. Discredited in catching the big game, these same advisers to the powerful remain undaunted and are eager Chicken Littles pointing to new falling skies. But, which sky . . . and for what reason? Now that East-West tensions are slackening, some experts in France say that the "CIA and possibly other U.S. intelligence agencies are feeling embattled and so are exaggerating the [current alleged] industrial-espionage threat in an effort to win new clients," reports a *Wall Street Journal Europe* article.

Much of the analytic misinterpretation of the future comes from trying to seat data in the wrong context. Angelo Codevilla, the Hoover Institution researcher, has written an alert book titled *Informing Statecraft.* In it he maintains, "Since World War II the U.S. government has made 'stability' its highest, indeed its overriding, goal. It has assumed—contrary to all teachings of history—that long-term stability is possible. Hence the U.S. government has been the most avid consumer of 'end of history' theories." Many of us still look for those last few crises that need mending before the world settles down to a "natural state" of harmonization. We anxiously monitor these crises thinking that they are the final steps on the way to world tranquillity. Pending catastrophes are titillating, but powerful people don't misdirect resources in preparing for crises that are unlikely to happen. In the 1992 presidential election, for example, it was the vogue to predict that no candidate would receive an electoral majority and that the election would end up in the House of Representatives with neither Clinton, Bush, nor Perot chosen but some dark horse compromise candidate being elected president instead. This was never the most likely alternative, but it was certainly the most interesting one. The smart money was with those blander but bril-

liant pragmatists like Merck CEO Roy Vagelos, Sara Lee's John
Bryan, or then-Apple Chairman John Sculley, who figured Bill
Clinton would win.

In the same year, a fascinating study was published by the
Institute for Crisis Management tracking 31,500 news stories that
covered the two principal types of business crises: operational and
managerial. Between 1989 and 1992, the number of operational
crises covered (then the most frequently reported on type of crisis) fell 29 percent, while the number of managerial crises rose 25
percent. The three leading trend conclusions that Adam Shell
draws from the data as reported in the *Public Relations Journal*
are these: "Operational crises will decline in importance. . . . Top
management decisions in both corporations and non-profit organizations will be subjected to more news media and public
scrutiny . . . [and] Government will be an increasingly pervasive
source of negative business news coverage [criminal investiga-
tions, indictments, fines, etc.]." To me, this says that not only
were managerial crises of growing frequency and climbing media
interest, but also that companies were doing a better job of anticipating or predicting *operating* crises . . . and were neglecting the
necessary preparation for managerial disasters, which in the
meanwhile had really captured media interest. Seeing that company management had almost routinized their defense strategies
for oil spills and chemical accidents, media attention has turned to
juicier prey like boardroom squabbles and CEO firings.[1]

Prediction remains a very difficult business. William R. Rhodes,
Vice Chairman of Citibank, wrote a 1992 article for *The
Economist* that was a revelation. Titled, "The Disaster that
Didn't Happen," it's publication just about coincided with the
tenth anniversary of those ominous forecasts that the Latin
American economies were collapsing in an insurmountable debt

---

1. Not only is this an example of the perils of operating in the wrong context (in
this case, a faulty definition of what constitutes a crisis worth preparing for), it also
shows that the media are targeting powerful individuals as villains, especially as we
continue to move further away from an industrial economy and more toward a knowledge one where the serious "accidents" are both human and judgmental.

crisis. In the last decade, what *has* happened to Latin American debt? Argentina has been on a steady comeback path, very much because its currency has been rebuilt and given a basic predictability. The Peruvians have locked up Abimael Guzman in a breakthrough. Mexico is booming. (Who would have thought a year earlier that the department store chain Dillard's and the discounting giant Wal-Mart would have plans to open stores there?) Even the impeachment turmoil in Brazil could not shroud the steady progress the Brazilian economy has made in recent times. The fact is that few really believed that the Baker and Brady refinancing plans would work as well as they did, even though the evidence was clear that they would.

Badly analyzed projective data regularly warn of impending crises, and these crises regularly end up *not happening.* Such ominous events are being hyped all the time. In the days immediately after the Tienanmen Square uprising, few, if any, experts "predicted" that China would be materially prospering less than two years later under a capitalist dictatorship, generally called consumerism, while the Russians would be swallowed up in a constitutional and economic catastrophe that thrusts the ruble's value lower every day. After the 1992 Los Angeles riots, urban experts were predicting a wave of civil unrest in the United States that would swallow up the cities. It didn't happen. In the Middle East, the pundits said that Iraq was poised to collapse and that Saddam Hussein's days were numbered. Perhaps they still are. But, like it or not, the physical rebuilding of Baghdad has been an impressive achievement—probably more impressive than the first so-called democratic elections held in Kuwait.

The best example of a cataclysmic prophecy that didn't happen was, I think, the year 999 A.D. Expectations for the year 999 actually aligned power expectations in Western Europe as deeply as the catastrophic vision of the scholarly Club of Rome report did a few years back in our time. A couple of years ago, the *Utne Reader* published an excerpt from Richard Erdoes' book *AD 1000: Living on the Brink of Apocalypse.* In it, Erdoes writes: "On the last night of the year 999, crowds of people singing and praying, waving torches and palm branches, filled the streets and squares of Rome. . . . In the old Basilica of St. Peter's a mass of trembling and weeping worshippers awaited the end of the world." The account goes on to register that many even feared looking up at the host as Pope Sylvester II raised it above the congregation . . . and, people died of fright just waiting for the midnight bell to toll. What's the record for such predictions? Better as literature than as research. Most of Aldous Huxley's *Brave New World* has yet to emerge, if it ever will. Most of the totalitarian vision dramatized in George Orwell's *1984* was probably behind us in that year and certainly seems a distant memory now. In fact, Orwell's work had more to do with the world of 1948 than with 1984. And, the probability of a thermonuclear holocaust—forecasted in Nevil Shute's *On the Beach*—is lower than it has been since the mid-1950s.

Whatever it brings with it, we at least know exactly how long it is until the year 2000. With the make-things-happen bent of the powerful, the greater risk comes from events that take longer to happen than we expect they will, so that the anticipation becomes dulled by boredom. For two years, experts in Europe predicted that Yugoslavia would come unhinged. Finally it did, on a bloody and rapacious scale that the world's powerful were unprepared for because events had moved too slowly to capture their full attention. With measured determination, the conservative *apparatchiks* who once ran Soviet industry appear to be circling back to power, while the country seems to inch forward under the guise of democratization (perhaps because the conservatives know it would be unwise to seem to do anything else if they still want Western aid). Likewise, I think we have never been closer to a significant trade spat with the Japanese since World War II, and that has implications for every powerful person in the world today.

On the anastrophic side, Libya could have all the vacation allure of Morocco if it reformed its politics. Even apparently conservative and well-reasoned forecasts can go awry. A futurist scenario by a business adviser that appeared in the Conference Board's *Across the Board* in the spring of 1990 speculated, among other things, that Honda would take over a large part of GM by 1991, that Gorbachev would be under arrest in Siberia in 1992 (the last time I saw him he was taking in the Rockettes' conga-line kick at a banquet in the Waldorf-Astoria), and that Mexico would be defaulting on a $100 billion of global debt by 1995. But even now, things are changing markedly. I can't speak for Mexico (where the article's author *does* project a major turnaround by 1999). But the economic resurgence of other Latin American countries has been pronounced. Brazil, for example, has already been a major international creditor when Poland was unable to pay its debt.

Plenty of good money and time is invested in brain-storming speculation about the future. It may be an amusing mental exercise for a Saturday night dinner party, but I don't really know the good these Doomsday visions do in the world of business, government, and large organizations. Dun & Bradstreet's chief economist Joseph Duncan says that the smart powerful today look at forecasting that emphasizes "paradigm shifts." This technique does not focus on a particular number or extrapolating a present trend, but instead identifies underlying changes that are likely to cause other events to ensue. If one examined, for example, the appalling crop statistics in the Soviet Union from 1985 to 1989, it would have been impossible to imagine how the Soviets could have continued their grip on Eastern Europe. Similarly, the smart powerful have been quietly investing in China (whose trade surplus with the United States is now growing faster than Japan's), Latin America, and the Democratic Party because they reacted to essentially irrefutable fundamental information.

Everything *can* be studied, but not everything should be. Also at the border of the quantitative limits to information is to know when to stop studying. When it comes to decision-making using advanced research and development, what distinguishes the most powerful from the also rans is knowing when to stop. Some of the companies with the leading reputations in research overspend because they don't insist on a close relationship between research and practical business needs. They also end up making suboptimum decisions. Analysis always begets more analysis. Only trained intuition and experience can define and declare when the analysis must stop.

Guy de Jonquières in an article he wrote for the *Financial Times*, described the new attitudes toward research that are causing such a revolution at Nestlé, the global food giant. A Nestlé research manager conceded: "In the past, people here didn't get their hands dirty dealing with food. . . . Everybody was busy publishing papers. They were trying to compete with universities." The article describes how Nestlé "cut the salt in Lean Cuisine dishes by 30 percent without using substitutes or changing the taste." Instead of resorting to pure science, the Nestlé researchers used practical modelling and turned a traditional five-year laboratory project into a two-month study. Werner Bauer, who has been a major figure in Nestlé's research revival, says: "In research, there is always a will to perfect. But a company can't afford that. . . . Stopping at the point where learning curves become incremental is what I see as my major job." For many powerful people, this conflict between getting things perfect and getting things done gnaws deeply and constantly at them.

Useless or misapplied knowledge can strangle power more easily than ignorance. The information age has made too many firms and individuals see research as an imperative for its own sake: "If information is king, then the more discovery of information the better." This unbridled philosophy is a real symptom of weakness. Powerful people managing information know the wisdom of Werner Bauer's strategy of putting a stop to incremental learning curves. *If power is getting things done, then only* useful *information matters in the end.* And, there are specific symptoms to search for. One is insisting that issues be endlessly studied and restudied even when the basic options are obvious. A second symptom is a researcher's aversion to practical problems or realities and an inability to sum up clearly where any learning expedition stands at key points in time. Being intimidated by what a rival appears to know as opposed to measuring what rivals *do* with what they know is a third. A relentless drive to be innovative in areas not a part of an organization's or a person's mission is a fourth. All these are symptomatic of compulsive analysis.[2]

So much for the risks of quantitative management. While I've pointed out some of the most important risks in using and requesting data, I've regrettably been far less thorough in advising how to use data well. Only an expert statistical adviser can truly do that, but perhaps the above cautionary list can suggest some questions to help manage the process. Careful statistical study is surely one positive discipline to recommend, and controlling the impulse toward impatience and quick conclusions is another. The how of the statistical analysis of power problems is often unappealingly boring, but this part of power is as indispensable as any intuitive flash of genius.

Information's Value Betrays Power

Intuition is not solely within a powerful person's genius. Nor is it without guideposts and directional signs. Intuition often reduces down to acting on a hunch, but to act on a hunch you must have one first. And, there is a method to flushing out hunches. Aspiration and information are bloodbrothers. If you want to trace, for example, the pattern of power in commerce—who's hot and who's not—simply look at where the action is in industrial espionage. Today it's in microelectronics, genetic engineering, advanced polymers, and fiber optics. Several years ago, it was in defense and synthetics.

Industrial information is not only a clue as to which sectors are hot, it also is a clue to which processes are hot and which, like the false pursuit of quality, are really a *fata morgana*. One behavior pattern that I find amusing is how Western managers are now imitating Japanese behavior in taking notes at meetings. The Japanese take and review copious notes and distribute back-

---

2. Peter Drucker offers highly perceptive advice on research in two essays—"The 10 Rules of Effective Research" and "R&D: The Best Is Business Driven"—both to be found in his book *Managing for the Future*.

grounders before making decisions. I once asked a trade envoy in Japan why the Japanese top executives didn't like the tight, one-page summaries that their counterparts in the States were so fond of. "It's very simple," he said, "in the U.S., you have to get their attention. In Japan, you already have it." Similarly, the world business community knows that the Japanese are avid consumers of information, but—as a distinguished international economist once pointed out to me—the Japanese are, in fact, terrible *managers* of information. There is a great difference between being an information manager and an information consumer. So what if the Japanese consume endless reams of information or capture every nuance and gesture of a meeting? This is generally useless information, and it makes no contribution to power. Duncan's position has convinced me that Japanese information collection may be a cultural reflex, perhaps a school behavior carried out through adulthood. Outside of the systematic management of data on quality, I doubt whether the Japanese appetite for information ranks with these other formidable success traits: their sense of craftsmanship, their ability to focus on issues important to the customer, their individual loyalty to the firm and its goals, and their competitive tenacity. The real revelation comes when one asks a senior Japanese manager how much all this note taking is relevant to making the right decision and getting things done. One will probably receive an elliptical Cheshire cat grin. Misunderstood endless note-taking and information-gathering can be the meeting attendees' intuitive counterpart to never-ending research.

Another simple intuitive tip-off for power is pressing through the Byzantine explanations and determining the simplest technical reason why something may be true. One thinks, for example, that the world's military intelligence centers would be utterly invisible from the public eye, but they are actually easily known to any who care to think about finding them and doing a little library research. Because of its strategic geographic location, Oman is a plausible clearinghouse for Middle Eastern military intelligence. But the real reason the CIA, MI-5, the Surité, the Bundesnachrichtendienst, the

Israeli Defense Force, and the KGB are all there is because Oman has the region's best satellite uplinks. Muscat, the capital of Oman, is a high-tech telegraph office surrounded by date farms and oil fields. The presence of modern technology in certain geographic centers can also distort information, as it did in the war in Bosnia during the early 1990s. Because Sarajevo housed the only workable uplink facilities in the region, reporters focused on the conditions there. They were terrible, but the situation in electronically unreachable outlying cities was far worse.

A third and reliably important intuitive tip is that the powerful should consciously resist *interesting* information. Important information is generally mundane (truck production output or an abrupt change in the flock grazing patterns of sheepherders), while scintillating information about a head-of-state's mistress or the corruption in a country's commerce department is rarely of any importance. Tobacco baron Zino Davidoff recalls that in 1911 his family's store had become a congregating point for the Russian opposition. Had the Czar's secret police really paid attention to where the radical ideas were being cultivated, would the course of the Russian Revolution been the same? In November 1992, everyone was watching the controversial voyage of the Akatsuki Maru from France to Japan fearing an exotic maritime disaster, but very few people were paying attention to the far more compelling underlying trend (as *Time* did) that Japan's plutonium stockpiles to feed its fast breeding reactor program would climb by a factor of twenty by the year 2010, putting Japan not far behind the plutonium reserves in the United States or the former Soviet Union, making Japan a potential nuclear threat of awesome dimensions. It takes a keen eye to distinguish between information voyeurism and truly informative intelligence.

If you want good hunches, certain kinds of behavior will identify them better than others. The most effective powerful people give others around them good hunches as to what *they* are thinking. There are individuals who institutionalize themselves (and the positions they constitute) so clearly that their power is acknowledged as a continuous presence at meetings, even though they may rarely attend. Exclusive and demanding, Bill Ylvisaker, the former CEO at Gould, did not suffer fools gladly. He rarely came to meetings and might have been physically thousands of miles away, but everyone knew that he was "on the other side of the wall." Like Topper or the Canterbury Ghost, everyone talked about him and dealt with his agenda as if he were present. To have such an aura can help steer the hundreds of individual ships that make up a corporation in the same direction by dint of character, and it did that at Gould. But, the stratagem can also misfire by making certain topics taboo "because the boss doesn't like to have that kind of thinking talked about," and the ships can all go toppling over the same waterfall as a result of serious unresolved problems.

Suemitsu Ito, the former CEO of Sumitomo, is just the opposite of Ylvisaker at Gould. Ito makes himself physically present at meetings but absent as a personality or identity. I mentioned earlier that the Japanese are vastly overrated as managers of information. One exception certainly is Ito. His data-collection technique is to consciously withdraw his own managerial presence. Not long ago, I presented to Sumitomo on the attitudes that the Americans hold toward the Japanese firms operating in the United States. The audience was Sumitomo's top executives, including the then-CEO Ito himself. When Ito came into this meeting room at the Waldorf Astoria, everybody was already seated in carefully appointed places, but he acted as if all this careful preparation was a shock to him. As the meeting started, Dick Wirthlin—one of the finest pollsters in the United States—began passing charts around that showed emerging trends. Some of the data was sensitive and unexpected and said that the underlying American attitude toward the Japanese was not as benevolent as many other public surveys seemed to indicate. During the presentation, Ito never said a word. From right and left, his underlings fired questions. There is a great lesson here on power. Many top managers have adjusted to the practice of having others taking notes in a meeting (and, probably too many notes, if they cast an adoring glance toward Japanese methods). Few have learned how to conduct a meeting *through others* so they can simply sit back and listen, not taking charge. The person who liberates himself or herself to become effectively absent as a conversational force demonstrates far more power than those who must actively assert themselves to somehow *prove* that they are powerful.

Strongly present or seemingly absent, the modern powerful have been collecting data in a decentralized way for a long time. Anyone who has had a conversation with the likes of Jack Welch or David Rockefeller and has been interesting enough to tingle their intellectual curiosity for whatever reason is likely to walk away exhausted. The powerful are information cannibals, voracious for genuine expertise whenever they find a mind worth picking. When retail consultant Kurt Barnard met Sam Walton for the first time, "he introduced himself as Sam Walton from Arkansas. I didn't know what to think. When he meets you, he looks at you—head cocked to one side, forehead slightly creased—and he proceeds to extract every piece of information in your possession. He always makes little notes. And he pushes on and on. After two and a half hours, he left, and I was totally drained." Although Walton was also a passionate collector of intelligence from his own and from competitors' stores, this is quite different from "management by walking around" as practiced by most managers. Walton insisted that gathered information always be related back to a central mechanism of decision-making, action, and motivation performed weekly in only one place—the firm's Bentonville, Arkansas, headquarters. Walton's legendary and peripatetic vacations with their stops in America's campgrounds and parks was to some extent a statement of national fervor, but it was also a thoughtful strategy to learn the small retail markets of the United States, where Walton spent his "vacation" days painstakingly measuring stores and shopping centers. Walton reminds one of the disguised Roman general Sertorius, described by Angelo Codevilla, acting as his own intelligence agent sizing up the Celts.

When collecting information, the powerful ponder very hard to find some intuitive pattern to it. The complementary skill of organization comes into play, not the organization of desks or papers (the powerful can often be hopeless in the mechanics), but in the adjacency of ideas. The powerful organize information well, and they are especially good at categorizing information. I'm not talking about trivial or straightforward distinctions such as those between analytical and subjective information. Rather, they see information flowing in patterns and understand the power that those patterns exert at a given point in time. Nestlé executive vice president Alexandre Mahler once told me "Nestlé has basically two sources of information: the more operationally geared information patterns provided by the different markets and the more strategic information patterns of the headquarters. The combination of both should help shape the long-term future of the company." Correlating external marketing realities with a central and focused worldview enables Nestlé to run such a successful global business.

It always pays to know if higher allegiances exist, and corporate cultures like Nestlé's are one such type of allegiance, but there are others. With greater and greater frequency, conglomerates fail as power structures because they have been unable to build a higher loyalty. But, the U.S. Navy has that institutional loyalty and because of it held together through the Tailhook scandal. In Europe, one reason that hostile takeovers are so hard to achieve is because of the cross-holdings of companies interlocked through family relationships. It is in some respects a throwback to the aristocratic era. In Paris, for example, being a graduate of one of the grandes écoles (like the Polytechnique) is much more important in defining power cliques than being a Socialist or Conservative. In London, everything is defined by the luncheon club to which you belong. American business and government leaders who have been to the Bohemian Grove retreat in northern California and have bunked in one of the camps like "Moonshiners" or "Poker Flat" often build friendships with one another that transcend old-school ties such as those found among Ivy League alumni. In America, one of the great defining consciousnesses is simply being Texan. For many Texas natives, being Texan counts for more than being city- or country-bred, Baptist or Presbyterian, Republican or Democrat.

What Binds Atlas?

The powerful should vigilantly study what is imposing limitations on their power. Those threats and barriers are often that which appear to the untrained eye to be harmless, irrelevant minutiae. Rarely is power challenged today with such obviousness as a gentlemanly slap of the glove and a seconded call to the dueling grounds. No longer is it so simple. There are limits to the exercise of power that may result from the prosaic subparagraph of an accounting rule. A provocative article in the *Financier* by Robert K. Elliott of KPMG Peat Marwick contended "the movement toward an information-era accounting paradigm is irreversible." We must adjust, but we haven't yet. Elliott points to MIT's Lester Thurow: "Thurow has noted that, of all the major Western developed nations, only the U.S., where R&D is charged straight to income, has an R&D curve that rises and falls with the business cycle. This suggests that R&D that meets the definition of an asset should be recognized as such, rather than being automatically charged against earnings." Elliott also makes a very practical suggestion that we should "compare the information top management actually uses to make decisions with what is made available through financial statements." Accounting standards drive financial reporting. Investment analysts and company managers generally end up using the same standards to measure a company, but the official reports that the companies write and the analysts read do not.

Robert Kuttner has described another below-the-water power hazard this way: "The underlying problem is that commerce today is international while regulation is national, and regulation itself is out of fashion." The lead-in to an article he wrote says it all: "When global banks can pick their regulators, the logic of regulation is undermined." Former SEC Chief Accountant John C. Burton puts it this way: "The way you keep score determines how you play the game." It's hard for me to imagine that a global economy can or will want to live with transnational "regulator shopping" much longer into the future, but that is what is happening and it circumscribes the range of power in very real ways. There is a heartening aspect to all this, which is that existing laws and regulations can be changed with the power of an idea. To the powerful, those people who enjoy getting things done, the opportunity to make a change can have great appeal.

The powerful must also have excellent intuition about why things *don't* get done. This is the intuitive side of the "tyranny of choice." With so many more things people can choose to do, I think powerful people of all sorts better improve their understanding of why people *don't* do things—from not polishing their furniture to not voting in elections to not changing prosaic rules. The most common reasons are sloth and inertia.

Walking Nowhere

The powerful today are being victimized by what I see as a classic form of bad intuitive input, one of the most overestimated management pastimes of the past two decades: the principle of "walk-around-management." To promote flexible and labile leadership, advisers to the powerful have deified spontaneity in recent years. The spontaneous gathering of information seemed the ultimate weapon against massive, sclerotic bureaucracies. But, while certain kinds of firsthand knowledge contribute to power, aimlessly wandering in pursuit of the grail of intuitive knowledge and reckless spontaneity can pose grave dangers to the exercise of power. I have seen a number of world-class virtuosos in the art of "management-by-walking-around" (MBWA) preside over failing organizations. They did so because they believed leading management consultants who decreed that slumming—either inside or outside the organization—in the real world of employees, customers, and suppliers was how to seize and hold power. While the counsel made consultants a pile of money, it also played on the weaknesses of managers in nonauthoritative power structures. The managers overestimated their need to be fluid and nomadic and actually harmed their communications, the very thing MBWA was supposed to improve, principally by causing their organizations to lose a sense of center.[3]

As I scan the "accident reports" of the powerful who have stubbed their toes stalking reality on plant floors and in customer service centers, it's certain that leaders who get the biggest highs from MBWA usually hate the administrative parts of their jobs. Their wanderings are a legalized recess from dull, gray days at headquarters, corporate or otherwise. Managers not only dodge their own administrative duties, many fail to make sure that someone else would be handling the indispensable administration needed to run a company. Second, "walk-around" companies tend to lurch from priority to priority. When the boss learns from the front-line troops that a faulty ball bearing or badly designed government policy is "costing millions," the top team will often go into orbit for days until they think that they have solved the problem *or* until the players unearth some other more scintillating investigative bombshell and a new chase begins. "Walk-around" organizations have a tough time limiting and sticking to their priorities. Third, most powerful people are poorly trained to seek and absorb spontaneous input properly. They may invest thousands to underwrite focus groups managed with clinical precision. But, at the same time, an offhand comment by a volunteer shelter worker or consulting engineer can be elevated to an incomprehensible level of importance. Fourth, in businesses especially, employees are more and more cynical about generals in the trenches. Employees resent the invasion of high-priced cheerleaders from headquarters who patronize the rank and file with ten minutes of sweet talk. In one instance I know of, rank-and-file workers systematically misled their leaders on productivity issues by kibitzing them with bad information. Today's Luddites are *on* to management and know that they can do more harm through misleading

3. A "center" or homing point is not the same as the top of an organizational pyramid, and even the most fluid organizations need to have a sense of center to define themselves.

input than through hurling a monkey wrench into a drill press. Fifth, and most important, MBWA only really worked as a *corrective* strategy. MBWA is a guerilla tactic to attack frozen hierarchies and faulty communications. Any organization that tries to live off MBWA as a daily regimen is admitting that its routine communications are unreliable. No outfit in that condition will last long.

Chaining the powerful to conference tables is binding Prometheus. A pure commitment to viewing the world from headquarters is not the solution either. A certain amount of MBWA will always be healthy, but it's a poor choice as the centerpiece of a management power strategy. MBWA has become a cult and an addiction, endowed with fictitious powers. It is easy to lose one's bearings spending all one's time stalking yet another morsel of "reality." A crusty but perennially successful executive said to me recently, "If my executive committee had intended me to spend most of my time tumbling ass-over-teakettle through two million square feet of conveyor belts and development labs, they wouldn't have bought me a twenty-square-foot mahogany desk and a PC that can talk with every other work station in the company." I think he's probably right.

While "walking-around" and other intuitive contact strategies can be limiting or dangerous, there is no denying that the repositories of information are decentralized. The challenge is in absorbing that information and keeping it in the context of a central focus. Today, information experts say there is five times as much computing capacity in personal computers as in mainframes. Mainframes were analogous to centralized courts of power. Part of IBM's struggle has been the attempt to make a centralized decision, as it had always done in the past, to abet the creation of a world which would no longer operate by centralized decision-making. The metaphor "It's not showing up on my screen" is telling. We are not all watching the same central signal any more.

❁   ❁   ❁

Brute Instinct—Electronic and Otherwise

Even in the electronic age, there is precedent for going with instinct. Roger Ailes, Ronald Reagan's communications guru and Rush Limbaugh's producer, observes people very intensely as he talks—with good reason. "I tell leaders to go with their instincts. Their instincts are quite good. Leaders are not naturally wooden and frightened although the camera may inhibit some of them. Good media training is getting people to be themselves. Although TV editors sometimes distort meaning by the way they cut up a taped interview, people growing up today are remarkably video literate, as a result of watching thousands of hours of television. They know when a piece is unfair and when it's not." At the same time what restrains the power of organizations is often that they fail to let people use common sense the higher that they rise. The organization will compel the use of too much data in making decisions, it will stipulate too many counter-check reviews, it will smother its leadership in excessive advice.

Married Mastery

If putting together intuitive common sense with the ability to absorb and utilize quantitative knowledge is the exercise of power, then who qualifies as a modern master of power? Certainly, Peter Ueberroth is one remarkable example of such finely honed power skills: successively a business person, baseball commissioner, Olympics head, and reconstruction czar for the city of Los Angeles, he has proven that power can be portable. His personnel organization skills have been documented at length by others and need no recounting by me. He was able to build the second largest travel empire in the United States because he understood that the information age had come to the travel business, particularly in reservations systems. Despite the 1984 Soviet boycott, he was able to turn a perennial money loser like the Olympics into a triumph that netted more than $200 million, in great part by restricting the number of sponsors and increasing their fees while he simultaneously managed to increase the value of the Olympic

TV-rights sales. Even though he is remembered as the enthusiastic, congratulating, and inspirational leader for that event, it was his simultaneous knack for securing the right numbers on the right issues that permitted him to be successful. Ueberroth has an uncanny ability to break up problems into their component transactions. The way that he wants to build 57,000 jobs in overhauling Los Angeles is through small companies and small steps. He dignifies the small step, but he is still able to situate the small step in the context of a master plan—albeit a plan that is supple and flexible like well-played billiards. Right and left lobes of his brain humming, Peter Ueberroth has already demonstrated his mastery of the transactional nature of power in four major arenas and has shown he knows how to play the right "game" to match the scorekeeper's standard. And, with an Awe Factor of his standing, one should anticipate a run for national office as the right fifth star to fill out his epaulets and honors.

THE MASTERY

Information and economic realities drive the structure and organization of power in today's secular society. Power today is a unified discipline. It is more scientific than it was two decades ago, but it is not exclusively or even predominantly scientific today. Exerting significant power can only be achieved by reconciling the intuitive and quantitative approaches to leadership.

4

The Organization of Power

Stoking the Structure

[In interpreting a movie,] the public knows more about the director than anyone else because film critics, in order to be able to write reviews, apparently have to personalize and channel the creative forces into one person.

—ERNEST LEHMAN, SCREENWRITER

Is power rendered through individuals or groups? How is power organized? What distinguishes powerful people from weak ones?

Are powerful individuals really individuals? Look at the most powerful individuals in the world, and it's hard to believe that they *are* just individuals. Alexander the Great may have untied the Gordian Knot with a stroke of his sword, but at least he solved the problem on his own. Few powerful people could make such a claim today. The White House staff that surrounds the president is an entourage that produces almost everything for which the president is ultimately credited or cursed. Even the staffs that serve the press corps that cover the White House are entourages. The secretary general of the United Nations has a brigade of trained talent working for him—although it is probably not enough, given the task with which he is charged. The think tanks of scholars and researchers behind many business leaders are vast. The truth is that power has to leverage a lot of people to help create ideas and get things done.

In the practice of power, it's not surprising, then, that what works for individuals generally works for countries or organizations, too, because most powerful people are simply the nucleus of a sometimes vast organizational maze that surrounds them. That maze is only partly formal and often scarcely visible. The reason that some powerful people seem so protean, so superhuman, is that they are really *multihuman*. Seemingly lone and starkly visible in the streaming canoe, they are really propelled by an extended team paddling away below the water line. The screenwriter Ernest Lehman, who scripted Alfred Hitchcock's *North by Northwest*, once observed: "The public knows more about the director than anyone else because film critics, in order to be able to write reviews, apparently have to personalize and channel the creative forces into one person." Historians practicing a "Great Man" or "Great Person" theory of history generally conceal the supporting cast, overwhelmed like the string pullers who guide the huge balloons in Macy's Thanksgiving Day parade; and they turn their Roosevelt or Stalin into an all-purpose convenience to explain away complicated power dynamics as well as the accomplishments (or atrocities) of a great many other people.

That the supporting cast of a powerful figure will generally include their management team and administrative staff goes without saying. The board of directors is a different matter. A business board can be friend or foe, depending on the last quarter's earnings. Other members of the cast include catalysts to fire the imagination of the powerful when their inspiration runs cold and lightning rods to cool them off when their image sizzles in the press. There are beacons to help them navigate emerging issues and elder statesmen to remind them of the hidden reefs. There are backers and fans to keep them high, and reality-checking mirrors to keep them honest. There are also figureheads to perform their ceremonies—figureheads who the powerful pray to God every night will not come to life and meddle in policy-making.

Plenty of instruction manuals have been written on how to staff one's board of directors or organize a management team. My intention in this essay is rather to highlight the issues involved for powerful people in organizing their resources given the modern realities of little hierarchy and no command mode. Structuring an organization is smelting the boiler drum, and staffing it is really stoking it with power. "Solidifying power" and "solidifying one's power bases" are often-used expressions, but they are not merely that. Their truth goes back to the importance of the power structure surrounding the individual. Even though roles are far less clear today and the medium for power has become transactional, true power cannot be spotty or haphazard if it hopes to last. For individuals, optimum power demands a shrewd alignment of the forces around them. As with any structure, its basic components must be firmly hardened before it can withstand testing, but organizational fortresses with rampartlike divisions of turf belong to the past. What does structural strength mean in the shifting contexts of transactional power? The answer, ironically, is still to be found in military analogies. In the latter stages of the Cold War, both sides invested increasing amounts of their hardware into either missile-armed submarines or other mobile launch vehicles. That is what the structural strength of power must be today: maneuverable, portable, at times unpredictable, but in no sense haphazard.

The official organization structures of power have become more elastic. Alvin Toffler rightfully describes them as becoming "closer to the biological [and like living systems] . . . only partly deterministic." The members don't serve a clearly preset goal, and they pursue multiple responsibilities and maintain a variety of reporting and "contact" relationships. If today's formal organizations are more elastic, informal organizational links to the peers one must keep motivated and advised (and even connections to "relevant outsiders") are even more so. There is great danger, however, in confusing *elastic* with *relaxed*. There is nothing relaxed about the complex new structures. In fact, they are very demanding to sustain, maintain, and—most of all—to adjust. Since so much rests on the quality of organization, few things are more important for a powerful person to study than organizational science. *A fascination with organization is not only a giveaway trait of powerful people, it is also an essential part of their continuing education program.* It especially behooves the powerful to study organizational structures in totally different realms, because that is where fresh ideas can be found and exported. A wisely appropriated structure from another world, for example, can serve to elevate an issue to new importance. Bill Clinton knows this. Clinton was elected president to address domestic problems, especially economic ones. He was shrewd to create a National Economic Council modeled after the National Security Council and to place investment banker Robert Rubin at its helm. This gave economic coordination both a new seriousness and the flavor of a military campaign. While Lyndon Johnson could launch a unilateral War on Poverty (and break the bank doing it), Clinton had to reconcile a number of diverse priorities—hence an integrated council of advisers setting the tone. (This step also responded to attacks on the earlier days of the Bush White House as lacking rudimentary order and sufficient depth: "John Sununu and a thousand interns," a Bush staff member told the *New York Times*.) In fact, Clinton's opponent, George Bush, in the later days of the campaign, intimated he would take the same direction and create a single domestic economic czar, suggesting that James Baker would fill the leadership role in domestic economic affairs if Bush were reelected.

Clinton's deployment of economic advisers may be an important breakthrough for government. Of all institutions, however, business has surely done the best job in exploiting structures found in unlikely places and is light years ahead of government in both the extent and the boldness of its innovations. Proof of such innovation is the most exciting manufacturing plant in the entire General Electric system, Bayamón (outside of San Juan), where surge protectors and arresters are made. The personnel structure is a blend of ultramodern manufacturing principles with knowledge incentives (having roots in academia). In this factory, *Fortune* reports, workers "declare a major" in a particular manufacturing discipline and are then paid premiums for successfully completing courses that strengthen their chosen skill base. Power is so decentralized at Bayamón that there are only fifteen managers, and these are simply called "advisers."

With all of the innovation occurring in organizational thinking, it's important to distinguish between the personal power of people and the power of the structural role that they discharge. At Bayamón, General Electric has all the right leadership factors meshed together: properly defined roles for the guiding team; effectively trained people in key posts; an energizing organizational concept; and the overwhelming momentum of a winning corporate umbrella. The stars are not always aligned so favorably. A powerful person can be (or more likely, can newly become) a proprietor of a weak power structure; but if it's weak, it's crucial to get at the reasons why it is weak and to fix them fast. It is possible to be a strong leader in a weak organization . . . but not for long, if the organization must be competitive and if its constituents have normal human needs. However, this situation can have an appealing upside for the powerful: An organization weak in the right ways can be like low-hanging fruit. Powerful people often choose to join weak organizations in order to rehabilitate them, and a seemingly weak organization whose power is deeply discounted or underestimated can become a better springboard to glory than an air-pocket basketball shoe. The important point is to accurately assess the present power of a potential organizational home and its dormant promise for recovery.

To strengthen the weak organization, power must declare itself for one of two essential defining categories (or modes of leadership) before it launches its agenda: Does it wish to be a change

agent or a stabilizer? Or, using the principles derived from
Drucker earlier: Does it want to use its knowledge to *innovate*
(reform or change) or to *make more productive* (stabilize)?
Certainly, every powerful organization leader wants *both* innovation and stability, but a powerful person is generally compelled (by
the agenda expectations of the constituencies that person is serving) to cast a directional lot that emphasizes one option over the
other. There is a vast difference between the mission of the
reformer or change agent and that of the manager of a stable
organization. The former derives power from overhauling a disap-
pointing or oppressive present; the latter from continuing (and
progressively enhancing) what is basically an acceptable current
reality.[1]

Today, the technical requirements of the reformer versus the
stabilizing manager in most complex organizations are so vastly
different that the reformer is jolted by peace every bit as much as
the stabilizer is unhorsed by conflict. This has led to considerable
and increasing migration by the powerful to other venues if the
signals on the organization's agenda change, and this in turn also
weakens organizational loyalty overall once the tune at the top
becomes "run for your life." Generally, when powerful people
relocate to "fresh challenges," they are shrewd enough to see
that they are no longer useful to their present organization's
ends (that is, either the era of reform or of stability is over) and
are, in fact, quite likely to be sidelined or eliminated if they
don't take the initiative and move first. Former Avon CEO
Hicks Waldron, who was at the time a member of four boards,
was once quoted in the *Wall Street Journal* describing the reality
of many board-CEO partings: "No one is happy to say, 'We
fired the bastard.' It doesn't do the company any good. . . .
[Yet,] there are a lot of (former chief executives) 'pursuing per-

---

1. Ruling through perpetual reform (à la GE's Jack Welch) is a new dance step:
An eighteenth-century king might have waged occasional war, but, unless he
presided over periods of sustained peace and stability, or could show his bankers an
eye-popping "return on plunder," odds are high that a palace or popular revolt
would cut him down, as it did Charles I in the England of the 1640s.

sonal interests' who are pursuing them on an involuntary basis."

The power structure is not just the structure of an organization table. It is architecture in time. And, the powerful must organize time every bit as much as roles.[2] Every significant power structure has its ritual temporal pattern, and each cyclical year has its high point. For the president of the United States, it's the State of the Union speech. For the President of IBM, it's the annual meeting of shareholders or of its 100 Percent Sales Club. For the president of Princeton, it's commencement. For the Bishop of Rome, it's Easter Sunday. In addition to the predictable dates, the powerful also do their best to bend the calendar to their advantage. Says Mike Walsh, CEO of Tenneco, about the architecture of time: "If you look at people in leadership positions and do a time analysis of what they do, I submit you'll find a great deal of the time they're doing somebody else's job rather than shaping the concept and the structure by which the concept will be implemented across the board in a large, complex organization."

Even in an age of astonishing communications (forget about gabbing office to office, Sweden, which is the world leader in per capita mobile phone penetration, is adding ten thousand mobile phone registrations a month!), geography remains a crucial factor in determining structure, even though some of the reasons behind geographical decisions have certainly changed. As already pointed out, part of geography's importance reflects the need for every organization to feel that there is some center or coordinating point for its mission and leadership. The value of face-to-face dialogue, also highlighted earlier, is a second important drive, but the basic limiting issues of time and distance remain fundamental factors. The further separated an organization's outposts are, the more it may need to lean on advanced communications to overcome time and distance barriers: Bridge games in the Stamford-bound club car of the New Haven railroad were once the site of things getting done by industry moguls on the Eastern seaboard. Now, different

2. For a more comprehensive discussion of time and power, see the chapter titled "The Power Clock" in my book *A Briefing for Leaders*.

kinds of communications devices are needed and are emerging. ABB in Sweden has a large commuting population, many of whom live in Stockholm, which is one hour and twenty minutes away from ABB's main Swedish facility in Västerås. The firm has equipped a rail car that can be used during the commute called the business coach with phones, modems, and PCs for its knowledge workers. Technology is an increasingly important force in shaping organizational design.

In some cases, the technology actually allows organizations to *centralize* their decision-making, rather than decentralizing it. Decentralization was particularly vogue in the 1980s (in keeping with the eighties enthusiasm for shoveling risk outward in almost every sense), but thinking that all sophisticated companies are highly decentralized ones is an illusion. Distance may actually *increase* the need for centralized thinking, rather than diminish it. If you elect a course of decentralization over long distances, you must rely heavily on communications and a strong culture to sustain the centralized framework. Centralization and decentralization are as much a function of the kind of institution or organization as of the excellence of managers or the quality of their principles. Rather than allowing geography to justify decentralization, American Airlines and other carriers fight hard to make their product uniform across the globe. "Geographically, our industry is very diverse," says AMR CEO Bob Crandall, "thus, we are very reliant on the motivation of people. A good leader must motivate in a way which overcomes the problems of geography. The goal is to provide a consistent, uniform product worldwide." When you don't have geography on your side, getting an organization to function properly requires a far more active commitment to principles and values. Crandall said to me, "A service business must be *explicitly team-oriented.*" In my view, a global service organization must be especially so. An explicit team orientation demands clear principles and values and a sharp definition of the products the customer is looking for. That's why Crandall and his colleagues clock so much time traveling. "In the airline business," he explains, "it's important for management to spend a lot of time talking with front-line employees—checking attitudes, behavior, and understanding of mission."[3]

For years, it was thought that service businesses like retailing were the opposite of airlines, a truly border-locked phenomenon. Indeed, some are, and the more complex the retail concept, the harder it is to transplant to foreign soil. "Boutiques cross national boundaries well," retail genius Stanley Marcus once pointed out to me, "department stores don't. Complex bodies don't. Takashimia tried to do it on Fifth Avenue. Seibu tried it in Los Angeles. Harrod's tried it in Buenos Aires. Galleries Lafayette tried it in London. They all lost." Nordstrom, Neiman-Marcus, and Macy's have successfully built outposts within the United States, but that is because of the growing homogeneity of taste among the economic elite in America's large cities. Whether these stores would succeed in other countries is another matter. Often, department stores—like many forms of print media—are too closely linked to the local culture. In some senses, we are now seeing that it's possible to have certain retail businesses succeed as global chains (witness Toys-R-Us in central Europe and Japan, with thirty-seven stores in Germany and Austria), where their product offering and operating principles are sharply defined and restricted to focused categories, and therefore they are much more like an airline or a fast-food restaurant than a department store.

Technology can bring the extensions of an organization in closer touch with its center. On the other hand, moving the geographic center of an organization can reapportion its organizational power by forcing knowledge workers into greater contact with the constituents who define their agenda. J.C. Penney's headquarters move to Dallas helped "cut travel time considerably," says Chairman William R. Howell. But, he adds an argument that I

---

3. Management by flying around? Maybe. But, an airline's center is different from that of most other organizations because the business literally is in motion. Perhaps it has three "centers"—the cockpit, the transportation hub airports, and the computer network that handles its reservations systems.

think is even more important: "A major benefit has been to get our people in the home office out where their ultimate bosses are.... When we were in New York, it became increasingly more difficult to attract management from our stores to transfer to the home office.... Now there is an increased willingness on the part of managers to come into the home office as part of their career path." Dallas was both a more hospitable and a more pertinent center for Penney's. The sense of "center" in the American retail industry, to continue the example, has shifted dramatically westward over the past two decades. Twenty years ago, while Sears and Montgomery Ward were based in Chicago, critical buying functions of both firms were situated in New York. Penney's headquarters, of course, was totally there. Now the retail powerhouses are in Bentonville, Arkansas (Wal-Mart); Columbus, Ohio (The Limited); Troy, Michigan (K-Mart); Minneapolis (Dayton Hudson); and Dallas (Penney's).

In designing structure, powerful people weigh the components of their personal mission, asking such questions as: "What resources are available to apply to my greatest needs?"; "How much time have I been granted to realize which objectives?"; "What innovations must underpin my reform?"; "What imposed or self-defined milestones exist to measure my performance?"; and "How does the physical scope which I must master affect both the structural and cultural design of the organization?" All these issues involve shaping reality—physical and otherwise—to adjust to the needs of people. Adjusting to contours and not *commanding the landscape* is the modern portrait of power: No longer does an organization unfurl itself from the seat of power like a cloak billowing outward from the throne.

The Confederacy Rises Again

The team—not the officer group, "management", or any other fiction cooked up by the personnel department—is what drives organizations today. It is the principal structure of applied power. The team at the top is more than the officers. It almost always includes key administrators, planners, and gatekeepers, and sometimes outsiders.[4] Outside counsel, management consultants, and investment bankers often have a surer path to the CEO than many inside officers. But, what really is a team? Is it a win-driven juggernaut like Vince Lombardi's Green Bay Packers, an ant colony to be studied from "the Tower" over the practice field like Bear Bryant's Crimson Tide, or, the twenty-four-person Team Bandit task force that Motorola established in 1986 to create the world's most advanced radio-pager? Future Super Bowls are likely to belong to the Motorolas. The Motorola team, and any other successful knowledge team, is a union of persons. A confederation implies both independence as well as solidarity. Nestlé, one of the world's most successful global organizations, is fundamentally a confederation. As Nestlé Executive Vice President Alexandre Mahler once explained it to me: "Both the Swiss political structure, and our organizational set-up at Headquarters and around the globe, have made us get used to confederate thinking."

Confederate or collegial power—the leading of peers or near peers—will be the approach to power in greatest demand in coming years. What goes into it? The first step for any powerful person is to steep themselves in how the knowledge work team functions. Knowledge workers are the elite troop—the Green Berets—of nearly every organization that can contribute to the objectives of the powerful. There is only one way for the powerful to survive in a knowledge economy—where the widespread and reliable support of knowledge workers is so indispensable—and that is to become unabashed advocates and students of the team habits of knowledge workers. The shift to this relatively new form of environment and outlook can be disorienting, especially for powerful people coming out of more traditional organizations. When John Sculley made the switch from Pepsi to Apple Computer, he wrote that "within days . . . my Pepsi experience

---

4. Gatekeepers (and supporters in their gatekeeper role) are excluded from this discussion of the power structure, because they do not directly contribute to getting anything done. Rather, if they are good, they prevent valuable time from being squandered on stupid projects or ideas.

seemed out of another lifetime." The team of knowledge workers at Apple was also driven by other motivations. As Sculley puts it, "At Apple, you would rarely hear the word 'win.' At Pepsi, you would rarely hear anything else."

Collegial power is complex and demands deep trust among the partners of the team, especially on the matter of risk. If the Japanese understand one thing about collegial power (and they understand many), it is that risk must be shared rather than forced down as an individual accountability. Comparing American-style risk management with the Japanese philosophy, Arthur D. Little consultant Bennett Harrison has described the American risk pattern as the "hot-potato" approach: Dump it somewhere and pinpoint responsibility for the record. The Japanese teams hang on to risk, and one reason that they do is that their teams are generally more mature and invested with more powerful people. In contrast, U.S. teams may be full of enthusiasm but are rarely as solid or steady and have a tough time withstanding accountability pressures.

Accountability witch-hunts often ensue when routine risk goes awry. This was demonstrated when Navy Secretary Lawrence Garrett III resigned in 1992 over an incident of sexual misconduct by Marine pilots at a Las Vegas hotel, the so-called "Tailhook Scandal." The behavior took place during a gathering that he attended, although he did not observe the misconduct directly. In the information age, top managers are blamed for misconduct or judgment errors that occur during their watch—even though they may not condone or be personally aware of what's going on. They are held accountable for the necessary information and control procedures being in place. Lack of awareness about subordinate conduct then poses a serious potential threat to power.

The Japanese have a special reverence for the group because they know what a group can do. For Westerners, the group is more a device than a natural pattern, and this has obvious effects on how the powerful staff and treat teams. As a general rule, specially chartered teams, such as task forces, succeed chiefly through their coordination, not because of their consensus; but such special teams do not work equally well in different cultures.

Populist teams constructed to include every level and walk of life generally fail at a serious business mission. Teams need ballast. Many American firms have emulated the Japanese in building cross-functional teams to accelerate the development of innovative new products, but American teams have not been nearly as successful as their Japanese counterparts. Why not? In the research of two Harvard Business School professors published in the book *Revolutionizing Product Development*, Americans were found to create very egalitarian product development teams of about 1,500 employees, including plenty of low-level participation. Frankly, they have a lot of "lightweights." In contrast, the Japanese teams had an average of 250 people and were more heavily skewed toward senior management. The key is to train and position enough senior people to be serious guides, not bureaucratic dictators, but motivating forces. The most important special teams should not be a proving ground for "high potentials" but an operating arena for proven performers.

The fine hand of power in team management is seen in the skillful alignment and distribution of resources and the weaving of a sound and resilient emotional fabric. An organization's size and its stage of evolution greatly influence how a team should be built. The smaller the company, for example, the more professional managers must balance out the remaining mix of entrepreneurial geniuses. Although Scott McNealy did a phenomenal job of building Sun Microsystems as an entrepreneur, he under utilized the leverage inherent in his company until he brought in the management professionals who could build external strategic alliances and further develop Sun's own organization. Alignment is as much a matter of focus as of makeup. The focus should not be on balancing power within the team (politics) but on concentrating the team outward on the organization's mission. This, to me, is the heart of what Bob Crandall means when he strives to make American Airlines "explicitly team oriented."

Solid internal communication is the core of effective team management. Crises and directional change are always the real tests of power within team structures. Because power is so easily distrusted, team members are forever on the lookout for any feeling of betrayal. Team members can be easily disenchanted if they are not trusted and brought into major decisions or crises early with a thorough and frank explanation of what is happening. That includes the broader, organization-wide "team" surrounding the inner core of power and is particularly true in knowledge and service-based companies. In the information age, it is important to deal with negative internal issues more quickly than external ones because the team is increasingly transparent to the media and other outsiders. (And, as Chapter 3 points out, the likeliest crisis any management must now combat is organizational and internal and not technical.) As pressure increases and the public record is colored by arguments, it's easy for leadership to hedge in uncomfortable explanations to the troops—or even to find reasons why explanation is altogether unnecessary. I saw this happen once in a law firm that took on the business of an African country with a questionable human rights record and promptly disaffected its entire cadre of junior partners, a number of whom were people of color. Internal ignorance and misunderstanding incubate and breed with incredible speed and are the primary reason team members can turn against team management. The powerful can also often sabotage a team's commitment simply by their own personal style. Some powerful people are convinced that team dynamics and processes inhibit their own individual decisiveness. Teamwork does, but trying to prove that one is a decisive leader *despite* the team proves nothing. What such insecure but powerful people overlook is that their own personal decisiveness is unimportant. What *is* important is the decisiveness of their organization's agenda.

In today's frequently downsized organizations, one of the worst handled constituencies is the "survivors." If improperly managed, they can become some of the most dangerous adversaries to the top team and its goals. When the powerful prune their organizations, they often project a generous and indulgent attitude toward those they fire and a dangerous and ambivalent manner against those who "made the cut." An excellent *Industry*

Week article addressed the frustrating problems of survivorship. The powerful can communicate disdain to the survivors of reorganizations in many ways. If not in words, then in looks and tone, the "Lucky you have a job, aren't you?" message echoes out as cuttingly as if a nobleman had flung a half-gnawed table scrap in front of the castle peasants. This is no way to motivate a workforce. A Boston consultant group officer describes the psyche of such workers as the "doom loop." People who feel doomed are prone to act with the condemned's sense of desperation, which can drive them to become confidants of perceived *ombudsmen* such as the investigative press. There is an old saw among financial analysts and business journalists that goes, "If you want to gauge the seriousness of an organization's problems, look at the *level* at which information leaks to outsiders take place. The higher the leak, the worse the internal difficulties." And, a common tactic for individuals close to or even within the top team (that is, those with information that has the taint of credibility) is to pit the CEO against the second in command. Sometimes the conflicts have their roots in sincere differences about management philosophy as between Joseph Canion and Eckhard Pfeiffer at Compaq. The tradition of pitting power against itself, often used by boards in creating management teams steeped in psychological and cultural checks and balances, is fortunately giving way to a less antagonistic era of "complementary resumés." Power cannot afford to either be or be seen as being divided within its own house.

Bonding Agents: Networks and Strategic Alliances

Sometimes, the team inside an organization is generally just not up to getting the tasks at hand done. That's when the powerful turn to networks and strategic alliances to leverage their power. Networks and alliances are alike in that they are both built on reciprocity, and, without the mutually useful trading of favors, they wither away. As I define these two kinds of bonding, their principle difference is that a network is an informal tie between individ-

uals, while a strategic alliance is an official bond between organizations. While the powerful are often judged by the quality and
size of their networks, building vast networks just to have a contact base of great size is akin to collecting string. Having a huge
Rolodex is an unlikely tipoff to real power. The Rolodex, the most
frequent measure of a powerful person's networking, should be a
well-manicured garden, not a wild jungle. When a powerful person thumbs their Rolodex and assesses their network, they should
be thinking as much about who *isn't* there as who is. A tangible
example helps: It is imperative that the head of a large real
estate company should know the city and state heads of economic
development. He or she should know the mayors' and governor's
right-hand persons. Being on a first-name basis with the real
estate chiefs of the big companies in the area is essential to developing credibility in the professional fraternity. Knowing the
bankers who finance property deals and their economists, who
project the lending climates, is an absolute must. Acquaintance
with the real estate editor of the local papers and the real estate
expert most often quoted in the papers increases the chances of
themselves being quoted or consulted as an authority. If residen-
tial real estate is a major business for the firm, the personnel
directors of all the major employers in the community are the
most direct source for housing needs. These are the people who
have the influence and who can sign the checks that will make a
difference to the business. The preferred list also contains *stretch
contacts*, higher level contacts than even powerful people in real
estate management would generally think of pursuing. Knowing
them is an indirect investment that speaks of long-term relationships rather than instant opportunity.

A board should be used as a connection of networks. Later in
this chapter, I'll talk about the intricacies and difficulties of
board management. But plying a director's network belongs here
because the biggest value a powerful person gets from a board is
access to the network connections of the directors. Astonishingly,
when candidates are considered for a board directorship, their
networks are often not analyzed. The network of relationships

offered by a prospective director should be diagrammed as precisely as the layout of a printed circuit. A nonprofit organization, the Institute of International Education, manages networks superbly. Their central board oversees a half dozen other boards across the country. The regional boards are interlocked with one member of each advisory board serving on the central board in New York. The central board maintains a relatively low profile because the local advisory boards don't overlap geographically and thus feel very select. The bottom line is that the Institute gets the active participation of several hundred networks rather than the dominating participation of twenty to thirty (possibly overused) networks in the central organization.

To be able to create multiple networks simultaneously is a true signal of power. Barry Sullivan, former CEO of First Chicago, is now the deputy mayor for finance of New York City. He recently took a group of more than thirty business people to Europe, where they made calls in London, Paris, Frankfurt, and other financial capitals to spur investment in New York. Sullivan was literally orchestrating a network exchange that will be as good for business in America as it is in Europe. And, each committee member has added a valuable and powerful credential (as well as a focused network of contacts) as a result of participating.

There is a certain protocol to the use of networks. When you borrow a network, you should plan for repayment.[5] Never ask for a favor when you're doing a favor. When you need a favor, probe for an open line by stepping out to selected members of your network and say you wish somebody could help you on this matter. Never expose a network to embarrassment, legal action, or exploitation. When you tap a network for a third party or outside organization make sure that they are principled. An unscrupulous outsider can actually take over another person's network and short-circuit it. This is sometimes done in nonprofit boards, where

5. Networks generally work on barter. People who donate money, generally want prestige, social access, or intellectual capital back. Those who confer dignity and respectability may need a research grant for a friend, etc.

the mailing lists of prospects are filched and milked for rival charities. Those lists should be carefully guarded and not released.
Another rule, absolutely fundamental: Know what you need, but
build your networks one by one based on what you can contribute
as opposed to who you want to use. And, there is a world beyond
networks, too. Sometimes, consciously *not* using or referring
to one's network is a stipulation for dialogue with the powerful.
For example, everyone attending conferences like the World
Economic Forum in Davos or the Business Council's meetings
at the Homestead in Virginia has immense networks. But, to clear
the air of horse-trading and to test the personal mettle of others,
the participants are generally so powerful that they agree to hang
up their networks and not even to refer to them in meetings.

Alliances or strategic partnerships are the official and organizational counterpart to individual networks. They *lease* access to
competence, knowledge, market position, and other intangibles. It
is the emphasis on intangibles that often makes these unions different from mergers. Mitsubishi and Daimler-Benz, Ford and
Mazda, and Renault and Volvo have established global-scale joint
ventures in the automotive industry. Through their twenty-two
bilateral economic agreements, the Czech and Slovak Republics
are now a joint venture, replacing what was a country for more
than seventy years.

The Atomic Building Block

More than any other one factor, powerful people are distinguished
from weak ones by the quality of their informal, individual power
structure—so much so that I deem that structure the atomic building block of power. The informal, truly personal power structure is
called by some the private board of directors; by others, the
kitchen cabinet. It must be as thoughtfully designed and staffed as
any other human support for power, but there is no generalizable
organization structure for this advisory group. It doesn't hurt,
however, to have a strong financial mind, a creative marketer, an
alter ego who knows your personality weaknesses and can help lift

you above them, a truly trustworthy confidant with whom you can share your deepest frustrations, and one or more well-connected people at whatever community level you deem your playing field (metropolitan, state, national, or Mother Earth). Surround yourself with success and with experience. Second, you will advance faster and further when you learn to shift needed constituencies of support *before*, not after, you are promoted to a larger role. You benefit from the forward thrust of closest advisers picked with this in mind. Third, it is by no means necessary that the personal board ever meet. Fourth, these are people genuinely committed to your personal success and in seeing you optimize your power. The majority of the board should not be drawn from the organization over which you preside.

Personal boards provide networks, objectivity, access to sources of capital (especially career and intellectual capital), technical advice, continuity, and assurance. The loyalty of the personal board is terribly important because you are likeliest to consult its members when you are under threat or siege. Their dedication permits you to overcome setbacks such as being passed over, fired, or compromised. The personal board epitomizes the voluntary orientation toward power.

The personal board can be pivotal in career planning. First, they can help one to isolate the true power component of what you do and to identify deliberate ways to expand it or market it. And, they can help you weigh if you are looking at career opportunities in a fresh and fertile way.[6] They can help you groom a consistent image and show you ways to talk beyond the narrow sphere of your technical competence. And, they can help you define if there is an oncoming crisis that should cause you to accelerate or alter your career planning.

---

6. In this regard, good advisers can help protect against the many misleading assumptions that exist. For example, even sophisticated business people still think that there are great opportunities in the smaller companies, but statistics show that small businesses may, as of this writing, have a difficult stretch ahead. This is exactly why I would take a serious look now at opportunities in the Fortune 500 businesses. A candidate who can present ways to make a Fortune 500 company more entrepreneurial or who can clean up bureaucratic remnants offers a very powerful credential.

Propping Up Power:
Backers, Sponsors, Endorsers, and Spokespersons

The official top team of an organization normally includes individuals who are personally and emotionally committed to the success of the organization's leader. There is also an entourage of backers—who factor in the success of the powerful—who are not necessarily part of the team. I've already mentioned that trusted outsiders, such as attorneys and management consultants, are commonly part of the team. They can also be part of the entourage. Other backers in the entourage can't be defined so predictably or easily. One powerful CEO's roster of backers included a management recruiter charged with defining and staffing the optimum organization of the future. (In this case, no friend of the present team to be sure.) The list also had two major suppliers, who knew that their own company would be on the skids if the firm in question failed. A fourth backer was the firm's founder, who was determined to show that his successor (who was also the CEO's predecessor) was a bungling idiot responsible for dragging the company into the swamp. Powerful people must be especially wary of questionable backers like the latter who provide backing for the wrong reason. They generally can invent other reasons to quickly cross agendas with their new "allies."

The power structure requires the consent of those backers it touches deeply. When you change your identity as a power structure, for example, you must have the consent of your backers. For an enterprise, identity may simply be a trade name. An automobile may be a Ford or a Toyota, but lift the hood and you will see a battery and other electronic components with the well-known names of other manufacturers. And the tires you kick surely are not branded Ford or Toyota. In Europe, Siemens may build a television set, but the maker of the picture tube could be Philips. When the Minneapolis Symphony Orchestra changed its name to the Minnesota Orchestra, it certainly broadened its fund-raising constituency. It also became the only major American orchestra not linked to a particular city and jeopardized years of international prestige built up as the Minneapolis Symphony Orchestra with conductors like Ormandy, Mitropolous, and Dorati. When one of the biggest companies in Japan and in the world was intending to change its name, the most important advice I recommended to them was to ask its biggest customers how they felt about the prospective name change. I know of companies that thoughtlessly changed their name, sacrificed their reputation and their brand power in the eyes of their customers, and actually lost their lifeblood business as a result. Identity is not always so simple as a name, especially in politics. When Margaret Thatcher tried to implement the poll tax in 1990, she was changing her political identity and disenfranchising the populist element that had been so important to her rule. It sparked her downfall because she didn't match her intuition about government revenues with adequate statistical analysis of the agenda points of her constituencies.

The powerful must understand the motivation of their followers, especially if they want donors to provide financial backing for a nonprofit organization. The powerful must especially understand what causes adherents to join or increase their commitment and what provokes them to leave or reduce it. Former Republican National Committee head Clayton Yeutter notes that "you have to understand the motivations which underpin political loyalty. Just why do people pound in campaign signs on their front lawns?" It's just as important to pore over the causes of disloyalty, such as the attrition rate in major donor programs. Yeutter believes that you also have to understand what's troubling ex-donors if you hope to win them back. Important, though much less so, is what causes people to *remain* loyal. The principal reason for loyalty is sheer inertia. So often powerful people mistakenly read the donations of those remaining loyal as an endorsement of present policies and rhetoric, when it just as often is a matter of people not caring or not being inspired enough to make a change. To be willing to make a positive change, to start or meaningfully increase giving, financial backers must feel rewarded, in the very least through a specific grasp of an organization's goals. As Red

Cross President Elizabeth Dole puts it: "To encourage international support for the Red Cross, we need to present discrete projects rather than call for contributions to a central pot." Financial backers, of course, can be rallied by psychological as well as intellectual means. The powerful, dependent on contributions, also know how to give others a momentary taste of visible power. Richard Daley, Sr., Jane Byrne, and Harold Washington filled the coffers of the Chicago Democratic Party this way with political fund-raisers in the ballrooms in the Palmer House and the downtown Hyatt in Chicago during the seventies and the eighties. Surrounded by loud bands and even louder paper hats, nondescript foot soldiers would march up to the awesome rostrum, showered in spotlights, as they pledged a union's or PAC's $5,000 or $10,000 to the campaign war chest, their amplified voices booming over the roar of the stomped plank-and-iron platforms. Every four years, Walter Mitty the Backer got to savor his great public moment.

You have to know where to get backers. In the eighteenth century that meant the town square or the village tavern. If you're the YMCA, the Peace Corps, or the Young Republicans in 1990s America, you recruit the youth market in shopping malls on Saturday morning and other places where their focus is already trained and available. Medical research fund-raisers can hit the bull's-eye through controlled distribution magazines in doctors' offices. Impatient professionals (and many other audiences, too) waiting in line at banks and supermarket checkouts can be approached through a new Ted Turner broadcast network. In fact, carefully thinking about the access channels available to reach backers can trigger new ideas about potential backers worth reaching. Never stereotype a potential backer. Participating in a business panel discussion in Turin when communism was rampant and considered an active menace in industrial circles, I spoke with Umberto Agnelli—then-incoming chairman of Fiat—during the break and said to him, "You and your brother Gianni are the two greatest capitalists in Italy and you are also the greatest forces in Turin. If this is true, how can Turin be governed by a Communist mayor?" He looked back at me with a smile and said, "Ah, Mr. Dilenschneider. He may be a Communist, but he's my Communist."

A last word of advice on backers. Cultivating backers is costly. Always ask what kind of quid pro quo is expected? How much time must be surrendered? Is pro bono work in the cards? Some backers can be too expensive for the clout they dish up. If so, the graceful way out is to illustrate to them that *you* really can't help them very much. The best way to rid oneself of an unwanted backer is to demonstrate your own weakness.

Sponsors can be of two general sorts. The first group are the supportive mentors who guide junior leaders-to-be through their career development, and this relationship has been examined from every slant in business literature. The second type of sponsorship is when a powerful person shares his or her patina to materially add to the power of an aspirant. That experience can only really be described through sharing an anecdote. It was December 1979 when I first came to Chicago. My mission was to revive a dying public relations agency. Prowling for business, I made it a point to join the city's most exclusive private club, the Chicago Club. On the first Sunday of each year, the club's members gather for the annual New Year's dinner. William McCormick Blair, Jr., saw me wandering around the fringes of each little conversational circle and sensed that I was anxious to join in but didn't know how. This seventy-five-year-old man came up to me and spent ten minutes chatting with me. Through watching his eyes, I could tell that he was gathering all the vital statistics about who I was and what I was doing in Chicago. Then, because he held the keys to each important conversation, he shepherded me around the room's five largest circles. In less than twenty minutes, he had converted me from wallflower to centerpiece, and I have never forgotten Blair for it.[7] Blair's sponsorship

7. In fact, Blair did a better job for me than he did for Adlai Stevenson, when Stevenson was running for the White House in 1952. Blair—who traveled with Stevenson during the campaign—was able to get the Democratic contender, an unmarried divorcee, an introduction to Greta Garbo but even the charmer Stevenson couldn't land Garbo's phone number. For an interesting account of Garbo and Stevenson, the reader is recommended to Ronald Brownstein's *The Power and the Glitter*.

was a business epiphany for me and the closest personal experience I have had to those legendary tales of J. P. Morgan placing
his arm around the shoulder of the head of a new philanthropy or
college and walking them around the dining room of New York's
Metropolitan Club. After the symbolic stroll, the newcomer could
collect money from anybody.

Endorsers differ from backers and sponsors by being official,
visible, and very often *paid*. Endorsers are a seal of approval
stamped on the mantle of power. They must also be carefully
chosen. What empowers a spokesperson to speak on your
behalf? Travel around the country and you will see scores of
actors, often actors who played doctors or nurses, endorsing
medical care facilities. What do actors know about appendec-
tomies or pacemakers? However, if Dr. C. Everett Koop were to
endorse a medical institution, I'd be inclined to listen. First,
Koop has vast and proven medical experience. Second, he maintains a hard-won professional reputation that he would only risk
for a matter of great principle. Third, he repeatedly has proven
his personal integrity. Endorsers also have to fit with specific
niches. A *Harvard Business Review* article described that Nike,
for example, grouped one part of its tennis products into "rock
and roll tennis" formulated around endorsers like Andre Agassi.
(When Nike's sports marketing director first saw Agassi, he
described his game approach as "hit the ball as loud as you
can.") Agassi is an endorser for the more irreverent *Challenge
Court* Nike niche, while John McEnroe and David Wheaton
appeal to older tennis players through *Supreme Court*—an
assortment geared to "tuxedo tennis." Some endorsements can
be expensive and yet unintentional. Ironically, one of the things
that may save Detroit as an auto center is the fact that the
Japanese now have such an enormous presence there through
strategic collaborations and are so intimately connected through
joint ventures (for example, Mazda and Ford). Wanting to or
not, Japan has endorsed Detroit.

A spokesperson is a particular type of endorser. When a
spokesperson is injected into a controversial situation, integrity,

multidimensional experience, unassailability, and ecumenical access are premium traits. After Johns Manville was nearly overwhelmed by its massive asbestos problem, it hired Paul Kotin to be its spokesperson. His credentials were Awe Factor–caliber. He was director of the National Institute of Environmental Health Sciences—part of the National Institute of Health—and was then the dean of the medical school at Temple. An environmental expert once told me, "Kotin was a first-rate scientist in his own right, and that was very important. Even at the height of the controversy, he could walk into a room and he would be respected for his authority and as a person." Exclusivity is a tangibly valuable trait for a spokesperson. Cliff Robertson's association with AT&T was a highly effective example of this. When Charlton Heston endorses William Buckley's *National Review*, you know it's unlikely that Heston will be boosting *Rolling Stone* next week. And the hunt is ever on for a fresh mouthpiece. There are people who have great credibility for one reason or another but have never been politically active in their past. These virgin endorsers can have tremendous authority as a spokesperson for a political candidate, a social cause, or even a product. Their endorsement states that they have finally found a product, person, or idea that has moved them to speak out. Eleanor Roosevelt got plenty of attention as a first-time spokesperson when she made a margarine ad late in life, even though her fees were donated to charity. Some apparent virgins aren't as chaste as they pretend. A stellar list of chic actors—activists and purists—who turn up their noses at pitching products on American TV are or have been spokespersons on Japan's TV channels. One can scarcely imagine Woody Allen doing ads for Saks or Macy's but he has appeared on Japanese television representing a department store there, according to the Associated Press.

The Fire and Light of Power:
Catalysts, Lightning Rods, Mirrors, and Beacons

Returning to the relationship of energy to power, the powerful hunger for energy, imagination, and intellectual capital, but they often need insulation from excessive controversy. One imposing and often neglected role in the informal organization structure of power is that of catalyst. It is best known in the arts, but it belongs in every form of power structure. In the twentieth century, it would be challenging to find the equal of Alma Mahler, married in turn to the composer Gustav Mahler, the architect Walter Gropius, and the poet Franz Werfel, and a paramour of the painter Oskar Kokoshka; she energized the imagination of each. The critic Friedrich Torberg writes: "She was a woman of colossal artistic understanding and intuitiveness. . . . She was a catalyst of incredible intensity." Catalysts are today more likely to combine analytic skills with their intuitive strength. Peter Drucker, Tom Peters, and Alvin Toffler are such effective executive catalysts because they understand analytic rigor as well as they do intuition.

Even the most inspired ideas require pretesting and refinement. Powerful people often need lightning rods to float trial ideas or absorb controversy. Some positions are almost crafted to be that, and one of them is the White House Chief of Staff. These aides irritate public opinion so often that they are generally kicked out of office on a trifle. Dwight Eisenhower had an extremely capable chief of staff in Sherman Adams, a former governor of New Hampshire, who was hounded out of office because he accepted a vicuna coat as a gift. The coat was only worth a couple of hundred dollars but became a national *cause celebre*. Ronald Reagan's chief of staff, Don Regan, was pitted by the press in a rivalry with the First Lady. Under George Bush, John Sununu was assailed on the matter of personal travel. Since powerful people need lightning rods, mighty allies, who acknowledge the job they do and the risk they take, can and do often exchange emotional "letters of credit" with those who take on this kind of high-risk assignment.

The *mirror* is a power figure who keeps the powerful honest by not letting them ignore the reality of others. Studs Terkel is the archetypal mirror. R. E. Allen, Chairman of AT&T, once said in a Chicago Economic Club address that Terkel was someone who "harnessed the technology of the tape recorder and the printed page to let America know what Americans are thinking."

And there are beacons who help light the way. Former Lyndon Johnson aide Bill Moyers has had a remarkable knack for early identification of emerging themes. This gives him considerable power with the nation's intelligentsia as a relay station and decoder for "incoming" ideas that makes him of special interest to opinion leaders. That knack is also what keeps opinion leaders carefully studying his books and TV series.

Back to the Past

In the circle of power, no contrast is greater than that between power's fire-and-light contingent and the dusky world of figureheads. Figureheads are to power the opposite of what Pygmalion is to statues. Instead of beauty come to life, figureheads are power turned to stone. Turning a powerful figure into a figurehead was once a graceful way of shuffling him or her off the stage of events. Just recently though, the mummies have sought their revenge and the currently powerful are finding out more and more often that they must deal with power out of the past.

As two eminent examples, the Queen of England and the President of Germany were supposed to be seen but not heard. Or *if heard* then comfortably mouthing safe, noncontroversial platitudes. That began to change in the early years of this decade. In 1992, Britain's Queen Elizabeth mildly criticized her countrymen's Westminster politics in a speech before the European Parliament in Strasbourg. More important, her presence in Strasbourg was a potent message about Britain's own sovereignty. Just as Britain's royalty has effectively ceded its sovereignty to democracy within the country, the Queen was signalling Britain's willingness to cede its national independence to a greater Europe. Analysts say an element of Elizabeth's journey to Strasbourg had been blocked during Margaret Thatcher's tenure as Prime Minister and had only become possible with John Major's election.

Since World War II, the German president's post has traditionally been that of a figurehead—the chancellor really holds the power—with the president appointing the majority party or coalition leader chancellor, hosting foreign dignitaries, and addressing congresses of world charities. In the early 1990s, Richard von Weizsäcker (a former president of the German Lutheran church and one-time mayor of Berlin) shocked post-unification Germans on two scores. First he staunchly came out for Berlin as the site of the new German capital, and then he lambasted German politicians for being obsessed with their powerful status and perquisites while they failed to define a new German agenda.

The same phenomenon—is it too strong to call it "The Day of the Living Dead"?—is happening in business. These days an executive kicked upstairs or officially "retired" may land with a nuclear thud on the head of an unsuspecting CEO, as board director John Smale did to GM Chairman Robert Stempel (even though Smale was himself an outsider to GM). What's causing the widespread animation of figureheads? As more and more issues become deadlocked in democracies or in bureaucracies, the press and other watchdogs taunt any sources of power to help break the bottlenecks. Note carefully that most figureheads *do* officially have power. Historical precedent simply dictates that they don't *utilize* the power that they have. Figureheads today are listening more intently to the needs of the present than to the dictates of the past.

Four Truths About Formal Boards

The powerful find the boards of public companies and very visible public institutions to be even more of a power nuisance than figureheads. The demise of reliable hierarchies (a reality that is good for knowledge and bad for orderly control) is truly at the root of much antagonism between boards and CEOs. How do you deal with accountability absent the traditional authority structure? In corporations, this has recently led to boards of directors having a much more visible role in the management of presidents and chief executives. Ironically, the board-CEO relationship is one of the last remnants of classical hierarchic reporting relationships, and the board itself was not taken seriously as an instrument of power or control in corporate affairs until the last decade. Boards, and especially the executive-committee directors, were often the CEO's hand-picked cronies, who created a club of interlaced if not interlocking directorships. Not wanting to have the board apply real pressure against them as CEOs, CEOs serving as directors on other boards politely refused to demur regarding the recommendations of their host CEOs and so on. What resulted was a passive system of no real control, which gave the CEO great operating immunity in the world of American business.

Today, the financial culpability of directors in badly managed businesses can be enormous, and they will find themselves drawn away from their own affairs if they must conduct management searches to replace a company's leadership or fend off takeover campaigns of hostile litigation. In effect, the shift in director attitudes has been achieved by making the threat to personal power weightier than the luxury of letting each CEO be the lord and master of their own manor. A good example of a board turned adversarial is that of General Motors hand-picked directors turning against Robert Stempel. There are warning signs. When the board forms its own outside committee, for example, it's a sure sign that the canary just dropped dead in the coal shaft and that power is in trouble.

Why do most boards now distrust CEOs? Primarily because most CEOs view internal successors as dangers: "Let's get them ready, but not too ready," is the way that most CEOs see things. If an internal successor is poised to advance and the organization stumbles, it is too easy for the board to change partners. But potential successors face risks too. Governmental vice presidents and corporate vice chairmen are vulnerable to the problems of a bobbing transactional profile. Technically a heart-beat away, they often seem a mile away from the true exercise of power. What undermined former Vice President Dan Quayle's authority and credibility was putting him alternately in high-profile situations and then thrusting him into low-profile assignments. At one time he was chairing national security meetings. Later he was the White House emissary to local rallies and spelling bees. It is particularly hard for a powerful person to position a successor credibly without giving them a certain levelness of transactional dignity at the right plateau, but that doesn't happen often. In big institutions, this lack of a reliable backup strategy always causes anxiety. That's why the Pope's smallest sniffles cause anxiety. There *is* no succession plan for the leadership of the Catholic church, and the entire liturgical and political direction of the religion can gyrate in an instant; and, indeed, it did in 1958 when John XXIII succeeded Pius XII, embarking on a major course of theological reform.

The shareholder/director paradigm has become so automatic in addressing accountability that "boards" that are mere phantasms can spin into large organizations like invading starships from outer space and operate as if they have taken on a life of their own. In 1992, if you studied the rhetoric of Republican contrarians Patrick Buchanan and Richard Nixon, you saw how they really depicted themselves as disgruntled shareholders/directors of the Republican party. Nixon's foreign policy memo "The Challenge We Face in Russia," published by the *Wall Street Journal*, was a masterstroke of combative thinking and had all the air of a special study commissioned by a hostile executive committee.

Earlier I commented that what boards offered CEOs was the access to important networks. It's equally important to understand what boards offer to directors, and this is the first of four vital truths about boards. Heidrick and Struggles recruiting expert Pamela Hayes says: "Directors don't do it for the compensation, which is generally token compared with their salaries. They don't do it on a whim—not the way liability insurance premiums for directors have soared. One of the biggest motivations must surely be to contribute their skills and knowledge to an organization: A prime directorship is an excellent way to be visible to other powerful decision-makers." In this sense, the directorship is an opportunity to perform and demonstrate competence and insight to a highly credible network of powerful individuals who could be of enormous use if one is thrown out of a job or stewing in the middle of a heated public controversy.

The second thing that powerful people recognize about boards is that every board has a leadership contingent within it. Consulting the fancies of that contingent is essential to survival. I recall when the head of a major communications conglomerate wanted to fire the president of his biggest advertising agency. He called up the most influential outside directors and asked (a) Do I have your vote? and (b) Is there anything that I must do with respect to the other directors? The outside director said he would lobby the other outsiders in advance to make sure that the vote is wired, and the maneuver was nearly effortless. While this maneuver was implemented by one contact, most CEOs assemble their board with two or three stalking horses. Wise leaders routinely canvas their board (and especially its stalking horses) before the board meets. Ed Woolard at du Pont and John Reed at Citicorp are very good at working their boards. The fact that Henry Schacht withstood all the heat he took and ultimately triumphed in his drive to make Cummins a premier manufacturer of diesel engines indicates how well Schacht built support among his directors.

The third and fourth boardroom truths are that the leader of an organization learns a paradox: Formal boards cannot afford to be a formality, and they cannot afford not to be. They must get real advice flowing into the organization. Recent articles have pointed out that corporations are worrying too much about creating rainbow coalitions in boards without instilling enough outside technical, marketing, and international expertise. That said, no powerful person can afford to treat the directors casually or to make the director meetings brainstorming sessions and retain real control. For example, board meetings and board agendas are painstakingly orchestrated. Annual meetings and board meetings become so calculated that they can make the entire tone of an organization seem contrived, making difficult if not impossible to seize real opportunities. Anyone who has shared in preparing for a Fortune 500 company or a national charity's board meeting knows the amount of theatrical preparation these sessions receive: All of it is calculated to enhance predictability. Even that doesn't always work. I have heard of a director on the board of a major financial institution who flies in from London each month. Between Heathrow and Kennedy his positions will somersault. Even during the meetings he'll change like a chameleon. His colleagues think he's a knave, and the CEO doesn't know what to think; but the chairman of the executive committee is already shopping for a director's retirement gift. When you are entrusted with power, constancy is a very important trait. If you don't have it, you can become a significant risk and a royal pain in the neck.

Thoughtful business leaders like Sir Adrian Cadbury in the United Kingdom have been grappling with business governance and the board/CEO schism. In the highest industry circles, there is a growing move toward making the chairman and the CEO separate positions as in the European style of organizational governance. But until American management style adjusts better for true teamwork at the top, I doubt that much progress will be made. In general, it's hard for an institution to tolerate two sources of ultimate power.

Cleaning the Power House

The most dramatic way the powerful purge their adversaries or potential adversaries is to allege that a palace plot is about to take place. Hitler did so when he rid himself of Ernst Roehm and several hundred other foes one evening in 1934 in what is now called the "Night of the Long Knives." Although a Nazi ally, Roehm proved too "moderate" for Hitler's tastes. The powerful can clean house in lots of ways and give lots of different reasons for doing so. Former CBS Chairman William Paley went through his share of top executives. The French president can turn over prime ministers faster than the *Coutouriers et Créateurs* shift skirt lengths. And, Saturday night massacres of presidential aides didn't just happen in the Nixon White House.

Literal and figurative bloodbaths do the powerful no good. But, the systematic and justifiable expulsion of anyone in the support structure—including even donors, endorsers, principal fund-raisers, and guiding lights—may be necessary from time to time for the sake of the organization's agenda. Just as a Rolodex needs premeditated shaping and regular review, so does the supporting cast. Tough questions must be asked: Is a person and his or her image consistent with long-range objectives? Does he or she have similar stature to the endorsers supporting other institutions with whom one must compete for capital, government aid, or professional regard? Is the person really an "inheritance" rewarded for their past giving or personal involvement but now leaning on those historical laurels? It's easy to overlook someone in the cast: The review should include commercial spokespersons, motivational speakers at company meetings, special-interest and regulatory advocates, and political figures. I know, for example, of at least ten politicians, some of them very liberal Democrats, who are terrified of being endorsed by Jane Fonda. One suspects that handshake photos with Congressmen Jim Wright or Barney Frank came down from an awful lot of office walls as these politicians became embroiled in controversy. Part of this behavior makes sense and part of it is phobic, but a legitimate aspect of stoking an organization with power is finding where the energy is seeping out and patching up the leaks.

THE ORGANIZATION

Modern power does not function through hierarchy, nor is it realized in a command mode. Power is a social act and increasingly a collaborative one. If power is their goal, individuals must consciously

manage themselves as power structures and develop an ample cadre of human resources, because
authority and the force of power is no longer
invested by directive, can be quickly crippled, and
needs plenty of fresh ideas.

5

The Management of Power

A Guide to Heavy Lifting

They had these grand e-mail votes on things, but nobody had any authority to do anything.

—CAROL BARTZ,
AFTER TAKING OVER
AS CEO OF AUTODESK

**How is power seized and increased, lost and weakened?
What feeds power and what undermines it? How is
power conferred and how is its continuity preserved?**

We have become very discriminating about how power is allowed to handle itself. Certain behaviors fit a proper mold of modern power and others don't. For example, order-giving used to be what power was all about. Today, order-giving is often dysfunctional, since most people in organizations can solve their own problems and are expected to do so. Similarly, the powerful have been revered and feared as sources of arbitrary change. Today, a powerful person can easily overdraw the "change account," as people demand to know what benefit all that change had.

Defining and defending turf were once tantamount to defining power over an organization's geography, but the modern organization won't work without its players being able to slide over the arbitrary boundaries of departments, sectors, and commands. Playing general inspector was once a favorite power pastime. If today's leadership has to inspect to get results, then the organization is already failing.

Buffers, Barriers, Flanking, and Choke Points

Some of the management prerequisites of power have remained the same, and one of these is the need for a fundamental stability. In simpler times, power usually ruled in an orderly way over a relatively orderly universe. Today, powerful people are darting in and out of transactions constantly. Their role and authority is continually challenged by an often changing cast of adversaries. With all these complications, underlying stability becomes that much more precious a commodity. Any large-scale change threatens stability, and it is a serious and essential challenge for the powerful to determine what contributes to stability and what threatens it. Those forces are often concealed and hard to isolate. Cavalier growth or expansion, for example, can undermine that stability and unhinge the very power it seeks to expand. The moorings to support growth must be strong and tested. In reality, some of those moorings are often misjudged or even overlooked.

In his autobiography, former **IBM** CEO Thomas J. Watson, Jr., points out that barriers to or from power can act as buffers as well. Buffers can also turn out to be supports. When a barrier may be nothing more than it seems to be, power must find its way around it. For example, because the business situation in northern Europe is so firmly established and all the players are well known, competition must shave margins to a tenth of a point. Some northern European firms have stopped banging their heads against the growth barriers and have moved the heart of their new business development to southern Europe and South America. They have no established strength there, but the relative openness of those markets holds more opportunity than their former position in the established markets. However, the tactic doesn't always work, and is especially risky when a paradigm shift begins in the home industry, profession, or market. Then the growth barrier can function as a buffer that keeps aliens out while giving domestic players a power advantage. It can also be a buffer against poor internal decisions and can help prevent drifting from the main agenda. In this case, a domestic player romping abroad with a new venture at the wrong time, and dedicating its best resources there, can undermine its home core.

To illustrate, the Hong Kong–based conglomerate Hutchison Whampoa justified its excursions into aggressive foreign investment (such as its stake in Canada's Husky Oil) on the basis of limited investment opportunity in Hong Kong and the imminent return of the Crown Colony to Chinese authorities in 1997. But Hutchison's expansion went amiss and was compounded by apparently diminished attention to businesses back in the Colony. Even worse, the entanglements abroad seemed to have hamstrung Hutchison's penetration into the People's Republic of China just as free market dynamics there were taking hold. In the end, expatriate Chinese families operating from distant centers like Manila, Los Angeles, and Vancouver may make more of the Chinese economic evolution than Hutchison may, even though it is probably the most powerful single company in Hong Kong. Had Hutchison Whampoa simply lived with the temporary growth barriers in Hong Kong and waited for economic opportunities in its own region to evolve, some observers think that it would have been much better off. Instead, its attempt to elude barriers created new ones.

Barriers can be created by faulty information as well as poor judgment. Camouflaged information about the strength of a force or about that force's true motives can present formidable barriers to the powerful. In my discussion of Awe Factor, I mention charlatans who try to bluff the expectations of others to create a sense of awe. In combat, concealment of strength is a major strategic advantage—a point that von Clausewitz develops admirably. To prevent

German intelligence from detecting the site of the Normandy Invasion, Eisenhower created mock air fields with decoy clapboard airplanes. As contests have become less bloody and increasingly economic, the principle remains the same, although the methodology changes. The manipulation is generally for economic gain. Some experts, for example, suspect that the Republic of China systematically understates its economic output. Why would an emerging economy *understate* its economic productivity? What concessions on trade or its obligations to the international community as the world's largest nation could it hope to earn by *overstating* its economic performance? Such a manipulation can only work for a while.

If a large organization's evaluations are important to the powerful, it can camouflage the fact that it has its own particular agenda, but not forever. The League of Women Voters, an organization that has done considerable good over the years, is today a force that has evolved a definite political agenda while it remains technically nonpartisan. Writes Robert V. Pambianco, who edits the *Organization Trends* newsletter of the Capital Research Center: "With no agenda other than good government; [the League] is prevented by law from endorsing candidates. In reality, however, the League is a potent political advocate whose positions on issues are anything but 'strictly nonpartisan,' as its literature declares." Pambianco goes on to mention a number of controversial topics where the League has political positions, including gun control, voter registration, and the environment. More politicians will step forward to challenge the League as a barrier to fairness if its purported neutrality continues to lose its defensibility.

Other obstructions to power are limits imposed on operating latitude. As one has more authority, the more volatile the management of power becomes. The traditional pyramid surrounding power generally used to offer security (except from assassinations) and the semblance of stability, now advancement means plunging ahead into a broader river and even more turbulent white rapids. As we saw earlier, boards of directors are often anxious to control the prerogatives of a CEO who takes too much risk, takes the wrong kind of risk, or is simply struggling with complex problems. I call this kind of control "flanking" and the ultimate form of flanking is establishing an "office of the president" or "office of the chairman." This step may seem prudent, but is often ineffective, because it substitutes an officially empowered committee for true leadership. That committee will be more interested in exerting control than in getting things done. An interim flanking strategy is to recall retired executives to "help" supplement management during a particularly tough time. At the end of 1992, IBM did exactly that when it brought back Paul Rizzo and Kaspar Cassani to aid John Akers. Since Rizzo was a major rival of Akers, it is unlikely that Akers came to this conclusion alone. Outside sources speculated that the board was at least a partner in this action, if not the source. (Akers, of course, was ultimately replaced by Louis Gerstner.) On a more prosaic level, a form of software that limits the range of options (called "groupware") is being used more often to contain the power and risk-taking of executives in financial organizations. This is a mechanized form of the flanking strategy.

Flanking creates barriers or limits for the powerful within their own organizations, while choke points are generally limits imposed by bottlenecks or gatekeepers external to the organization. Choke points may often seem and may in fact *be* petty, but they can be enormously aggravating strategic barriers. Also, choke points, in this discussion, are different from the mere situational inconveniences of surly drivers or uncooperative phone operators. The people or processes who form these choke points are generally highly skilled and can exert an influence that materially affects decision-making, and the powerful constantly scan for the choke points that govern a situation. Many choke points are hard to detect, but some are blatantly advertised. A certain head of state in the Middle East is consistently more powerful than his peers because he successfully links business and politics and promotes his control of certain strategic choke points. "Do you want to impose sanctions against Iraq? Pay my nation certain concessions or my border will be like Swiss cheese," he says in effect. Power

learns where the choke points are and how to control them, just as
a knight in the Middle Ages knew where the chinks in his armor
were if he wanted to stay alive until his retirement. Wherever
power is curtailed, refined, or slows to a crawl, one can generally
spot a choke point. In many industries, to cite a very different kind
of example, there are just one or two analyst symposiums each
year that present the leading companies in a given industry to
major institutional investors. Control of that agenda is a choke
point to power, and the organizers of these seminars know it.
Zoning commissions are choke points for real estate developers.
Dogma committees can be choke points to a religious organization's scope of action.

Choke points that control property rights have an enormous
bearing on the pursuit and exercise of power. In years past the
powerful may have chased gold, oil, spices, or salt, and in time each
of these kinds of treasures developed their own choke points.
Consider how many movie westerns revolve around registering a
claim with the assayer's office, the government geologist, or the
bureau of deeds. These were the power choke points of the Old
West. In modern Japan, it often takes between five and seven years
to process and establish a patent. Patent office examiners are a
choke point to wealth rights and knowledge because knowledge in
intellectual property law is certified in Japan on a first-to-file standard rather than a first-to-invent basis (which is the norm in the
United States). But the Japanese liberate the knowledge contained
in the patent, publicizing it eighteen months after it is filed. They
do so intentionally, ostensibly so that others can contest the claim,
but probably—in the spirit of Michael Porter's analysis of national
competitive advantage—also to help feed the knowledge pool that
has become such a strategic advantage for the foremost Japanese
industrial segments. In a comparative sense, Japan as a nation owns
the power advantage of its resident knowledge more collectively
than the does United States, and that can be a critical stimulus to
innovation. How the Japanese regulate the process of establishing
idea ownership has an obvious impact on Japanese competitiveness
worldwide. A Japanese patent office examiner is not only a choke

point of power in Japan, but equally one for any firm wanting to do business worldwide *versus* a Japanese competitor. The Japanese practice is a choke point with a profound impact on how people invent or disclose in the rest of the world.

Choke points are generally manned by flesh-and-blood people, but not necessarily. In one European country, the mere twenty-six physical seats in a parliamentary hearing room control the number of voices and viewpoints that will be aired on a given issue. Toll gates helped fund the fiefdoms of Europe's feudal culture, and its aristocratic class derived considerable income on exacting fees for passage through the choke points of narrow river bends and mountain passes. Bribery and political corruption are choke points of the most primitive form. Generally, the powerful should respect choke points (no easy matter, since choke points by their very essence provoke impatience) and, at the same time, should avoid influencing choke points directly. People who attempt to wield this kind of influence are perceived as influence-peddling, bribing, or manipulating. That means working through what is euphemistically called an "agent" in the Middle East and much of Africa and Asia. Regulators bring choke points into being the world over. What *baksheesh* is in the East, lobbyists are, in a more legal and refined way, to the West. Global businesses are confronted with this issue all the time. Once while I was on an assignment in Europe, the prime minister of an African nation told me that he would throw another firm out on its ear if Pepsi would give his brother its bottling franchise. Clearly, Pepsi wouldn't and couldn't entertain such a deal, and I didn't even present them with the proposition. Uniform global ethics policies are a real constraint on power in the West, but often go unrespected by some of the more energetic international competitors.

Paying for Power: Plunder and Pork

Putting aside the official top team, the wages and salaries paid to those supporting power are rarely exceptional and hardly consonant with what the loyalty, time, and pain of the job demand. Outside of titles, roles, notoriety, or participation in the power structure—all the trimmings that go with the organizational structure treated in the last chapter—the most direct way that the powerful have rewarded loyalty and service historically is through plunder and pork. The general distinction I make between plunder and pork is that pork comes from the domestic public or community trough (or, in the case of a company, from the assets of the business) and generally funds jobs while plunder is appropriated from abroad, usually during military or colonial campaigns. Plunder is more primitive and deals more expressly with riches.

First plunder. For ages plunder was a critical medium with which the powerful paid personal debts and rewarded their loyalists. Plunder meant invading another country and taking spoils for nothing or next to nothing. There is no doubt that the Dutch settlers who bought Manhattan Island from Native Americans for twenty-four dollars worth of trinkets were practicing the "next-to-nothing" school of plunder. Other plunderers were outright thieves. Historian Paul Johnson says Napoleon looted the "art collections of Germany, Italy, and Spain for the Louvre. . . . [And] when the French plenipotentiary Brune left Switzerland for Italy, the bottom of his carriage collapsed with the weight of the stolen gold he had stacked in its boot." Such colonial powers as Great Britain elevated plunder to the status of both a political system and a civil religion.

Plunder is very much out of fashion today. In fact, plunder—while still extremely important to power—is chiefly of modern interest on a national or societal level, and its underlying dynamics have changed dramatically. Plunder was truly a straightforward concept in an age of undercapacity, that is, for the lion's share of human history. However, the modern world's overcapacity of production and a new hierarchy of values significantly complicate the problem of plunder. Assuming an advanced industrial society such as the United States needs intermediary ingredients like steel and computer chips to make its wares, traditional economic sense says it would want those ingredients at the lowest price and the best quality available. Certainly in 1900 it would have sourced raw materials and intermediary goods strictly on those terms. But, in a world of overcapacity, buying too cheap abroad—plundering at the invitation of the plundered, in effect—costs jobs and the very existence of companies back home. The powerful in the United States risk disaffecting their supporters—labor and other special interest groups and even shareholders and segments of big business—by favoring what look on the surface like absurdly smart economic decisions.

Pork is the domestic or internal counterpart to plunder. In some respects, pork is also an evolutionary step beyond plunder, truly establishing itself at the time of the Second World War and just as the last big grasp was being made (the Soviet seizure of Eastern Europe). Pork is most significant as subsidized employment (which also, of course, leads to revenues for service and manufacturing firms), and there is no better place to study the art of pork than the budget of the U.S. federal government. A private sector crusader against pork, the industrialist J. Peter Grace, is the foremost expert on pork. Grace's Citizens Against Government Waste (a public group of which he is cochairman) has actually printed an exposé called the *Pig Book*, spelling out the most egregious pork-barrel projects. The phrase "power pork" is used in analyzing the different kinds of political patronage doled out, especially by federal elected officials, to the constituents back home and a feature article in *Newsweek* points to "the rehab of President William McKinley's *in-laws'* home [and] studies of whether tequila will make fish drunk." *Newsweek* maintains that only a few members of Congress can get away with "brazen political spoilsmanship." Not quite, but with the media sifting every appropriation, that's getting truer all the time.

Pork was once the staple of the power diet in both industry and politics. Of course, large slabs of pork were generally purchased for hefty political contributions, but changing realities are changing the rules.[1] The former Wisconsin Senator William Proxmire

1. Even though the contributions that bought pork were massive by political standards, the purchase price of pork could never compare with the millions and billions of dollars in economic benefits that the pork itself supplied.

used to publicize "Golden Fleece" Awards, which brought glaring public pressure down on spending taxpayer dollars for studying the mating habits of obscure animals and similar exotica. Reforming the process is damnably hard, especially when the special interest and the elected official have a long-standing relationship. On a company and industry level, no one has formulated the problem of pork better than the economist Murray Weidenbaum, when he says: "New and growing firms may be economically strong, but they are usually politically weak. They lack a record of financial contributions to political candidates and a knowledge of lobbying techniques. Old firms, in contrast, may be economically weak, but they are politically strong. They possess well developed relationships with key political figures." This fact does more than hamper reform. It is also disadvatageous to innovation in two ways: Because dynamic new firms (those likeliest to contribute to the wealth of a knowledge economy) don't have the power investment built up over years, and because these firms must abide by newer and tougher moral standards before they can cultivate the relationships.

Because pork has been such an integral part of modern power, the powerful face a formidable problem, especially if they want to take a stand for values. Some members of their personal or official board might accept intellectual capital or prestige as reward enough, but most want their pork—either for themselves, their allies, or their own organizations. If they don't get it as a reward for their intellectual or emotional capital or sweat equity in one place, they are likely to find another place where they will. The solution is to reform pork oneself and hopefully the constituency with it. Instead of presenting esoteric projects, supporters should only be allowed to advance projects that are sensible and have some plausible tie to the commonweal. Constituencies should develop meaningful strategic strengths that can serve as the skeleton upon which future projects can be arrayed. If a state or university has a legitimate and acknowledged leadership in heart disease or Alzheimer's research, one's odds of commanding generous appropriations are higher than others. When the taxpayers' dollars are at stake, there's no substitute for an eye on the trends that affect the average person most.

Often the hardest part of the challenge is getting subordinates to accept developmental pork in lieu of lightweight work or goof-ball research projects in the Bahamas. This is a matter of training. Supporters should welcome developmental pork as the clearest kind of support for the enlightened self-interest of the knowledge worker. They will *if* the powerful merchandise it properly. On the organizational or group level, legitimate job-training programs or investments in free-enterprise zones are likely to be seen much more positively than pointless public-works projects. In corporations, training and advanced management programs are the healthy pork alternative to many executive perquisites. Above all, smart power avoids the "pig in a blanket," that is, hiding pork in unrelated appropriations, a ploy as often attempted in corporate budgeting as it is in Congress or statehouses. Its backers—when they are unmasked by auditors, the media, oversight committees, activists, or adversaries—are generally criticized on two counts: first, for the project itself and second, for its conscious conceal-ment.

Pork even functions in the world of economic diplomacy. Enlightened pork is what lets countries advance economically and socially. How does a country develop and change its status in the world economy? How does it become strong and powerful? Studying countries like South Korea, which has only recently become powerful, is instructive for both individuals and organizations. The most important powers a less developed country can exhibit are 1) a hospitality to new investment, 2) meaningful access to the power centers of developed countries, 3) the ability to protect itself from exploitation in the process of being developed,[2] and 4) a focused and tenacious dedication to a clear and

2. The third point can have devastating impact on the evolution of power. When I visited with Soviet leaders in the spring of 1991, they were already wary of how the West might exert power if they admitted that their economy was underdeveloped. Ideological conquest—the advocacy of free speech and market economies—quickly became commercial conquest (buying up assets cheaply and looking to launch mar-ket-dominant positions). In such instances, concessions to powerful expansionists are

limited agenda. At least partly because South Korea has been determined and successful in achieving this agenda, it has won substantial financial subsidy from the United States over the past fifty years—chiefly in the form of generous military aid.

THE EVOLVING MODALITIES OF POWER

Most contemporary books that address the management practices of power have a black-and-white reformist character to them. They tout consensus as the absolute solution to hierarchic management and/or empowerment as the only real alternative to order-giving. In truth, like "management by walking around," most of the acclaimed new modalities of power are really transitional and corrective and are often no more certain to solve problems than preceding methods. Intelligent powerful people regard them as a direction rather than a method. Generally, it is more important that things be done than it is that leadership be incessantly preoccupied with *how* they are done. Authentic power today should not try to make manipulation *more enlightened.* Rather, it should look at more meaningful ways to give people an opportunity for a piece of the action or at least a say in determining how the pie is cut. What has made many people very angry at power during the beginning of the nineties is that the powerful have begun preaching these humanistic homilies about management at the very same time that they have taken away the pie. In the fall of 1992, *Industry Week* turned a gimlet eye on the effectiveness of all this psychology of joy and liberation being infused into management. It simply asked workers if they were having more fun. They weren't. In fact, 67 percent said that they were not having fun in 1992 versus 63 percent in 1990. What is especially dramatic is that 61 percent said that "we're not a team" was the reason for the funless world of organizations—versus 49

---

generally the very worst thing to do. In the 1880s, Lobengula, chief of the Matabeles in Africa, thought he could get rid of Britain's African imperialist Cecil Rhodes by granting him mineral rights. Instead, the concession simply opened the door to full-tilt British colonization.

percent two years ago. By the way, it isn't just the proles and the punchcard workers who are disgruntled. More than 60 percent of the vice presidents and middle managers surveyed were unhappy too. Faulty efforts to reform the management practices are often at fault in causing this shocking erosion of attitude. Some of the chief New Age management practices should be looked at method by method.

1. Intimidation Versus Voluntarism

The recent literature on power has mostly emphasized the use of intimidation as the tool of power. In advanced economies, with today's modern social nets, intimidation is not as genuinely threatening as it may often sound. People allow it to have its effect because we have essentially become lazy and cowardly about losing our basic social comforts and incremental wealth. We treat them as entitlements. Intimidation touches our jungle instinct of fear, masquerading past threats for real ones. Intimidation is not the practice of power but the play-acting of power. (I treat intimidation here and not in the section on emotions of the powerful because intimidation, when used by the powerful, is almost always calculating and only seemingly emotional. It is emotional on the side of the victim.)

Only the naive would say intimidation is no longer a factor in power. The powerful use intimidation when they believe that someone under them could somehow thwart the agenda of the powerful or the organization. Intimidation remains a weakness of the powerful, although a waning one, and is generally only effective when the powerful exert "bogey-man" strategies about what *could* happen if one is disloyal or too independent. Nonetheless, the language can still be richly bombastic, as in the case of a screenwriter who contends that a very powerful agent said his "foot soldiers who go up and down Wilshire Boulevard each day" would blow the screenwriter's brains out if he switched agencies. One obviously assumes the terms are not meant literally but as a professional metaphor. Public exposure controls intimidation such as this, whether it is figurative or literal. In the West, we think of the magnitude of the Tienanmen Square massacre as being great. The real fact is that, without the relatively easy availability of pixilators and fax machines to feed back nearly instant images of what was happening, the repression would have been far more massive and much deeper.

Another form of intimidation that is still used is something I term the "moving freight train." The powerful invoke this tactic to buffalo members of their own team who fail to show sufficient enthusiasm. Organizations fight very hard to develop sales momentum, research momentum, and quality momentum. Skepticism, lethargy, and a host of other factors create enormous inertia against momentum, and even the most dignified power figures can become petulant and childish if the sense of momentum is blocked or extinguished. It is certainly true that the powerful person is right on a practical level. Anyone who retards momentum is actually more destructive to modern power than an external villain. It is the pursuit of a power structure's agenda that matters far more in getting things done than does a perceived adversary's attack. Offenses against "momentum" are combatted by making the subordinate feel either too small or too big. If the goal is to make the subordinate feel impotent, the momentum itself is magnified—the size and energy of the momentum distorted to make it seem far bigger than reality—turning pushcarts into thundering freight trains. Potential opponents, the powerful suggest, could be flattened by forces that are bound to overwhelm them, and *no one would want to see this happen,* the powerful benevolently add.

The second tactic is to portray an internal adversary as powerful rather than powerless. This person could *indeed* upset the upbeat atmosphere and might even destroy the organization. Here the target of intimidation is drawn mental pictures of the needless despair and torment other colleagues will suffer if they—the adversaries—don't button-up the criticism and play along. The first intimidation tactic coerces through warning the person not to become a victim. The second depicts him or her as a saboteur.

Both tactics are most effectively executed if 1) momentum is projected as some magical gift of the gods and not something that the aspiring manipulator can control, and 2) the threatener is positioned as a *helpful* ally trying to warn the unreflective of the dangers that surround them.

Jacques Delors and the European Commission used what was commonly referred to as the "moving bicycle" theory to try to speed Europe on a path of relentless momentum toward unification. Don't get in the way of destiny, Delors seemed to caution all the Common Market members. Then came tiny Denmark's brick-wall resistance to the Maastricht accords and a decided downturn in "1992ism" in such countries as Germany, France, and the United Kingdom. In our time, intimidation tactics will continue to lose luster because, as power becomes more and more of a social act requiring consent, it doesn't take long for other members of the team to see that manipulation, and not authentic power, is being used to prod them along.

The opposite of intimidation in the knowledge economy is motivating workers to want to produce and to surrender their intellectual capital willingly, enthusiastically, and loyally. Knowledge workers are smart by definition, and, with good reason, they distrust power and distrust putting much stock in loyalty to companies. That's why progressive firms like 3M reward their scientists who are "good at the bench" with attractive career advancement opportunities even if they don't have the interest in or the experience to be top-level managers; why real-estate baron Trammell Crow encourages his people to become wealthy in their own right so that they will stand up to him and help him to make the best possible decisions; and why Sam Walton was so pleased to see cashier and stockroom "associates" become millionaires.

2. Belligerence Versus Mediation

Belligerence once meant physical aggression. Now, it generally means relentless litigation, but the objective and the end effect are the same: to inflict damage. Just as Dwight Eisenhower was the first great tipster on the military-industrial establishment, it was the Manhattan Council and other farsighted study groups who exposed the fact that the only real benefactors of litigated belligerence are the attorneys for the warring parties.

Mediation is the only corrective alternative to belligerence. However, because of their penchant for taking charge, powerful people are prone to overlook an important attitudinal reality in mediation. Unless a special circumstance prevails (as I will describe in Chapter 8 with regard to Rabbi Schneier) the powerful are not called in to mediate a conflict. Instead, professional mediators are used. The powerful are at least one force in the conflict that is being mediated, and that position calls for different skills than being the mediator oneself. In this sense, being an effective figure in mediations really begins with the skill of listening to one's enemies effectively. One learns this from dealing with adversaries, where the subject being mediated is the "truth." Power must withstand the interrogation of congressional committees, brilliant attorneys, and penetrating journalists. These antagonists have really created an entire art form of how to make powerful people vulnerable, which often first requires putting the powerful person at ease. To do that, one must know how to make the penetrating, probing question look harmless. An outstanding investigative reporter like Jack Anderson or Brit Hume will generally come to an interview with a list of nineteen rapport-building questions and a seemingly harmless twentieth one. It will be sandwiched somewhere on the list, and it is the only question that they really want answered. For the respondent, the key is to reflect on each question thoughtfully, trying to spot what hostile agenda might be housed within its meaning. Another coping device is to use relationships as a buffer against hostility. Advance contact is often an excellent way to build up mediation reserves "on account." When the powerful talk to the editorial boards of the *New York Times*, the *Wall Street Journal*, or the *Washington Post*, it is often to create a preemptive sense of dialogue. Even if one is later attacked, an adversary attacks a conversational partner in a much different way than a total stranger. These tactics are not just of use in dealing with journalists; trial lawyers, Congressional oversight committees, and shareholder activist groups can all be managed better through listening to potential adversaries honestly, thus setting a groundwork to make them more receptive.

Just as the structure of power is rarely the lone individual, the powerful can dub emissaries to help in the mediation role. Dave Osborne and Ted Gaebler's recent book *Reinventing Government* describes how Madison, Wisconsin's city officials deployed that city's meter monitors to become the initial level of police community relations. Instead of just writing out parking tickets, they formed the first line of community relations and intelligence. Here the representatives of potentially hostile authority serve a mediating role. (If more powerful people would only use their administrative assistants and secretaries in the same way!)

Listening to enemies is not just important when one is under attack or scrutiny. With the right skills, it is possible to encourage an adversary to confess their agenda and to preempt the ultimate need for mediation. How can one inspire one's adversaries to open up? Observing Sir Geoffrey Yeend, the deputy assistant to the prime minister and the number-two man in the Australian government, one could learn important tactics in this regard. In any conference or committee debate, Yeend would always commend his enemies for their viewpoints and would insistently ask them to explain their positions. They would feel flattered—especially as he took copious notes—and he was generally able to draw them out and expose their position and tactics. It was because of the way that he conducted himself that he was able to draw them out. Although he was genuinely trying to understand their position and his sincerity beamed through, he had no intention of changing the government's position because of their argument, and this irreversible singleness of purpose was undetectable. He is a true "invisible man" (because of what he does not reveal). Yeend's personal style helps enable this; he's unassuming and doesn't make a big impression when he walks in. Once I saw him before a group of scholars debating an issue that was later taken up by the Australian parliament. The scholars were obviously entranced with the intellectual elegance of their own battle plan; but, before the meeting adjourned, Yeend had learned their agendas and tactics to the point where their entire scheme was for nought.

It is both hardest and most important to listen to those smart challengers who try to define power with great precision and to anger it at the same time. John Wyclif, the fourteenth-century Oxford scholar, was forever splitting hairs and reigning in power: "No, communion was just bread and wine," he would say. "No, the Pope's business is just church business." The Chicago community activist Saul Alinsky reminds me of Wyclif. Indeed, Alinsky, who died in 1972, called himself the "kosher cardinal." What made Alinsky so hard to deal with was his relentless anger, but Chicago journalist M. W. Newman points out that Alinsky had some remarkable friends, too, like the theologian Jacques Maritain and the millionaire philanthropist Marshall Field III. I'm convinced that what allowed people like Maritain to make contact with Alinsky was that they engaged his intellect and compelled him to a dialogue above emotions—no easy thing with someone who has a driving emotional agenda, but absolutely essential if one is to preserve the power stakes.

Jesse Jackson is certainly one of the best powerful figures to study as a role model for a participant in mediation. Over the last three years (remembering the flap over the Nike shoe boycott in 1990), Reverend Jackson has shown more and more poise in advancing the agenda of his supporters and has even been requested to mediate for organizations beyond those he generally represents, as when unions asked him to intervene in the 1990 strike against the *New York Daily News*. In the summer of 1992, he scored a major moral victory when candidate Bill Clinton had to apologize to Jackson for an emotional outburst. One hallmark of Jackson's new mediating style is to put emotional outrage to the side and to concentrate on economic objectives and issues.

3. Order-Giving Versus Empowerment

It's hard to imagine a more committed order-giver than Saddam Hussein. He has made the command mode so automatic that his people may assume it is almost a fact of Iraqi life. In the words of Jafer al-Barazanji, an Iraqi civilian official: "If President Saddam Hussein says something, the whole nation says the same." In the modern West, we recoil from such blind obedience and are constantly asking the people to speak up. But, how often do we truly want employees to do so? We *say* we do, but the people who *aren't* having fun don't believe it for an instant, especially if we throw the word *empowerment* into the message. In no management theory has looming hypocrisy been so manifest as in the concept of empowerment. On its own, empowerment is a wonderful theory. In reality, it has been disastrously mismanaged and has often fallen on it's face. I'd even call it the *fool's gold* of personnel policies in the 1980s. One human resources executive described it to me a little differently, as "the dirty little secret" of personnel management. Rarely defined with any precision, empowerment has been presumed to mean decentralizing power to the lowest levels possible and giving individuals the authority to get the job done. Why hasn't it worked? Because the constructive goal of decentralizing power was not the real reason that empowerment was pursued.

British Petroleum provides an excellent example. In June 1992, *The Economist* reported that British Petroleum's nonexecutive directors asked for the resignation of its CEO Robert Horton. Horton had only been on the job for two years and, according to *The Economist*, had instituted an aggressive program for renovating BP in which "empowerment" was an important concept. But that's not what some insiders perceived happened. "Instead of feeling themselves 'empowered,' some BP managers are described in internal memos as being overburdened by work that has not been reorganized to suit the slimmed down hierarchy."[3]

---

3. It should be pointed out that British Petroleum has made recent and important performance improvements under its present CEO David Simon.

∘   ∘   ∘

It's no accident that empowerment and downsizing emerged as management concepts at the same time. A study done by Wyatt Company found that "downsizing firms may not bring profitability." Most companies tackle the problem of reductions in the wrong order. Rather than eliminate "low-value work" first, they cut jobs instead. They never really get at the inefficiencies, and empowerment is used to cloak the reductions. Too often empowerment has become a convenient explanation for staff cuts. Before any leader pursues a course of empowerment, they need to pose hard questions: Is my goal to really push power down the line or to license the creation of fewer positions? Does my plan for empowerment specify how the mechanics of decision-making will change inside the organization? Have those to be empowered been readied for the change, or are they simply being told to "sink-or-swim"? What power is top management actually foregoing and how will this change its use?

But empowerment can be genuine. When it is, a leader must usually assume meaningful risk, as when rivals are enabled to resolve differences without authorities intervening. Ulrich Roloff-Momin sits at the helm of the cultural budget for the city of Berlin, according to John Rockwell of the *New York Times*. (This is nothing to sneeze at, Rockwell points out. Berlin's culture budget is $600 million a year, more than three times that of the National Endowment for the Arts' for the entire United States!) When Berlin was united, Rockwell describes how Roloff-Momin was confronted with two rival singing groups each of whom saw themselves as an heir to Berlin's famed Singing Academy. A cagey diplomat, he didn't grind them through the state bureaucracy. Instead, according to Rockwell, the culture czar invited both groups to dinner. The inevitable impromptu songfest followed, reconciliation bloomed, and the groups came up with their own merger plan. In this case, genuine empowerment was providing access to the actual right to decide.

The most interesting and potent form of empowerment, like

most evolving management techniques, deals with control over assets. In the industrialized countries, this has made pension rights and the portability of pensions hot topics. Empowerment may also include restoring to people their rightful assets to make them fully vested players in a market economy. Such is Vaclav Klaus's program of giving ownership vouchers to the citizens of the Czech Republic and thereby returning to them property that was appropriated by the state. Deng Xiaopeng has practiced true empowerment in China by dumping communes, reforming agriculture, and giving poor people the chance to earn a relatively decent living on their farms. The Chinese decision has created a primitive prosperity that lifted up the entire rest of the society at least economically. Jack Kemp's proposal to give public housing tenants ownership vouchers was a program of true empowerment.

4. Decree Versus Consensus

Consensus differs from empowerment, in that consensus targets everyone into helping make the same roster of decisions. It is upside-down centralization and slower than a lumbering tortoise. In *A Briefing for Leaders*, I contended that consensus management may be one of the greatly overrated management tactics of the last decade. When Compaq's board ousted CEO Rod Canion (the unofficial embodiment of consensus management) in October 1991, American industry got a clear clue that consensus was no longer to be given its former esteem. Consensus was downgraded for one simple reason: There's not enough time to agonize through the vast number of decisions that need to be made for an organization to stay on course. Consensus is a victim of the " Tyranny of Choice" problem outlined in Chapter 3. Too much choice and too much reflection are simply enemies of getting things decided and done. A consensus-ridden company is somewhat akin to a computer with a virus—it loses control of its operating program. Describing the conditions in the computer company she was asked to revitalize, Carol Bartz, CEO of Autodesk, told the *Wall Street Journal,* "They had these grand e-mail votes on things, but nobody had any authority to do anything."

On the other hand, the same destructive effect occurs when diverse people simulate a consensus that has no reality. Generally acting without reliable information, a mandate is delivered upward to answer a popular need, often for a white knight to provide refuge or leadership in a vacuum. The upward endowment of power, as with making the movie director solely responsible for all the creativity in a film, can lead to political stampedes. Ross Perot's huge popularity, when he first announced his interest in the U.S. presidency, was a direct consequence of Perot's being undefined. He was like a vast soap bubble and a diverse throng of voters willingly projected onto the surface of that bubble their own political beliefs, thinking that they were looking into a mirror. People, many with wildly contradictory political beliefs, resonated with Perot's attacks on Washington and party politics. They projected on him their confidence that Perot had an acceptable solution, even though they didn't really know what that solution was. Such a wished-for consensus is generally short-lived because adversaries will demand facts and concretes, and the *endowed* powerful person usually lacks either the plans and/or the desire to produce either. A similar but more subtle problem occurs when a consensus is reached on setting a policy, but disagreements cause implementation to break down. When that happens, leadership has generally failed to forge a specific and real consensus in the first place. As I have written elsewhere, it is the selective use of consensus reserved for the most important issues that pays off. That use must be coupled with collegial leadership at the top and the very limited, but sometimes indispensable, use of decree to get the job done.

The Measurement and Merchandising of Power

There are more fundamental issues to managing power than the gimmicky new twists just discussed. They are measuring and merchandising. It's not possible to manage power well if you cannot first measure it. How do you measure how much power a person or an organization has? First, it's surely easier to measure other things than power. You can assess a management team on many different scales: how much does it make (profits); how much does it cost (salaries and purchasing); how much does it develop (promotable managers); and how much does it innovate (patents). The best quantitative analysis of management is always based on competitive comparison. What comparably sized institutions are most like mine? How do we measure up against this comparison group in funding performance, profitability, board strength, professional staff, acknowledged specialization, and any other relevant norms? Measured against the standing two, five, and ten years ago, has our institution gained or lost power and esteem? In which ways? For what reasons? Is the total sector of a nonprofit corporation, for example, gaining or losing share of community support? Is a community hospital, for example, losing ground to regional medical centers and other specialized hubs? Is that same hospital fully in step with demographic change for its constituency—for example, an aging clientele or a local population increasingly working for smaller vendor firms with poor insurance or without any medical insurance at all? These measures are all straightforward.

You can also gauge a management team's power, but it's rarely done. Just as corporations are measured for their profitability and productivity, it is possible to assess the *productivity* of power, the ability to get things done, and *innovation*, the volume of meaningful new tasks achieved. I describe this measurement as weighing the agenda's harvest. In *A Briefing for Leaders*, I wrote that a well-constructed agenda has staying power, only shifting its four or five fundamental points gradually over time. However, the productive tasks done to further the agenda are *countable* for quantity and *judgeable* for quality (their contribution to advancing the agenda). They can be an element of the organization or leader's formal quarterly or annual plan and could include: appointment to a steering committee of a significant trade or professional association; prevailing in a litigation that protects a valuable patent; developing an agreement to be an exclusive (and, thus, authoritative) source for the *Wall Street Journal* for certain sorts of technical information; or completing a licensing agreement with a strategic partner abroad to significantly expand a distribution channel. The achievements can also be part of a more personal and private plan, which still contributes to the development and strengthening of organizational power every bit as much as the formal steps: identifying a "beacon" for one's personal board of directors who can help spot incoming trends; striking an initial agreement with a retiring executive committee chairman to operate in a well-defined figurehead capacity; delivering an unexpectedly thoughtful and provocative talk before an industry council so that the Awe Factor is awakened; or having a measure-taking dialogue with an important executive in South America so that one's network is effectively expanded to a new continent. I call this *weighing the harvest of power.*

One can measure the number of achievements against various standards such as the number of planned supporting objectives in a particular time period and the competition ranked with other performance benchmarks. The latter is more difficult, though not impossible. Methodical study can tell you how many outside boards your counterparts in competing organizations sit on, how many major speeches they give and where, and—through a little intelligence work—who sits on their personal boards of directors. These quantitative tidbits generally add up to a convincing comparison. Put differently, it is rare when such pieces of data are combined that a person with a high volume and quality of output and contacts will be less powerful than a person who does less and does it on a lower level. But just as the networking potential of a powerful person is not often well studied, the comparative power output of rival organizations is rarely considered except by the most perceptive and disciplined powerful people. Not only neglectful, failure to measure power is fundamentally as dangerous as the failure to measure financial results or personnel turnover. It is too easy for power to withdraw inward and think in terms of its own style rather than focusing outward on the real standards for its performance.

Thus far the forces that try to smother or obscure power men-

tioned above represent specific challenges. Clutter, the next factor, is really just a general environmental problem. In this sense,
clutter refers to the unintentional snow storm of information and
competing images that can obscure or conceal one's power from
audiences who matter. Former Republican National Committee
Chairman Clayton Yeutter once described one aspect of the clutter problem for me this way: "Direct mail has become a mainstay. A decade ago, an excellent direct-mail campaign was a distinct advantage. The money would roll in. Now there is so much
competition of all sorts for donations that it is much less effective." At least in America, one has to merchandise to survive, let
alone to be powerful, and one has to merchandise according to
the most current techniques or one will fail to penetrate the clutter. For packaged goods products, U.S. advertising expenditures
have climbed three-fold to $75 billion in the last decade.
Marketing and promotion budgets for churches, charities, political candidates, and schools continue to rise—sometimes to
obscene levels, but it is impossible to compete without this
investment.

While power can generate awe, it must be known and recognized to generate anything. Power must have significant notice to
be leveraged, and to be noticed it must be merchandised just as
anything else must be merchandised. Merchandising is both what
confers power and what sustains it in our time. At the end of the
eighteenth century, says historian Paul Johnson, a technological
breakthrough spurred some of the first experiences in modern
merchandising. It was the development of plate glass in then-
mammoth sizes of two feet by three feet . . . and even three feet
by four feet. This glass enabled the first display windows in the
shops of Regent Street and Oxford Street. Merchants could now
create room interiors and exotic fashion scenes. They could entice
the pedestrians of London with the first three-dimensional fan-
tasies of consumerism, and they succeeded in creating a culture of
want. Back then, passersby would gape through those windows
with the same wide-eyes we reserve today for high-definition TV
or holograms. Since the eighteenth century, almost every succes-

sive improvement in power merchandising has had both a technological and a content element.

This book is not about the technology of power communication
(except to say that the powerful should have access to first-rate
technicians because messages packaged with lagging technology
or poor quality won't be heard), but about content. The first
principle of content is that power grasps its strength and range.
Knowing what you can deliver consistently is also the first principle of effective merchandising of any sort. While the powerful
may seek to inspire others, they also define their own limits. As
Sun Tzu wrote in *The Art of War:* "When in difficult country, do
not encamp. In country where high roads intersect, join hands
with your allies. Do not linger in dangerously isolated positions. . . . There are roads that must not be followed, towns that
must not be besieged." Because competence is so important to
modern power, it has become very important to merchandise both
one's command and the authoritative narrowness of one's skill.
Les Wexner has built an entire empire of apparel stores around
his flagship The Limited—and I've always thought his choice of a
name apt, because The Limited is as much characterized by what
it *doesn't* carry as what it does. H. J. Heinz has a broad assortment of categories in which it competes, but it stays out of some
product groups, experts contend, because it can't guarantee that
it would achieve the company's rigorous internal quality standards in every kind of food product. Individuals can also merchandise themselves using the same strategy. Senator Bill Bradley's
trump card is his knowledge of the Soviet Union, and his able staff
has deftly marketed this special competence to the media and
opinion-leaders, here and abroad.

Powerful figures in the not-for-profit world are the most likely to
underestimate the importance of merchandising their own power
and authority. Centuries ago, universities, hospitals, and museums
were fragile affairs that were supported because of their altruism,
their benevolence, and their charity. While their mission today is
unchanged, the criteria for selecting such an institution, for

endowing it, even for paying its bills or claims, and certainly for supporting its survival all relate to effectiveness. And, contrary to popular belief, that power doesn't speak for itself. In the information age, power is knowledge and proven skill. In medicine, more than in any other discipline, awareness of demonstrated knowledge and proven competence are the levers that attract all other resources and advantages a not-for-profit hospital can possess. For hospitals, power means access to government and regulatory ears, community recognition and leverage, recruiting and maintaining the best professional staff, and courting the best pocketbooks for fund-raising. Even for not-for-profits, power really means *comprehensive brand strength*—just as if the market position of a consumer product or service were at stake—as it is understood in today's commercial marketing world. For a hospital, that includes strength of the brand as a personal-service institution and health-care provider, as a forward-looking employer in a people-intensive business, as an ethically responsive institution in a medical world increasingly saddled with complex moral issues, and as an alert environmental force in managing vast amounts of hazardous wastes.

How power is merchandised is as important as the fact that it is merchandised at all. Flaunting power recklessly is a sure way to lose it. Capitalizing on power intelligently and extending it thoughtfully is the only workable approach. There are both subtle and garish ways to merchandise power. Of course, the subtle are the surer and more effective. Walter Olson's book *The Litigation Explosion* mentions a brassy Dallas law firm that has "adopted" the snake collection in the Dallas Zoo. At least then, this firm was spending sixteen hundred dollars a year, according to the *Wall Street Journal*, to keep the reptiles hissing happily. That kind of sponsorship is merchandising bravado, not merchandising power. Pretending to be competent or to have an expertise is another terrible way to merchandise power, and it almost always backfires. In this light, I recall an anecdote from *The Economist* titled "North Korea's Potemkin Hospital." This facility is in the capital city of Pyongyang. The hospital had become renowned as a leading-edge

medical center, impressing many foreign visitors. A knowledge-
able Western scholar now alleges that the doctors, nurses, and
even patients are played by actors in a sham put on to convince
foreign visitors that the state of North Korean health care is far
ahead of where it really is. The same actors, it is said, also turn up
on North Korea's showcase farms and in its star factories. When
Libyan Colonel Gadhafi personally bulldozed a prison wall on
television to symbolize his commitment to free speech, he was
performing a similar act of errant merchandising.

Another kind of faulty merchandising is to recklessly declare
yourself a threat. It is hard to shake loose a threatening agenda
because most power agendas are so fervid. Germany, for example,
still lives under the curse of Otto von Bismarck's 1862 declaration as minister-president of Prussia: "Germans do not look at
Prussia's liberalism but at her power. Prussia must keep her
power together for the auspicious moment. The great questions of
the age are not settled by speeches and majority votes, but by iron
and blood." Germany's neighbors are forever cringing that a
new "moment" may be on the immediate horizon. Although
anti-British hostility would appear to be the furthest thing from
Bonn's mind since German unification, Britain has been sniffing
for any hint of German aggression in everything from Bundesbank
interest-rate policy to the (ultimately canceled) plans to celebrate
the technology behind the V-2 rocket. Britain has been awash in
anti-German literature, theater, and political commentary, and the
popular press likes nothing better than to talk about those "Sour
Krauts." In business, any budding firm boasting it would like to
dominate any particular industrial sector will, if very successful,
almost always find itself on the agenda of the Federal Trade
Commission as a threat to free enterprise and competition. That
caused a stir just recently for one of America's most successful
software firms (indeed, one of the world's most successful firms,
period), partly because of aspirations it allegedly publicized two
decades ago.

It's obvious that power would be merchandised to the authorities we have already discussed who are so influential over the des-

tiny of the powerful: financial analysts, boards of directors, agenda committees for major forums like the Conference Board, or the governors of stellar institutions like Lincoln Center. These are visible and readily understood merchandising targets, but the powerful must also grasp a new kind of merchandising that is emerging from the broader world of marketing, and that is merchandising to relationships. "Can a relationship be a valid power merchandising target?" It's a worthy question, especially since power is a transactional phenomenon. As in retailing, it's important to merchandise power when people have a motivation to buy. Consider the imposing power of a Disney theme park and how it exploits the family relationship. The target here is neither parent nor child but the family drawn together in fun. Any parent who has been to Disneyland knows what a great equalizer this is in the American experience. And, there is probably no childhood vacation harder to deny a youngster than a visit to one of the Disney centers. That's why many firms do cross-promotion with Disney products and parks. Not surprisingly, most of these strategies are aimed at children. What *is* astonishing is that so few of the strategies are focused on adults, especially adults in their parental roles.

Even skilled marketers often seem blind to the fact that what is powerful for the future of children *is* powerful for adults because of the parental relationship. Most insurance companies, financial planners, educational services, and computer makers fail to understand the relationship focus of the Disney experience. Similarly, plenty of marketing is today aimed squarely at senior citizens, but many seniors are reliant on others for help. Not a great deal of communication focuses on the relationship between seniors and adult children, who are often partners in important decision-making—from housing to grocery shopping to favoring one brand of pharmaceutical over another. If the transaction is the target, then marketing becomes intercepting the relationship on its pathway to a transaction. Individuals are today defined by hundreds of different kinds of relationships.

As the world continues to become more democratic and less

sequestered, knowledge work grows to be a bigger portion of the economy. The powerful will need to address their targets in "slices," and this means creating appeals that speak to them in particular roles and relations and reaching them in particular transactions. Failure to market to relationships is one reason why the United States is so consistently unsuccessful in negotiating with Japan. We alternately target either Japanese industry or government, but not the relationship between the two. Roger Swanson, president of the U.S.–Japan Business Council, once pointed out to me: "In the dialogue with Japan, we are incredibly successful at the technical level." In part the problems may result because the American agenda is too fragmented, while the Japanese agenda is relatively transparent, assuming that what is in action is a governmental-industrial consortium of interests. "In Japan, the national corporate agenda *is* the national agenda," Swanson says. What we fail to speak to is the agenda which connects the business and governmental interests.

It is important to merchandise power in a way that makes sense to the audience being courted. *Forbes* has described how PepsiCo "earned . . . the enviable position of Mexico's largest consumer products company." PepsiCo created strategic partnerships with local bottlers. It studied the Mexican distribution system and now has powerful positioning in the candy and snack businesses. All this entailed governmental relations, vendor communication, and business-to-business marketing. Rather than seating themselves as either a luxury firm or a commodity business, one Pepsi exec calls the company's positioning "small luxuries"—the bag of chips that people buy themselves before they are able to buy a car or a stereo. That means understanding the buying motivations of each national market one at a time. Wily power sends people what they are ready to buy when they are ready to buy it.

In fact, the best power merchandising is usually informal. Public recognition through an official position is not necessarily a way to elevate or merchandise power. It is quite likely a future role in the Clinton cabinet for Rev. Jesse Jackson—outside of an occasional special assignment or the post of secretary of state—would actually *reduce* Jackson's stature rather than increase it. Political experts describe Jesse Jackson today as the President of Black America. To be the unofficial but generally acknowledged spokesperson for more than thirty million Americans has more weight and recognition than any cabinet post, except the secretary of state position.

Sometimes the goal of power merchandising is misinterpreted. Many think that Islamic fundamentalism, if it is merchandising anything, is advancing the ideological solidarity of a region's people under a religious banner. Far more basically and practically the movement is merchandising the power of the region's oil reserves in achieving an ideological goal. Iran and Iraq, both postroyalist, represent two options—one theist and the other secular—and both are anxious to harness the Middle East and its oil. In international diplomatic circles, it's nearly been an axiom that the Arabs will never be able to unify one another. It's not an axiom I would rely on. Behind the spread of Islamic fundamentalism is a recognition that the Middle East has a potent political weapon that they have not really used for years. One cannot forget that OPEC—the first modern incarnation of "oil is power"—was really a collection of individuals, many of them very wealthy, cut off from a sense of the popular mass beneath them. In the end, oil may provide a totally new sense of solidarity, particularly in the context of Islam. In Algeria, Saudi Arabia, and other Middle Eastern countries, Islamic fundamentalism is trying to connect a new agenda to oil, one of the world's few scarce and irreplaceable natural resources.

But the real action in power merchandising, as in every other aspect of power, is not in the advantages delivered by material things, either manufactured goods or raw resources. It is with knowledge and competence, and that means it is with people. And the true Charles and Charlene Atlases of power merchandising are high-capacity executives. They are power figures who get a lot done and are known for it, because they know how to merchandise their output. Or their staffs and/or informal boards of directors know how to merchandise on behalf of their high-capacity patrons. No trait elicits the Awe Factor more consistently than a reputation for being high capacity. High capacity is the stuff of legends. Mathematician John von Neumann held three full-time jobs at once and read encyclopedias to amuse himself. Helmut Schmidt is a former German chancellor, publishes the newspaper *Die Zeit*, and has recorded a Bach keyboard concerto on Deutsche Grammaphon. Wallace Stevens was an outstanding insurance company executive and simultaneously active as a poet who penned extraordinary verses. Jonas Salk is not simply a brilliant scientist in his own right but a remarkable organizer who has helped pioneer the very structure of research organizations. Capacity is truly an important indication of power. In an era of reduced staffing, the high-capacity executive is more desirable than ever before. Organizations stand in line to entrust such people with their agendas.

The high-capacity executive is not a drudge, not a muscle-bound weight lifter of the routine, but someone capable of creating intellectual capital in a whole range of areas that is usually distinctive and innovative. High-capacity people are also generally noted for their ability to manage a broad range of people (that is, to have excellent skills in handling diverse power transactions). Just as the well-toned athlete has rigorous disciplines, high-capacity executives demand of themselves that they regularly stretch for performance. General Electric is an entire culture of high-capacity performers. Wright Elliott at Chase Manhattan and David Scott at Ford are two worthy high-capacity role models, and their style is particularly noteworthy: Not high-capacity personal performers as so many biceps-flexing high-capacity types are, they are able to motivate the people around them to reach for high-capacity behavior. They understand the collegial approach to heavy lifting. The Red Cross, with 27,000 grassroots chapters worldwide, is a high-capacity organization. Its president, Elizabeth Dole, says, "as governments must reduce budgets, they are turning to organizations like this to fill the void. We are often the first to step into a problem when it arises." One example is the Red Cross involvement in creating housing for the homeless. People are confident that the Red Cross has the capacity to find solutions to problems.

MANAGEMENT

Instead of strong leaders, people want competent leaders in service to strong agendas, so modern power must work much more through assent and approval than through suppression or intimidation. Proof of achievement, competence, reliability, and a sense of direction create the confidence that enable power to be won and sustained. True empowerment, development, and mediation are replacing outdated power modalities. This makes power more fragile and more amorphous than it once was and requires that the powerful give continuous evidence of their power through merchandising it effectively.

6

The Communication of Power

Solidly Superficial

Why are mental models so powerful in affecting what we do? In part, because they affect what we see.

—PETER SENGE

How is power projected, recognized, detected, and acknowledged?

Power has had a theatrical bent ever since kings held court and waged war, and priests uttered rituals and executed sacrifices. Shakespeare gives us a seemingly endless procession of kings, queens, and the other power figures who populate his histories, tragedies, and comedies. The powerful can expect to find themselves caricatured and characterized in terms of Shakespearean models: an urbane Antony, a ruthless Richard III, an enigmatic Hamlet, or an ambitious Lady Macbeth. Shakespeare's grasp of power seems quite modern, as in *Richard III*: "Conscience is but a word that cowards use, devised at first to keep the strong in awe" or in *King Lear*: "Get thee glass eyes; and, like a scurvy politician, seem to see the things thou dost not." In our time, power figures have tilted toward the cinema rather than the stage. Hitler, Mussolini, and Stalin were all crazy about movies. Stalin sent FDR a copy of Alexandrov's movie *Volga, Volga* during World War II. FDR wrote a screenplay about the American Admiral John Paul Jones, while JFK lobbied for Warren Beatty to star in the biographical *PT 109.* (Beatty turned the role down.)

When we think of Hitler and Charlie Chaplin, what comes to mind is Chaplin's caricature of power turned absurd in *The Great Dictator.* But there are more profound associations and similarities. Frederic Morton once wrote that both Adolph Hitler and Charlie Chaplin, who were born in the same year and on nearly the same day, "tapped the need of the outsider to be let it. It is an old need, endemic to hierarchical society, manifest in the Bible and in fairy tales." Hitler and Chaplin were cunningly asking for permission to have their antics approved. In different ways but on a seismic scale, the resulting approval delivered enormous power. Both men also "understood spiritual drought and slaked it," Morton perceptively observes. Both Hitler and Chaplin, he points out, were driven by control. (Hitler's obsession with control stretched from architectural monoliths to maniacal mandates; while Chaplin supervised the production, direction, financing, scorewriting, and much else in his movies.) In an article in the *British Journal of Management,* Professor Iain Mangham actually pairs the powerful in organizations and actors as, in a significant way, cut from common cloth: "Actors and senior managers are involved in performing. . . . Stars, particularly in the theatre and within business enterprises, appear live before their audiences and must elicit appropriate responses moment by moment, *reading* the situation so that they 'get it right on the night.'" And both Chaplin and Hitler stuck with a similar and very clear commitment to the surface. Many critics and cinema historians have described how Chaplin's career, for example, could not withstand the more penetrating and intrusive world of talking pictures.

Power is "superficial" in the best sense of the word and operates through the idiom of symbolism. It roams on the surface but can be overwhelming when its instant symbolism is recognized (as in the New Deal, or General Electric's "We bring good things to life"). If power didn't operate smoothly on a surface level, people couldn't interpret it quickly or accurately. Power, one must remember, steers away from introspection and has an action bias, and that requires being clearly understood quickly. Contending that power is superficial is not to say that it is trivial, and this distinction is important. To say that something is simple is not to say that it is easy.

The most successful people distill their mission and that of their organizations down to a simple message whenever possible. No organization, certainly no business, has been the source of more complex ideas in modern America than IBM; and none has a shorter, richer slogan than "THINK." When Lord Nelson stood on the bridge of HMS *Victory* and spearheaded the British defeat of the French, the admiral signaled his fleet, "England expects that every man will do his duty." At this decisive battle of Trafalgar, the British averted invasion. The battle cost Nelson his own life. During his tenure as mayor of New York, Fiorello La Guardia displayed a legendary mastery of symbolic gesture. Keith Thomas, in his introduction to a book on gesture, points out that one could watch a news clip with the sound turned off and tell in less than a minute if La Guardia was addressing a Jewish, Italian, or Irish audience—he articulated ethnic gestures that well. There is a communication that surpasses words, code, and gestures—and that is competence. Competence speaks best of all. There is little to rival mastery decisively stated, as in the boldness with which Coco Chanel ripped a deep-red taffeta drape off the wall and instantly fashioned a new evening dress for the Baroness von Rothschild in 1953, just minutes before a major social event. At the ball the Baroness attended, admirers asked her where she got this marvelous new gown.[1]

---

1. Speaking of apparel, the symbolic communication of wearing grand clothing— I have always contended—is far more trivial and transparent than designing it. However, there is a certain power to carriage and *how* someone wears something, just as there is to gesture. A perfect case is the advertising legend David Ogilvy—a

The mantle of power is changeable—from business blazers to dinner jackets, from kitchen aprons to lab coats. It is also symbolic. Slavish attention to executive apparel is probably one of the most ostensibly ridiculous and exaggerated points in the entire repertory of alleged leadership and power skills. However, a thoughtful person can create a serious, inferential argument for certain kinds of clothing. One doesn't want to talk about lots of money while dressed in rags but dress must correspond to the occasion. However, dressing *to* the occasion doesn't mean a powerful person should try to dress in any way superior to the occasion. During the two weeks of the 1984 Los Angeles Olympics, Peter Ueberroth would motivate various key elements of the staff; he would dress up as a bus driver, kitchen worker, or usher on different days.

In contrast, suit-and-tie uniforms are often a defensive statement that defines the powerful as part of an elite. The *truly* powerful make the most skillful symbolic statements when they let their dress and manners exhibit a constructive diversity, shaped by their customers and their adherents. It is easy, if initially somewhat disconcerting, to project the Ueberroth attitude to the running of hospitals, museums, universities, and, most of all, other businesses. Certainly General H. Norman Schwarzkopf did this as he shunned his staff uniform for battlefield fatigues during the Gulf War. This consciousness also makes the Japanese simplification of "coveralls for all" more understandable.

What makes symbols such fast and agile communicators? First, they register with the dominant mental models stored in our minds. The mental models we permit ourselves profoundly influ-

---

precise, vain, contrarian, and brilliant man. He can say anything and get away with it because he is old enough to be deemed a legend and is the anointed dean of the ad industry. He also has a remarkable knack for gesture. The way Ogilvy puts something on must be exactly right. And, the way he takes it off must be, too. Once I saw Ogilvy shed his raincoat at London's Connaught Hotel, and it seemed that just exactly the right amount of water dripped to the floor; and then he lifted up his shoe at just the right angle so a footman could cleave the mud off the sole. Ogilvy leads by style—not surprising for the person who designed the aristocratic eye-patched symbol for Hathaway shirts.

ence both our potential and our potential understanding. In a provocative book called *The Fifth Discipline*, Peter Senge writes; "Why are mental models so powerful in affecting what we *do*? In part because they affect what we *see*." While they were only fictional characters, Raymond Burr's Perry Mason and Robert Young's Marcus Welby did a great deal to educate the public about lawyers and doctors respectively and to create forceful models of how these professions behave. We position figures in contexts, and some of those contexts are constraining while others are expansive. The characters Mason and Welby, for example, exude enormous confidence and personal power. Our mental models don't just govern our images of people. They also regulate forums in which we visualize how certain people or types of people are able to operate naturally. It is a kind of mental screencasting. The size and seriousness of plausible forums is kept in measure with the perceived scope of power and competence. African-Americans, for example, have had to expand the power forums that others will accept them in one agonizing step after another . . . from George Washington Carver as scientist to Marian Anderson, the first African-American to attain permanent status with the Metropolitan Opera Company, to Supreme Court Justice Thurgood Marshall. Although it was an important part of the developmental process of African-American rights and identity, many of us still link the most dramatic examples of African-Americans exerting power with the stadium turnouts to see a Michael Jackson perform or today's Joe Louis box, but those forums are anachronisms. What *is* important in our era is that Time Warner backed Spike Lee with $35 million to make a three-hour epic about Malcolm X and that Bill Cosby has been a rumored acquirer of NBC. Lee and Cosby are beyond performing for audiences. Their forum is the skeptical and far more serious one of cinema historians and Wall Street analysts; and their stature is all the higher as a result.

The right forum can also mean a platform that is poised to resonate back to the proper audience, even when it is designed to echo around the world. Not too many years ago, when Michel

Rocard had resigned as French prime minister (or more accurately, had been ousted by President François Mitterrand), he truly needed to find the right forum. Rather than reentering private life, Rocard's real goal was to prepare his run for the presidency. Officed in an elegant *belle epoque* building, the eighteenth-century interior decor of his suite was drenched in so many cut flowers it looked like a Matisse canvas. And for a reason. Twenty years earlier, Rocard was in the avant-garde of French politics, identified with the motorcycle set and reading Sartre—a little like Jerry Brown. He knew that he now had to prove once more that he had shed that image, and he did so with a *regence* desk, an imposing book collection, and stacks of signed correspondence in front of him—a collective effect that impressed any visitor.

Rocard was counseled to become known outside of France, that he must become a statesman whom the world respected and not be a bureaucrat known only within his own land. That didn't mean simply getting international exposure. Rather than attending an obscure conference in Brazil, he was told that he should be speaking at Georgetown or Stanford or meeting with the *New York Times* editors. He needed to create issues that would resonate outside of France, find prestigious and thoughtful places to address them, and prove to the French that he was a voice for them on international platforms, capable of statesmanship on a global scale—and he did.

Just as powerful people communicate *their* power effectively, so must countries, regions, and cities—if they are to attract the proper share of global prosperity to keep their citizens happy. If I were to evaluate a large city's prospects in the coming decades, my central challenge to its planners would be this: Can it satisfy the needs of a knowledge economy and knowledge workers? When British architect Richard Rogers was asked to design a new business center for Shanghai, his plan to develop Lu Jia Zui—an area that is nearly eight times the size of London's Canary Wharf—focused on transportation. It was a plan that could lift Shanghai from the bicycle age to the era of fixed-rail rapid transit, the right transportation medium for knowledge workers. Rogers knew that as long as Shanghai remained bicycle-bound, it would never be regarded as a modern commercial metropolis. As long as Shanghai, traditionally China's most cosmopolitan city, could not resuscitate its image, neither could the nation of China itself. It is hardly coincidental that Frankfurt is well on its way to becoming the financial capital of the new Europe, and that it is already established as the continent's air transportation hub. None of this is new: "All roads lead to Rome" was both a power statement and a transportation truth.

Symbols: Clashing and Cunning

Among cities, nations, and people, communication is increasingly competitive. Symbolic communication can easily become symbolic conflict among powerful people. The 1992 presidential campaign was marked by vigorous debate using media and entertainment symbols as surrogates for lifestyles or market niches. Rather than attacking real unwed mothers, Dan Quayle lashed out at the fictional TV character Murphy Brown, a female newscaster who, in the series' script, bears a child out of wedlock. Republican conservatives assailed media giant Time Warner for releasing a rap song performed by Ice-T that condoned violence against the police. The fictional metaphor has been no stranger to Republican communications strategy. Ronald Reagan dipped into the *Star Wars* movie lexicon to conjure up the Evil Empire in attacking the Soviets and to Clint Eastwood's movie legacy for the "Make my day" comment in vetoing a Congressional budget proposal. But these quips are not sure bets. In power contests, entertainment symbols can seem misleadingly efficient in attacking a position. The swipe against Murphy Brown didn't prove to be a neat shot against an unwed professional woman choosing to bear a child. It angered many women who were ambivalent over the pro-life/pro-choice debate and also seemed to be a thinly veiled attack on professional women in general. Whenever a media symbol is used as a surrogate for attack, the powerful should know that the symbol itself must be as one-dimensional and single-issue as possible.

Even though Reagan's symbols were starker, they were also clearer and wielded with a lighter touch. Pollster Dick Wirthlin has described how the Bush campaign spouted the "political mantra" of family values (which the electorate didn't buy, because only a minority of families could relate to it) rather than offering less heavy-handed "inferential cues."

The 1992 campaign also became a symbolic contest of another sort—a race of power vehicles, where the trophy went to the most relevant, not the fleetest. For years the power imagery of vehicles had centered on limousines and private jets. After the unsuccessful assassination attempt against him in 1981, Pope John Paul II has conducted most of his international visits transported through crowds in a bullet-proof "Pope Mobile." A similar vehicle protected Nelson Mandela in his 1990 parade through the streets of New York. In both cases, and beyond whatever pragmatic requirements justify these security transport vehicles, they instantly and tacitly state that the person protected inside is a treasured figure of rare merit and importance whose security is at risk from bigots and lunatics. On the other hand, these bullet-proof "cages" also demonstrate an aloofness that doesn't work well for politicians in their own land.

Vehicles became conscious symbolic devices in the 1992 Bush-Clinton contest. In August of that year, the *New York Times* printed two photos in dramatic counterpoint. One showed George Bush standing starkly alone and at the door of the massive-looking Air Force One. The caption said that Bush was "present[ing] himself as a 'moral compass'" at a New York rally. Below that photo, another pictured Clinton and Gore in front of a multiracial audience in East St. Louis, and the headline explained that the duo had just launched another three-day bus trip. The bus was a way of saying, "I am in touch. I travel like the people do. I will bring government down to the issues that are important to them." Clinton's bus became a populist symbol of the grassroots campaigner. In his presidential plane and helicopters, Bush, in contrast, seemed isolated and out of touch. Eventually, the Bush people tried to limit the president's exposure in front of Air

Force One, not just because it was an intimidating setting, but the plane was also an ominous symbol of incumbency as well. Instead, his staff mounted him on trains. Did it equalize Bush with Clinton in understatement? Not really. The train stage made the older Bush look like an out-of-date whistlestop campaigner from another era.

Misguided symbols are not always unintentional. At times and with great care, symbols are sometimes projected and institution-alized so that they will be misinterpreted by an adversary or com-petitor. It is disinformation of the highest art and can be a potent subliminal force in the power equation.

Symbols: Modest and Memorable

I call it "cheese-and-cracker" power—the leadership symbolism critical for nonprofit institutions. The drive to operate these insti-tutions more as businesses in recent years has created antithetical cultural drives, because hard-nosed business people are often motivated by luxurious perquisites like stretch limousines and flights on the Concorde even when they are working on behalf of crippled children or endangered species. As a member of the Board of Governors of the American Red Cross, I have had a chance to see firsthand how its president, Elizabeth Dole, runs her ship. She is exceptionally frugal and has weighed the value of every penny of every budget she's run since she's been in Washington. In this respect, her behavior seems very different from that of William Aramony, the former head of the United Way. Aramony's United Way office was opulent and overdone, graced with presidential seals and citations and the like. Dole's office is very small and spartan. Not long ago, a movement was underway to break ground for a new Red Cross headquarters because the present building is so inadequate. Dole has, how-ever, resisted this step until the financial situation is right, and the need is overpoweringly justified. I remember opulent United Way receptions with canapes and champagne. At the Red Cross, Elizabeth Dole would have soft drinks and cheese-and-crackers served at comparable events. Extravagance is yet another misinterpreted sign of power.

It's a great challenge to be both authoritative and understated, but that is what today's power game is all about. Instead of shouting to get above the clutter, it's a matter of orchestrating the two or three breathtaking but modest strokes that can brush the clutter aside. Another cheese-and-crackers virtuoso is A. D. Frazier, chief operating officer of the 1996 Olympics in Atlanta, who skillfully fended off an image issue. Initially, he was criticized for the tone he set by taking the job at such a high salary, even though he had always been a vigilant manager of expenses as a senior banking executive and his salary was probably modest compared to the task that he was expected to perform. But he didn't let his new stature elevate his lifestyle. Driving an economy car and brown-bagging it to work were personal evidence of his expense consciousness and self-reliance, and that built conviction among the people around him.

An old truism says that leaders can earn valuable loyalty if they are harder on themselves than they are on others. A Renaissance king could demonstrate that hardness by showering in ice cold water at predawn hours or by slogging through muddy battlefields swinging a broadsword at the head of his troops, while nursing an open wound from the last skirmish. But what exactly does *harder* mean in a world where knowledge is power? Showing endurance is still part of power,[2] but demonstrating knowledge in an exacting way is even more impressive.

When film director Michael Mann's *The Last of the Mohicans* appeared in 1992, stories circulated about how tough and uncompromising Mann was as a taskmaster, and yet he got both loyalty and results in making the movie. Why was Mann permitted to behave in the demanding way that he did? David Ansen wrote, "Long before [Mann] started on the screenplay, he studied the

2. Former Republican National Committee Chairman Clayton Yeutter told me once that the modern presidential candidate must be able to campaign in an afternoon the way candidates of previous eras would campaign in three days.

history of the American frontier, read the diaries of the time and consulted historians. He can expound at length on the colors and patterns of each tribe's war paints. 'The details make this movie ring true,' [Mann says]. 'Audiences today are more visually sophisticated. They know the real deal, and they know when they've been shortchanged.'" Mann's power over actors and crew—and, audiences, for that matter—stemmed from his authenticity, his knowledge, and his commitment to uphold what he knew to be accurate. For him the process wasn't an excursion into the fantasy of "let's make a movie." His direction was knowledge-driven, nudged up to the level of "virtual reality" cinema. A comparison of Mann's cinema with that of Sergei Eisenstein cuts a sharp contrast in the use of artistic power. Eisenstein was the dominant figure in film in the fledgling days of the Soviet Union, where discriminating knowledge then had *little* to do with making movies. As Soviet cinematographic experts have explained it to me, back *then* the masses effected change, and the job of socialist "realism" unequivocally was to create a person of the future. Eisenstein's mission was ideology; Mann's authenticity.

There are symbolic acts emblematic of the loss of power, and they aren't confined to the cinema or the theater. To cite one example, in the casinos of nineteenth-century Europe, servants would cloak a casino gaming table in black crepe or gauze if a gambler broke the bank. It signified that the power (and the mystique) of that table had ended for the evening. There are many important rituals that govern the loss of power, and they vary by organization and circumstance, but certainly the most important of them is the act of concession. A concession can be a speech, a letter of resignation, an apology uttered in a newspaper interview or a memoir, the gracious withdrawal from a market, or many other kinds of communication. No matter what it is, in all cases it is important to acknowledge failure. Even the victorious powerful may look back and rue the methods they used to win, as the late Republican tactician Lee Atwater did in apologizing about his campaigning tactics against the Democrats and Michael Dukakis in 1988. A team-spirited, fair-play society places tremendous weight on the proper act of concession. (Richard Nixon lost much sympathy with the media and the public when he scornfully told the media that they wouldn't have Nixon to kick around anymore after losing the 1962 California gubernatorial election.) The reasoning for the graceful departure is more practical than polite: Except for tragic cases such as Atwater's, effective concession is the first prerequisite for a return to power.[3] As Ellen Goodman puts it, "[Gracefully exiting] involves a sense of future, a belief that every exit line is an entry, that we are moving on, rather than out."

Power: Instant and Visual

Because of its symbolic potential, fame can be an important aspect in the organization of power but not, ironically, because of the fame of powerful people themselves. Most truly powerful people regard fame, when they have it, as an unfortunate price of being powerful. Much more important to the exercise of power is how the famous are used by the powerful to advance the interests of their power. My first book, *Power and Influence*, describes the growing importance of the "Favor Bank" in exerting influence. The premise: People can only wield sustainable influence if they hold hefty balances of favors that other influential people owe them. Since writing about the favor bank, I've become convinced that there is now a comparable institution that should be known as the "Fame Bank." Fame abets power because, as a famous Hollywood actor puts it: "Fame pulls focus;" and there are forces everywhere wanting to convert that power into cash, brand loyalty, or political initiative. Hollywood, of course, is to fame banking what Wall Street is to finance. When Washington limited individual political contributions to a thousand dollars, the political value of Hollywood soared. Political factions even invest in human research and development, meaning that they make a con-

---

3. The avenues to and rationales behind effectively regaining power are described in the Appendix.

scious effort to recruit promising actors and entertainers early in their careers.

While fame can pull focus and throngs of admirers, the quality of the throngs matters far more than their quantity. When *Wall Street Journal* editor Bob Bartley launched a new book, thirty or forty opinion leaders—business leaders, academicians, and journalists—were invited to the reception in Rizzoli's bookstore at the World Trade Center. From there, the group went to the TriBeCa Grill, where Paul Newman was coincidentally signing copies of his new book while being mobbed by perhaps five- or six-hundred admirers. The Bartley party may have looked like a humble splinter sect in comparison with the Newmanites, but there is no doubt as to which group had more power. While the powerful are still often (and erroneously) judged by the size of the entourage they can muster, we no longer live in a world of mass sentiment. Paul Newman does salad dressing, is a heck of an auto racer, and has a nice smile, but Bartley publishes one of the world's five most important daily newspapers.

Fame is not the only symbolic communicator that can grab focus. So can graphic design. Some editors snobbishly demean the visual versus print and contend graphics are only good for breaking up text. Jeff Moriber, a pacesetter among visual designers, is the master of bringing complex corporate stories to life with impact art. He was a pioneer in using pop-ups and diecuts to bring the sophisticated reader into a topic. Back in the early seventies, just when energy conservation was coming into vogue, he developed a poster for people to post on their refrigerators. It was constructed for reaction (not reading) and was really an actual game that you couldn't stop playing. It had an enormous effect on energy conservation in the South, and actually changed human behavior on a major scale through instantaneously effective symbols. Typefaces and graphics can unlock the imagination of power because trends often emerge visually before they are articulated verbally. Eliot Noyes's stark red-and-white design for the interior of the IBM 702 computer center, reproduced in countless ads and brochures, really helped establish IBM as a modernistic company. What is true for imagery is also true for intelligence on trends. Periodically I make it a point to visit with art directors and cartoonists. It's not because I need the cheering up: Cartoonists, art directors, or photographers can be very rich sources of incoming data. As to cartoonists, visual satire is power. The Mexican José Posada made satirical lithographs in the 1880s that said in pictures what he could not have safely said in words. Today *Newsweek* and *Time* are behind the curve on visual taste trends. One must really look at regional newspapers, the movies, TV commercials, Broadway sets, and advertising typefaces and graphics because trends often emerge visually in these domains before they are articulated verbally even in the best publications.

Visual symbols set expectations. The promised land is all about what people see or want to see because seeing is the route to having. People in less developed countries don't complain about open bus shelters. They complain about *open busses*. Until recently, Romania didn't have Germany or Italy as a base of comparison for living standards. Instead it was the relative wealth of still dingy Budapest and Prague that intrigued Bucharest. *The Economist* even uses the relative price of "Big Macs"—as measured in labor needed to earn the purchase price—as a serious economic standard in calculating the real success of an economy. The sets of the television series "Dallas" may have been knocked down, but their rerun images today are still exerting remarkable power in equatorial Africa and the hinterlands of the Indian subcontinent. Just as images of the Holy Grail fired the imagination of medieval Crusaders en route to Jerusalem, "Dallas" really articulated first a national, then a global standard for what it meant to be wealthy. The mythical Southfork ranch projected a complex pattern of tastes and comforts that have ignited revolutions across the globe.

Visual symbols can capture the power of a certain moral attitude, of course, as well as that of a lifestyle. The Tomb of the Unknown Soldier is a tribute to selfless patriotism just as the glitter of Trump Tower is a temple to the "shop-till-you-drop" cult. Visual standards are, however, ever more subtle. I remember a Bulgari desk piece given to one of the best connected lobbyists in Washington. Putting aside its elegant design and remarkable craftsmanship, the most distinctive aspect of the item was how minutely yet clearly the name Bulgari was imprinted on the metal. That really impressed the lobbyist, and I think that he found a similarity to his own work over the years—carefully crafted proposals and contacts for his clients that only slightly hinted at his own involvement. Steve Jobs achieved a comparable subtlety at Apple when he insisted, as John Sculley says, "that the signatures of forty-seven Macintosh creators be embossed on the inside of the computer's back panel."

In addition to the ears and eyes, power can speak to other senses symbolically. Researchers now tell marketers of the nostalgia value potential for the middle-aged in the scents of Play-Doh, Sweet Tarts, and Vaporub. Some European law offices try to bolster client moods with aromatized reception areas. Architects are talking about "furnishing" public spaces with certain aromas, and one expert even believes that fragrances can be used to temper fan aggression in the bleachers of soccer stadiums. If focus can be grabbed through the senses, it can also be shunted through them. It is not surprising that our most extensive knowledge of deflecting attention returns to the visible, since vision is the most studied of the senses. Researcher Carlton Wagner, an expert on colors—negative as well as positive ones—reports this case. "The government was requiring a company to rebate a large amount of money. . . . But, any checks that weren't cashed simply remained with the company. We created the colors for the mailer and they went out with the hope that as many as possible would be thrown away. The color we used is known to most people as yellow-ochre, a kind of baby-diaper brown. The result: 14.7 percent of the envelopes were opened." Getting something *not* to happen in design, as much as in lobbying, can have significant power consequences.

Media Trained Symbolism

Many of our habits in interpreting symbolic messages are governed by media experiences. Frequency of media presence should not in itself be confused with power: Many people mistakenly think that showing up on television is an indicator of power. Actually, television guests are just a fleeting detail in the enormous daily saga of a day's broadcasts. What matters is being effective and cutting through the clutter. This is especially true in politics. "Because of the media selection available to them, people want to hear dramatic, interesting, or entertaining things," says media expert Roger Ailes. Bill Clinton's saxophone performance on a Tabitha Soren-hosted MTV show recognized that 26 million (mostly young) Americans get their information from MTV. His staff, in effect, created an event to dislodge a statistical obstacle. MTV surveys had shown Barbara Bush as this viewership's "preferred" female role model, says *The Economist*. Quasi-news media like MTV, Arsenio Hall's talk show, and the countless tabloid journalism programs have amassed enormous power. In Latin America, a number of commentators like Carlos Palenque in Bolivia and Silvio Santos in Brazil are actually candidates and active politicians. Surely there is no more formidable host of TV marathons and spectacles in all of Latin America than Cuba's Fidel Castro.

With this constant crossover between entertainment and serious power, the discriminating media are justifiably cynical about how powerful people attempt to maneuver the electronic stage to project themselves. Regarding program guests, one of television's leading news commentators, Robert MacNeil, once told me that he applies this standard regarding program guests: Do they set all kinds of conditions to the interview? Are they forthright? Do they come to posture?

The media awareness is so intense today that viewers do much of the editorial work themselves and set their own high standards. As CNN's Lou Dobbs told me: "Viewers are far more sophisticated about television . . . and about investment. Viewers will make their own conclusions. I don't have to be a confrontational interviewer. My CEO guest may think that the viewers will have a reduced expectation, but that's not the case." The transactional nature of television has also sped up the process of communications and loaded each individual term with more meaning: "Back in the eighties, we had to *explain terms*," Dobbs elaborates. "We said, for example, the prime rate was the best rate. Today, we don't explain it. Instead, we emphasize *context*. I think that this gives firms an advantage in getting their message out. The stories aren't slowed down nearly as much by defining the terms."

Our symbolic sense is also trained to detect lapses—especially so because of the way that television accelerates our sense of time. In a transactional world, it is easy to be distracted and lose attention at critical moments. It may be easy to stumble, but people notice it all the same. When the powerful are merchandising their wares to adherents and prospects, they must themselves be focused on their jobs with the intensity of an expert salesperson and must be sure that the target is concentrating equally as hard. Retail legend Stanley Marcus once told me: "How many times have I seen a transaction fall apart because the salesperson lost concentration and started to 'look' through the customer when he spotted a better prospect getting off the elevator." On the prospect's side, it is equally futile to fight the natural patterns of how people receive messages. A powerful person must know, for example, how a live audience listens to a speech that is in turn publicized or else the audience will perform its desired role for the much larger downstream audience of the media. The general public has the same expectations of a political live audience as they do of the attendees at "The Tonight Show" or the laugh track of a sitcom.

Whole-Role Power

The media have a very strong influence on how we perceive power. Perhaps too strong. Unless the media back off from the fixation of turning every act, image, and issue into a symbolic milestone, the powerful simply won't get their work done, especially the job of global competition. Too intense a focus on symbolic communication can cripple power and leadership. We appear to lurch from one sensational incident to another and never seem to rise above them.

But many of the powerful themselves also have a job to do in proving that they are not just transactional opportunists, splicing together one photo opportunity or sound bite to the next. That requires projecting the "whole role"—a fundamental personal continuity that both surpasses and underpins the transactions. Paradoxically it is exactly the same public that wants depth of character and consistency in its leaders that is the first to swarm over the scent of the slightest hypocrisy or peccadillo in its leaders. The trouble generally begins on the consistency aspect of a powerful figure's comments and usually appears when a leader goes out of his or her way to stage transaction after transaction opportunistically, rather than skillfully intercepting genuine incoming transactions and turning them into opportunities. Hustling from one sidewalk sale to another is no way to communicate or merchandise power.

What goes into communicating the "whole role"? Having and using a regular public platform to stand back and size things up; properly summarizing the cornerstone events in one's life for the public record; regularly outlining one's values; constantly referring the press and other key outside publics to one's agenda and the progress being made toward achieving it; without overusing them, maintaining and applying a lexicon of key phrases; and having a certain structural pattern to one's life. Who are triumphs of "whole-role" power? Certainly among them are Abraham Lincoln, the president who probably gave more tailored speeches and political messages than any other chief executive in American history and yet is seen as the most cohesive leadership figure in our past; Henry Kissinger, who without a public platform in federal government for more than fifteen years is still considered to be the world's dean of foreign policy analysis; and Lee Iacocca, who, despite his very forthright personality and Chrysler's ups-and-downs over the years, has preserved a very clear image and an authority to speak out on a broad range of issues from America's immigration legacy to its import addiction. When powerful people look in the mirror of their own communications and can no longer figure out who they are and what they stand for, they should realize that the essential whole role needed for their power to abide stands on shaky terms.

COMMUNICATION

Power has credentials. It is also "superficial" in the best sense of the word and operates through the idiom of symbolism. Relying on interest-group assent makes power much more fragmented and fleeting. Among the powerful, far more contestants are competing to assert themselves as powerful while the volume of total power is not growing. Consequently, having a regular public presence or platform is much more important for exerting power than being in position in a structural sense. While their evaluators and critics react most strongly to individual results, positions, and decisions, the powerful must constantly poise themselves in a "whole role" if they are to have a convincing and sustainable identity.

7

The Emotional Fabric of Power

The Perils of Perfectionism

My power depends on my glory and my glories on the victories I have won. My power will fail if I do not feed it on new glories and new victories. Conquest has made me what I am and only conquest can enable me to hold my position.

—NAPOLEON

What motivates people to accept power or to want to possess it? How has the emotional constitution of the successfully powerful changed?

Napoleon's philosophy of power thrived in a world lean on productive capacity and nourished on noncollaborative, selfish, short-term thinking. Napoleon would have been temperamentally unsuited for the modern practice of power, but this is not merely a matter of our taste. It wasn't simply that Napoleon wanted to act like the *enfant terrible* of Europe. It was also that it once worked for him to become exactly who he wanted to be. That the conquest approach to power no longer works. Even in the Middle

East, which has had a steady supply of capricious dictators over history, conquest did not work for Saddam Hussein because world opinion would not allow it to work.

Even in the past, the powerful often also took far more credit for doing to others what others were already doing for themselves or what circumstance had already thrown into motion. For example, Britain was able to control the entire Indian subcontinent with a small number of Crown bureaucrats backed up by a largely Indian army, but what truly gave Britain that ability was the political weakness of India.

While many powerful people find it hard to dismiss the "hold they have over others," such arrogance is disappearing, at least in advanced economies. No by-product of true power, arrogance is in fact today a grave power weakness. *Business Week* did a cover story labeling the "CEO disease" as egotism. In it figures such as F. Ross Johnson of RJR Nabisco, Walter J. Connolly of Bank of New England, and Robert A. Schoellhorn of Abbott Laboratories are tagged for "losing touch with their companies." CEO arrogance is a major cause for rifts between CEOs and more demanding outside directors. In the *Business Week* article, Merck's Dr. Roy Vagelos and AMR's Bob Crandall, both widely viewed as powerful and innovative success stories, are given high marks for avoiding "the pitfalls of power." In an *Industry Week* interview with Wayne Calloway, CEO of PepsiCo, Calloway explains that arrogance was the leading reason why some fast-track executives at PepsiCo didn't achieve their potential. He calls arrogance "the illegitimate child of confidence."

Arrogance and power make a dangerous cocktail, and smart power abstains and even merchandises its abstention. The early nineties were dreary years for the House of Windsor in Britain, which was besieged by endless marital scandals. It was about that time when a superbly constructed biographical documentary about Elizabeth, *Elizabeth R*, was released. In it Elizabeth wheels around the back forty in a Land Rover, square dances Highland style, is a typical grandmother with the family toddlers ("That's my foot your standing on," she says to one kid in a stern, but friendly manner), and turns a welcoming address she delivered from a podium adjusted to George Bush's height and not her's (where she appeared to be nothing but a bobbing, babbling pink hat) into a triumph of self-effacing humor. If ever a piece of communication dispelled the whiff of arrogance, this video certainly did.

Putting aside arrogance, even the euphoric feelings of success can be a great emotional liability in managing power today. In fact, power must be most carefully and cautiously managed during the times of greatest success. The direst threats to power are reckless changes made during that rush of success, and dealing with success causes such problems because success is usually frighteningly unique and has few role models. Its own success hammered the designer jeans manufacturer Gitano in the early nineties. In the wake of its triumph, it expanded without a solid business plan, and its business mix shifted to more and more dependence on high-volume, low-margin retailers. Internal fiefdoms competed for precious expansion capital as an aggressive expansion was launched to open new Gitano's stores and buy another retailing chain. In short, there was a frantic effort to make the most of success, but there was insufficient competence in the organization to drive that success to the next level. Once healthy earnings became multimillion dollar losses. Since those troubles, Gitano has taken a diligent and effective reappraisal of its business. Exuberance is what generally prods powerful people to take incredible risks. It was hubris that led Napoleon to invade Russia. It was hubris that led Robert Maxwell to layer debt on debt in his publishing empire.

Powerful people frequently defend their own exuberant acts because they say such behavior contributes to or demonstrates their charisma. That's why some of them sweep through field tours with a vast and seemingly doting entourage, dominate meetings with their tirades, and imperiously reverse decisions. All of this has much more to do with the pretense of power and the charismatic tradition than with power's reality as both a responsibility and a burden. It's been my counsel to dismiss charisma in the pursuit of leadership. However, and in contrast, mystique *does* have a great deal to do with the exercise of power.[1] That power has a certain mystique—meaning that there is some alluring, undefinable attraction to holding power—is true but not significant. The correct formulation is the reverse: To hold power, powerful people have to demonstrate they *have* mystique, which I equate with the ability to remain not fully disclosed to the public or, put with more verve, to retain a certain mystery. Mystique is a conscious variant of the Awe Factor on a distinctly personal level. People who are fully known thereby define exact limits to their power and are more easily contained as a result.

There are many ways to create mystique. Mystique serves the purposes of power best if it shrouds a trait (or traits) that would be generally regarded as good—a trait that is complementary with, but not similar to, other skills publicly known about this person and that can be intimated in the closest circles so as to produce the heart of a legend. The anonymous, generous benefactor is the archetype of the powerful person with mystique. But just as the nature of wealth has changed, the people who freely spend their competence and not their money—among friends or with the general public—are creating the finest mystique in the most modern sense. A merchant banker I know is an Escoffier-trained French chef, but she only cooks for her closest friends and never mentions it during the business day. If people ask about her skill, she herself diminishes her prowess and labels what she does as dabbling. By holding back a special skill from the public eye, she makes people reflect on the richness of her character. It also makes her seem gracious and not preoccupied with herself—self-assured enough that she does not have to take credit for all of her accomplishments. Likewise, Winston Churchill's watercolor painting contributed a certain artistic depth that enriched public perception of his character.

Remaining exclusive about accessibility almost always enhances perceived mystique and power. Bain Consulting is a company that

1. Drucker also writes on the subject of mystique in management in his book *Managing for the Future*, and Korda advances a similar concept in his work *Power*.

for nearly a decade constantly got opportunities for major interviews with the most prestigious business press, interviews that other consultants would have never refused because of the publicity potential. Bain always declined. That was intentional and strategic. It made Bain the CIA or Order of Illuminati of the consulting business. The allure of mysterious modesty made them sought after. Mystique also marks Frank Lloyd Wright's architectural genius in Taliesin and other structures. Meryle Secrest, a biographer of the architect, extols Wright's ability to "conceal and reveal." Self-imposed seclusion can create mystique, as it did in the cases of Greta Garbo and Marlene Dietrich. Self-imposed exile from public performance can pave the way for a thunderous return, as it did for the pianist Vladimir Horowitz at the end of the sixties. But the seemingly opposite—ubiquity in the most distinguished power circles like Bohemian Grove, the Davos Symposium, the *Fortune* CEO Conference, and the retreats of the Conference Board—can also create a mystique, especially for someone not thought of as particularly powerful. Being freshly out of significant office endows mystique, but generally only for one reason: People figure that you have juicy stories to tell that you couldn't reveal while you were in office.

The powerful and their friends will sometimes go to remarkable extents to preserve mystique. A mere public handshake with the wrong person can be seen as violating mystique, and dogged efforts can prevent even an event like this from being immortalized for the public record, despite a herd of media in attendance. Václav Havel, the popular president of Czechoslovakia who stepped down in the summer of 1992 as that nation prepared to splinter, had his mystique defended from one such incident. One of Havel's presidential duties was to mend fences between Czechoslovakia and its World War II adversaries, one of these being Austria. In July 1990, Havel journeyed to Austria to make a speech opening that year's Salzburg Festival. Havel was received by Austria's president Kurt Waldheim, a former U.N. General Secretary and an intelligence officer on the German side during World War II. As the two presidents approached each other, Von

William Echikson has described how a trusted Havel aide, Karl
Fürst von Schwarzenberg, and his people rose up as a human barrier and moved the press photographers to the side, effectively
preventing a title-page photograph of the two statesmen shaking
hands.

Sometimes the powerful act in dramatically cryptic ways to do
just the opposite and bestow an issue or an event with great mystique. The nuclear physicist and "Star Wars" advocate Edward
Teller first had a "private audience" with Ronald Reagan in the
Oval Office in 1982 and began his dialogue in this way, reports
author William J. Broad: "'M r. President,' Teller said as he shook
Reagan's hand, 'third generation, third generation.' Reagan
looked confused, as if Teller was unexpectedly preparing to talk
about his relatives. Then Teller explained his nuclear vision as the
two men sat down on either side of the fireplace. It was a dramatic
start."

You can't be under constant public scrutiny and sustain mystique. In the past two decades, no player on the world stage rated
a higher *mystique quotient* than Mikhail Gorbachev. When the
world saw a weary and shaken Gorbachev return to Moscow after
the attempted putsch in August 1991, Gorbachev's mystique
vanished immediately. How could a man of Gorbachev's political
dexterity and awareness be undermined by his own closest and,
even worse, hand-picked advisers? George Bush's sudden weakness while jogging and his flu spell abroad, when he collapsed into
the arms of his Japanese host, Prime Minister Miyazawa, damaged
the carefully nurtured image of Bush's stamina.

Adversaries try to destroy one another's mystique at every
bend and corner. When adversaries lack compromising video
footage, the next most powerful weapon is gossip. It is a relentless
mode of assault. The aim of gossip is to slander the powerful person's mystique and to demonstrate that the target is vulnerable,
merely human. Mystique must withstand prying over a prolonged
period of time. Every compromising act or situation potentially
destroys mystique. Gossip columns make news more official than
any city hall registration. The likelihood that a powerful person

will be a casualty of gossip is higher now than at any time in history. But the probability that the target of gossip will simply be wounded and will recover has never been higher either. Writes Nicholas Lemann in the *New Republic*, "Walter Winchell, king of the old order [of gossip, who, by the way, carried two loaded pistols with him everywhere he went, as Lehman points out elsewhere in the article] was a creature of a structured, pyramidal society with a universal code of conduct, in which most people thought of themselves as just folks but admired those who weren't. Today's gossips reflect a fragmented, individualistic society in which everybody is, in his or her own self-image, simultaneously a victim and a star." At one time, after the taint of gossip, the tarnished hero would retire to a life of seclusion and perhaps repentance. Today the first steps are often to declare a press conference, negotiate a book sale, and haggle over movie rights. The best advice is always to cut down gossip hard and fast. People surrounding a famous person, even their closest relatives or members of their personal board of directors, will sell information to the gossip columnists under certain circumstances. One always has to look first for material motivations to establish where the gossip originated and why it is likely to be circulating.

Positively Negative

A constructive side of negativism in powerful people is relentless skepticism. A hunger for absolute authenticity drives many of the powerful. Often it is asked if a powerful person is hands-on or not. With regard to people, the powerful are always psychologically "hands on" no matter if they never touch someone. The face-to-face, look-me-in-the-eye reading the shrug-of-the-shoulder reality never happens by teleconferencing. There is still an instinct for the authentic deal-making that used to happen on Orchard Street or Maxwell Street. More than ever, people—the powerful included—want to deal with people they like, admire, and trust. As good as the world's phone systems are, you can't find that out over long-distance circuits. Periodic and direct human contact is indispensable. As Nestlé Executive Vice President Alexandre Mahler says, "An executive has to be on the road. As our President and CEO, Mr. Helmut Maucher puts it: Leadership is best exerted by looking in the eyes and not in the files." Just as a master chef can detect when the sauce is right, leaders must be able to detect the truth. "In a sauce," I once overheard a chef say, "each of the ingredients has its own agenda." If you don't taste, you can't find out what that agenda is or if it fits; and that is an indispensable, critical dimension in the character of powerful people. This is not "management by walking around" to me. Rather it is the more basic "management by contact."

Being positively negative has another equally important meaning. To generate an emotional tone that keeps character assassins at bay, to merchandise itself well, and simply to be more effective in getting things done, power should strive to be positive and energizing. One way powerful people commonly manifested their power in the past was to seize the final say by sometimes, or even often, saying no. It is no longer acceptable to arbitrarily say no. The vise of conflicting special interests and competing crises has intensified the important skill of qualified assent and confined denial. There is great public sentiment against negative forces and against people who gridlock and bottleneck initiatives. Lawyers have become synonymous with negativism, especially in the United States. They have limited what we can do and the constructive risks we can take. They constrain what we say, write, and even think. This is a challenge that must be overcome, and here is one way how that can happen: Leaders must demonstrate they mean "no" in much more constructive, positive ways than in the past. A superpower can say yes to humanitarian aid to a devastated and impoverished country, but still say no to military involvement.

Former Federal Reserve Chairman Paul Volcker excelled in being "positively negative." While he was a tough taskmaster, he also made Americans feel good about his brand of fiscal discipline. Setting clear limits and terms is often the hallmark of the constructive no. Negativism then becomes a matter of well-crafted detail rather than a clumsy wholesale declaration. Quaker Oats

CEO Bill Smithburg's "first job at [Quaker Oats] was as brand manager for Aunt Jemima frozen waffles." He could see that, although the product was popular in the South, the brand wasn't getting the necessary manufacturing and distribution support. He was instrumental in withdrawing the brand from the South "until a second manufacturing plant could be built," writes the distinguished executive recruiter Lester Korn. Afterward the brand reemerged in that region as a great success. Smithburg was careful to explain his logic to the people affected and to not make the decision seem doctrinaire or arbitrary.

Restrictiveness—a policy of "no"—can be made energizing. At General Electric, Jack Welch encourages his people to excel, but they must be in the number one or two businesses in their industry. This is a quality-driven "no," not an arbitrary one. A noted Washington lobbyist, unlike many of his colleagues, was careful never to have the typical autographed pictures of senators, cabinet members, or even Supreme Court justices on his walls. Only presidents were to be seen and that established a peer group for him.

Humanly Strong, Humanly Weak

Sometimes yes is more of a problem than no. It is particularly hard for the powerful to say no to ego, ambition, or flattery. There are adversaries and manipulative staff ever ready to use such emotional weaknesses to override power. Smart subordinates learn that it is foolhardy to assail many powerful persons directly (and especially in public) because of the strong defenses it brings out, even when the powerful person is dead wrong. Instead of saying that a powerful person's proposed course is foolish, they know it is always wiser to point out that other options may also be right. If *this* approach goes down, then the subordinates nudge along the notion that the other options may indeed have advantages. If the bait is taken, the staff generally praises the leader, serving a constructive end.

Subordinates and backers, on the other hand, can prove to be mischief makers. Not only does the problem of accountability, which was discussed earlier, pose many challenges to power, but it is mounted by the incompetence or the malice of subordinates or supposed supporters. One needs reliable human yardsticks to help determine if a challenge they identify is real and truly threatening. Is a purported crisis, for example, an unintentional canard created by an overzealous specialist who doesn't appreciate the big picture? Sometimes internal political agendas can actually activate the sabotage of power. Once I worked with an executive from a global chemical company in the Midwest. This manager had a cadre of executives in Europe. Whenever he visited them, the direct reports invariably plotted out agendas with which no human being could keep up. They were contrived to wear him down . . . and they did. At a highly sophisticated level, some subordinate top managers try to jettison their corporate owners because they don't feel that the corporate cultures of subsidiary and owner are compatible. That's what Duracell's leadership did in the famous "Exorcist Plan," when it motivated Kraft to sell this premier battery maker after six years of ownership.

With skillful manipulation, the powerful too often drop their shield when they are dragged down to a human, personal level. Telling a vice president or a secretary of state in a reception line that his wife is beautiful or that you knew one of his childhood friends will often get a calculating lobbyist a crucial minute more in the reception line. Sometimes this kind of manipulation may be fatal to the powerful. But usually it is not, especially if the powerful person discerns what's happening. After all, this is how the mere mortals rap on power's door.

The powerful suffer from many of the same flaws in human nature as the rest of the human race. Not surprisingly, the powerful often find ways to spend more time on what they like to do than on what they should do. High on the "like to do" list are "engaging in personal diplomacy," detecting paradigm-shifting truths and opportunities, stirring the pot, innovating, creating a legacy, and anointing new stars in the organization. These are the seductive and magical parts of the power role. Infatuated with these exhilarating and doubtless sometimes important ways to use time, powerful persons often neglect to energize the mundane, fail to demand basic competence, forget to put "developmental pork" on the table (see chapter 5), and don't seek to provide reliable continuity. Routine administration may be delegatable, but these latter power chores are not. They are no less delegatable than actualizing vision or demonstrating courage.

With power such a burden, how do the powerful keep their attitude high and straight? Humor can be a disarming mainstay of power, because it allows one to shut off the Awe Factor and to put the world back into the current context. Powerful people whose organization or nation is disadvantaged often use self-effacing humor with particular skill. When I first met Alexander Volsky, the real czar of Russian industry in the post-Gorbachev era, he pointed out that the last man who held his job in Russia and who also had the name Volsky was also an optimist and ended up getting shot in a cellar by the *Cheka* just like the czar had been in Ekaterinburg. One of Moscow's most prestigious editors boasts of living in a high-rise in central Moscow and staying fit by walking up the eighteen floors each day. That is the price of the view he commands in this elevatorless building.[2]

Even momentary setbacks for the powerful are often difficult, because they earnestly don't want to put the organization's agenda in jeopardy. The powerful are regularly haunted by images of the Ultimate Test and echoes of Churchill's "without victory there is no survival." I can recall a professional services firm that recently lost an account of enormous importance. They went into orbit over the defeat. The vendor firm's CEO called the CEO of the kingpin organization it had lost and demanded explanations. The vendor's corporate staff wrote elaborate studies of how

---

2. Eighteen is a magic number for power in Moscow and no sane Russian aspires to live on any higher floor because eighteen is as high as the fire department truck towers can reach, and that could spell life or death—since one can only imagine the condition of the interior fire escape systems in most Russian buildings. Just a few years ago, someone told me that, at least then, guests on the nineteenth and twentieth floors of one twenty-story hotel in Moscow could reach down and find parachutes under their beds.

unfair this all was, and the sales department was wild-eyed with misery. The result was that the vendor really *did* lose the entire account. Its client had been prepared to give an appetizing chunk of it back had the service firm just launched an intelligent, low-key protest. Instead, the vendor dramatically *over*reacted. Rather than matching accusations with incredible outrage, it is far better to admit, "There's no doubt about it, we have some definite problems here . . . and this is what we are doing about them."

When powerful people demean others and do so without true justification, it is usually because power believes that its genius or insight should overwhelm the concerns of a commonplace technician. In such a way, Beethoven angrily berated a violinist for thinking that the composer ought to be concerned about what a fiddle could or could not do while the master's focus was on sheer inspiration in writing a new score. Nuclear scientist Edward Teller, it is said, would insult scientists who left his fold as being mere "pharmacists." As Peter Hagelstein described it: "One or more of these physicists had decided to take the easy way out and go into pharmacy, where they could remove themselves from the battle and lead lives analogous to sheep. At the end of our discussion, Teller summarized his opinion of me in the most devastating metaphor he could think of at the time. He accused me of being a pharmacist." When the youthful Steve Jobs enticed John Sculley to Apple Computer, he chided Sculley with "Do you want to spend the rest of your life selling sugared water or do you want a chance to change the world?"

Power can still be seduced, and the rewards for doing the seducing can be sumptuous because the powerful still indulge their tastes, even though the prudently powerful are much more pragmatic—almost puritanically so—about the tastes that they permit themselves to indulge. Many things can be still sold to the powerful: We think in terms of yachts and mansions, designer gowns, and impressionist paintings. These are trophies, and the rich and powerful still yearn for them, but they are likely to detract from a person's power rather than enhance it if they become an obsession. What the modern powerful are truly willing to pay for are much more elusive investments such as settings, access, exclusivity, and assurance.

George Anders described the pitch KKR partners used to entice top management of prospect companies to undertake leveraged buyouts in *Merchants of Debt*, his study of the investment banking firm Kohlberg Kravis Roberts. It was crucial, Anders observes, that the subject of great financial gain was never raised *too soon*. "Chief executives melted at the speech. One after another, all the 'buttons' that motivated a CEO had been pressed by the KKR partners; first pride, then security, then a chance to overcome danger—and finally, pure capitalist lust for wealth. The KKR men had to be careful not to rush the mention of profits too fast. On one occasion, in England, an investment banker working for KKR mistakenly raced ahead to mention the financial payoff before establishing the right spiritual tone, and was told, 'Money does not concern me in the least.'"

Philippe de Montebello, Director of New York's Metropolitan Museum of Art, effectively *sells* settings to raise money for a great cultural institution. My Fifth Avenue apartment overlooks the Metropolitan Museum. Nearly every night, a caravan of stretch limos queues up there after dropping off guests for some banquet or benefit. There must be an equation relating de Montebello's museum expansion program to the length of those livery lines. It has worked, and *what* has worked is essentially marketing. I think de Montebello realizes he is selling a setting—decorated with the world's most stunning art—for the powerful rich to wage their dinners and soirees. Like a wily *maitre d'*, he collects the tips . . . and buys and builds. De Montebello couples this ingenuity with a natural gift for positioning. As he has put it in *M. Inc.*: "There is a time to praise and a time to ask."

What happens at the Metropolitan Museum also happens at the Kimball Museum in Fort Worth and in countless other venues. To the powerful who are without serious money and need it for their organizations, access is a lifeblood luxury. To raise money, there are three primary targets in the United States: Wall Street, Hollywood, and the Texas oil capitals. Often fund-raising campaigns visit all three. Seasoned political fund-raiser Liz Carpenter dubs such a three-pronged campaign "vacuuming the area." Texas oil money—particularly the Petroleum Clubs in Midland, Odessa, and Houston, and Houston's River Oaks Country Club, are musts, especially in vintage years, that is, those years when the clubs are so well heeled that their somelliers go cull French stocks *twice* in a given year and not just once. Politicians in particular know that this is their merchandising circuit. What they are seemingly out to sell here is not tonics but access. The politically powerful appear at these sites to barter governmental access with the powerful rich in exchange for cash. The politicos learn to solemnly utter the magic invitation "Tell me what you want the president to know." It is, of course, a hollow incantation. First, the political intermediaries have as little real intention of doing so as most presidents do of hearing the message. Still, the politicians will invariably have scribes by their sides to whom they give excited directions like "Get that down." Powerful nonpoliticians are so easily duped by this device because they are basically scared of politics and how direct political involvement could compromise them in other contexts—but they also know that politicians control the legislative and regulatory processes. The game is therefore played as though it were real.

Exclusivity is another siren for power. Exclusivity is a luxury that is more than an enticement. It is a *credential* of power. I once heard a popular and famous American actor describe this distinction as the "Do they know who you are?" factor. They do if you aren't charged for overweight luggage at the airport, get a table when there supposedly are none, are not asked to sign your credit card slips at your favorite clothing boutiques, receive complimentary subscriptions to key magazines, appear on the invitation lists for such events as the Masters, the Derby, and the U.S. Open, or sit in the owner's box at an NFL game, or most especially when you can say, "I don't need to worry about the flight timetable, I've got the *plane*." One shouldn't assume that these perquisites just belong to the powerful rich, for these luxuries are treasured every bit as much by noted activists who sit on the boards of large corporations, cabinet secretaries, senior clerics, and rear admirals. The justification for this kind of indulgence— just as with the other indulgences mentioned above—is almost always explained in notoriously selfless ways by the prominently powerful without money. As I've heard it often excused to me, "Being around this kind of wealth and luxury makes me feel terribly uncomfortable, but—if I don't keep these avenues open or maintain a proper parity for my organization—my board tells me I could do irreparable harm to the attainment of our goals." It's a sublime argument, one which is every bit as accurate as it is dishonest.

The surest weakness to exploit is the powerful's appetite for assurance, especially during a major transaction. The prey here is as easy as begging for table scraps at Christmas dinner, because the powerful are so scrutinized that they want definitive experts vouching that they are acting impeccably. They will gladly buy that assurance. No, the *courageous* may be self-confident, but the powerful are usually unsettlingly cautious. Lucre-scenting lawyers have learned this. As Kurt Vonnegut wrote, "In every big transaction . . . there is a magic moment during which a man has surrendered a treasure, and during which the man who is due to receive it has not yet done so. An alert lawyer will make that moment his own, possessing the treasure for a magic microsecond, taking a little of it, passing it on."

The Perils of Perfectionism

Perfectionism is a dilemma for many powerful people: It is surely a drive that helps them get where they are. But it can also be a straitjacket that hampers what people within an organization are allowed to believe or express. Perfectionism often leads to excessive control or anger. In Chapter 5, we saw how the control reflex shows up in traditional management practices. It can also regulate both the business and social agenda of organizations. Sometimes the powerful allow their organizations to be bullied by special-interest groups, figuring that it is better to be faultless than realistic. In the long run, the price is both power and credibility. *The Economist* writes "To ban 'inappropriately directed laughter', as the University of Connecticut did, is no way to change the attitude of the laughter." In an address before the Interagency Committee on Women Law Enforcement, Judge Maryanne Trump Barry said, "I stand second to none in condemning sexual harassment of women . . . but what is happening is that every sexy joke of long ago, every flirtation, is being recalled by some women and revised and re-evaluated as sexual harassment. Many of these accusations are, in anybody's book, frivolous."

Censorship is often a direct attempt to deprive reality of its power, and the powerful often accede to it for well-intentioned reasons. They support the underlying moral intention. This idealized strength of character can lead to weakness in reality. While truth may be subject to interpretation and bent to give certain goals needed emotional intensity (see Chapter 1), the intentional and obvious distortion of reality is a dangerous game and one that does not play well for long in a knowledge society. Unfortunately, with everyone intent on putting a spin on the facts, censorship of all sorts is enjoying something of a heyday. Former NBC News President Reuven Frank gave a passionate speech about censorship of the media in the Gulf War and the resulting coverage reaching viewers in their homes: "We saw no people. We saw no fighting. We saw 'smart bombs' taking out targets with great efficiency," Frank declares. "[Several months later, we were to] learn that no more than one-fifteenth of the bombs dropped on the Iraqis can be classified as 'smart' bombs; that the most effective planes were not the high-technology, high-priced Stealth fighters but the clumsy, lowly A-10 attack planes, from another generation." Frank pointed to a hero general, "saying over and over, 'I will not have you [the media] on my battlefield. 'My battlefield.' It's a challenging thought."

The alarming rise of self-imposed censorship really reflects a lack of courage on the part of even powerful people who cannot reconcile reality with social justice and the pressure of interest groups. In the *Wall Street Journal*, Irving Kristol wrote a provocative, actually daring, article titled "America's Multiculturalism Tragedy." He reports, "Recently, a journalist telephoned five leading professors of Egyptology, asking them what they thought about the claim of a black Egyptian provenance for Western civilization [the contention that Western European civilization is really the product of that cultural group]. They all said it is nonsense. At the same time, they all withheld permission for their names to be attached to this risky, 'politically incorrect' position."

Censorship rarely benefits the powerful. If anything, it merely avoids troublesome squabbles and pacifies special-interest groups. But the powerful are the ones who generally court censorship into their own organizations. They do so by having tantrums about being photographed at the wrong angle or wondering why a regulatory investigator brings up "that" topic once again. So the organization reacts by thinking there is a mandate at the highest level to control what is inquisitive, awkward, and external.

The curse of perfectionism often also leads to anger. A renewed interest in confrontation—in mixing it up—is making a comeback in the management repertory, but it is risky business. *Business Week* has marked the resurrection of "hop-to-it," bad-news memos that more executives are sending when they "feel a need to reach out and shake somebody. . . . Most often, the message is grim: Business is bad, and it's your fault." That's empowering the organization with blame and its unhealthy and unsustainable. Disputes are, of course, unavoidable, but great care has to be taken as to where and how they occur. When the powerful confront one another, it is important to remember who's in the audience—a truth every bit as important for prelates as for presidents. A Bruce Posner piece in *Inc.* in 1991 said, "Disagreements can be good. . . . But be conscious of where you have them. Understand that if you and your number-two voice your differences in front of other people, you'll lose control over how things are interpreted once a decision is made. No matter what the issue is, employees are going to look for a loser. "

President Bill Clinton has gotten some notoriety for his temper as an offshoot of his high expectations. Paul Johnson says John Quincy Adams was a "superb hater." He compiled lists of enemies throughout his life, and, at the end, created a list of the thirteen men who had done him the most harm. Revenge is a major motive of demonic power. Anger, when it is momentary and explosive, may just be a part of management style. However, there is little room for sustained bitterness in today's version of power. In fact, bitterness is a sure sign of weakness. J. C. Penney Chairman William Howell treats the matter well when he says, "Is the manager forgiving? He or she simply can't afford to harbor bitterness. It drains the manager's energy and takes focus off things that are important." John Milton's *Paradise Lost* is the archetypal study of bitter, demonic power. Milton's demons sue for war, "which if not victory is revenge." Yet there is ever a mesmerizing streak of goodness or refinement in the diabolical tyrant. The Hitlers and Husseins are always sharing cream puffs with youngsters or wiping away a child's tear with a tissue. Milton says of his Satan: "His form had not yet lost all her original brightness." It is that truth that makes so much vengeful thinking seem ostensibly righteous and dignified.

Another aspect of perfectionism is the throb of constant, superior performance. Much advice has been given about what constitutes peak performance, but peak performance can degenerate into a counter-productive arrogance of perfectionism in a world that is increasingly driven by long-term goals. Any powerful person is better off targeting really sustainable excellent performance. What diverts the powerful from this latter path is pressure. When power is under pressure and must measure and manage its reactions in the face of threat, there are four particular pitfalls that can be dangerously consuming: 1) not identifying and using all the available resources; 2) failure to deal quickly with negative issues on one's own team (discussed in Chapter 4); 3) overestimating casually promised support (generally by presumed "allies" in one's extended network); and 4) not recognizing fear and intimidation by opponents for what they are. Under pressure, the classic response of the powerful is to strive harder. The more productive course may be to scan for the classic pitfalls and react methodically. Von Clausewitz wrote, "All war supposes human weakness, and against that it is directed," a statement well worth pondering. And, perfection can be a formidable weakness.

THE EMOTIONAL FABRIC

People value competence, but in a democratic information-based society, they generally only endure power, and then only for the reason that people want to get things done and to have problems solved. Among a cynical population who expect to participate in decision-making, those powerful leaders who display arrogance, bravado, and extravagance are punished by public opinion while the image of understatement, rigorous consultation, and self-restraint wins praise.

8

The Higher Uses of Power

The Art of Getting Caught

Get caught doing something good!

—WALT SEIFERT

How is power best channeled to ethical ends?

Two central issues dominate the higher uses of power. One is using power for good ends and the second is being recognized for doing good things. I want to treat them in reverse order, however, to get the recognition issue out of the way and to put the emphasis on the more important matter, the actual accomplishment of positive deeds.

What people think about those in power was mirrored in the Robin Hood movie *Prince of Thieves* when actor Alan Rickman in his role as the Sheriff of Nottingham bellows out: "Cancel the kitchen scraps for widows and orphans!" The Robin Hood legend was grist for two movies in one summer, and no wonder why: Prince John is corrupt, the Sheriff is a knave, and King Richard ("The Lionhearted" and the only moral authority force) was so incompetent that the Holy Roman Emperor Henry VI kidnapped him en route from the Crusades and exacted a huge ransom from the British treasury in exchange for Richard's life. Thieving, looting Robin Hood, on the other hand, is deemed the pinnacle of virtue and is the people's hero. When the powerful are considered today, it seems that the balladeer Langland is still strumming the lute: Regulators, authorities, adversaries, competitors, the media—among others—are all constantly out to catch powerful people doing something bad. That bad thing could be violating someone's rights or ignoring a regulation. It could be behaving carelessly or saying something foolish. It could be one of countless things, as long as it seems intentional and can be interpreted as mean-spirited. This handicaps power tremendously, since it's very hard to promote or merchandise out of this problem because most proactive, positive image campaigns are simply neutralized by the cynicism and disbelief rampant today. Years ago, I had a professor named Walt Seifert who had a deep conviction that I now think was very prescient. He believed (and still does believe) that the smartest thing powerful people can do is to get caught doing something good. It's a clever idea, but not as simple as it sounds—although now far easier with today's much more sophisticated data and analytic resources. The latter point is exceedingly important. If you want to get caught doing anything, you also have to know where to hang out, and that requires good data.

Observers of the powerful, especially the media, generally believe only what they are able to dig up for themselves. When a big company or a famous figure talks positively about what they've done, the media generally assume that the message is a lie and try to unmask why this particular boast, bluff, canard, or whitewash is being spread. The challenge, then, is letting the press dig but nudging them in the direction of the right turf—turf that will help you get caught doing something good. Just how do you do this? One way is to stake out a location on the contextual map of information that puts you in the path of public attention. If you can relate the topics, trends, and themes of current interest to your own messages, your odds of getting positive attention are markedly increased. This works for dullness as well as goodness. Both have similar problems in getting noticed, and similar opportunities exist to overcome the problem. In fact, unexpected goodness is often a way to deal with dullness. Financial press expert Dean Rotbart once explained to me that being in a dull or dying industry is no excuse for the press to ignore you. A company may mold rubber or be in the tool-and-die business or in some other drab business-to-business commodity. Even the most vanilla of organizations can still be caught with a powerful presence if they sift what they are already doing *outside* of their daily knitting carefully enough. For example, *The Economist* recently had a feature titled "Throwing Things Away." In some countries, the costs associated with consuming a product—especially in getting rid of the packaging—are becoming as important an issue as the product itself. Firms that make less wasteful packaging aren't just doing something about the environment. They also make a statement about their values and stand a good chance of getting caught.

You can get caught doing something good if you speak to desirable new values or help sharpen the definition of ideas. The Ross Perot 1992 presidential campaign, especially in its early stages, was a landmark case of getting caught for taking a strong values stand. Some people have wonderful causes but fail to understand how they can be projected onto a national screen. But Perot succeeded at doing this because he made values so central and because he understood the chains Americans felt were constraining their spirit. Clinton and Bush talked about tax programs, but Perot's appeal was to the soul. Perot may have lost the election, but he is unlikely to vanish from the stage of great political influence and may prevail as a candidate at some future time because his values identification is so strong.

Generosity, even public-spirited generosity, has long been a trait of power, but it too is finding a new idiom. Public-spirited generosity with sophisticated technological information is a new and compelling power statement, as, for example, when Mercedes-Benz decided to share its safety technology with other automakers (as is discussed in the section on the Awe Factor in Chapter 2). When pharmaceutical giant Merck said that it would simply donate millions of units of a proprietary drug to treat human river blindness because the poor countries that needed the drug couldn't afford it, it got caught doing good and had buckets of praise dumped on it because it was the first to write on a new moral slate. Even though power is normally neutral, an opportunity to dramatically increase power exists through creating new positive values, as these two firms did in the sharing of knowledge.

Power Courageous

I said earlier that powerful people are often more cautious than courageous. There's a reason why. If people would be more tolerant of the powerful and realistic about getting tough jobs done, the number of powerful people who would step forward and courageously defend demanding principles would surely grow. Highly autocratic societies are rich in strong leaders but, by definition, weak in democratic principles. Pluralistic democratic societies, however, tend to be weak in leaders. Few knights of the roundtable are stepping forward anymore. While the standards for leaders in newly democratized countries are high (I have already mentioned Brazil), such countries also seem less obsessed with absolute perfection. Lech Walesa has blemishes from being arrogant to temperamental, but the public and the media still trust him. People must be more forgiving and tolerant if leaders are to step forward, particularly in the United States, because power is ironically more vulnerable and fragile than one thinks.

Yet some powerful people can be remarkably selfless. It is even possible to steadfastly refuse the means to one's own survival in the pursuit of power. In December 1992, the Nobel Prize—winning Myanmarese (Burmese) opposition leader Aung San Suu Kyi, who had donated her million-dollar prize money to a trust for the people of Myanmar, reportedly had nearly no spending money to buy food and embarked on a hunger strike—all to protest her forced detention on her family's estate near Yangon. The government wanted Suu Kyi to leave her country. She wanted to stay on and protest what she saw as political repression in her native land. Her power steadily grows as a result.

Some powerful people are also so selfless that they step forward no matter what, even when they seem to be doing the very opposite. On April 9, 1945, the German Admiral Wilhelm Canaris and the General Hans Oster, along with the Reverend Dietrich Bonhoeffer, probably the most distinguished Lutheran churchman of his time, were hanged by the S.S. in the Flossenbürg concentration camp for their resistance against the Third Reich. Five years earlier, Bonhoeffer and his friend (and later biographer) Eberhard Bethge were drinking coffee at a crowded outside café one afternoon when a radio bulletin announced that France had surrendered. The news led to a flurry of German patriotic songs and culminated in Nazi salutes. Bethge, like Bonhoeffer, was completely opposed to Hitler. "In the midst of this pandemonium, Eberhard remains seated," writes Jane Pejsa in her historical study *Matriarch of Conspiracy*, "as he and Dietrich have done on many previous occasions. Dietrich on the other hand is immediately on his feet, joining in the song while pulling Eberhard to his feet beside him. At the moment of the final 'Heil Hitler,' Dietrich whispers insistently to his dumbfounded friend: 'Raise your arm!' 'Are you crazy?' Dietrich then executes the most precise 'Heil Hitler' salute Eberhard has ever witnessed. When it is over, Dietrich turns to Eberhard and says, 'We shall now be running risks for more important things, but not for this salute.'" It takes great courage for powerful people to abandon their public identity and their personal values and to go underground in service to a higher agenda, but sometimes the situation demands that it be done.

Knowledge Wants Freedom

Perhaps the greatest moral benefit that the powerful can bestow on their adherents is to give them the right to do work that is not in conflict with their personal moral agenda. Knowledge workers place particularly great stock on not having to do work that they think compromises them. It's the obligation of managers to constantly check if the people in their organization feel morally compromised by working on particular business. Should data processing specialists be forced to create programs that abet bias in insurance cases? Should biologists be compelled to work on genetic engineering projects? Wherever possible, the powerful person must stretch to accommodate the plausible moral wishes of staff or the mutual understanding of truth that keeps the powerful person and his or her adherents together will be endangered. This is not just virtue. It is equally a safeguard against lethargy, poor quality, or even sabotage. Not that long ago in history, the local person of power *interpreted* morality for his subjects and even dictated which religion would be practiced in his home community. Many of the powerful would still have it that their first job in an enlightened business is to persuade the members how right the organization's position is, but we are leaving those days in the past. While not overlooking education, the powerful today have a far different role: It is to learn and accommodate, as far as possible, the moral preferences of collaborators on the individual projects that make up the flow of most knowledge work.

Feminine Power: Soft or Stereotyped?

Women are certainly more disposed to seeking power than ever before. As Elizabeth Dole puts it, women are not antagonistic to power: "women have come to realize that power is a positive force when it is used in support of a positive cause." But the stereotype that most women view power negatively is still to be overcome. Recent events and writings seem to point to improving conditions for women to exert greater power.

For women to be further empowered, what's needed is tangible and not emotional support, just as the truly empowered in China get farm land or those in the Czech Republic draw ownership vouchers for chocolate or crystal factories. If their power is to grow in a knowledge economy, what women really need is to have their time liberated, which often meets resistance. The treasurer of a British firm says, "Top jobs are designed for people with wives." Gail Sheehy certainly agrees when she writes in *Passages*: "If women had wives to keep house for them, to stay home with the vomiting children, to get the car fixed, fight with painters, run to the supermarket, reconcile the bank statements . . . just imagine the possibilities for expansion—the number of books that would be written, companies started, professorships filled, political offices that would be held, by women." A new trend in the management of careers for the most powerful people is helping acknowledge the need for tangible support. Pamela Hayes of Heidrick and Struggles, a recruiting firm geared to CEO—level placements, says that "help in finding a job for the spouse is a much higher consideration these days and has displaced other decision-making factors in importance." In time, that fact should help to obscure the meaning of spouse, which unfortunately still tacitly means "wife."

Also helping the situation is the growing number of female role models for power. Colorado representative Pat Schroeder has been a trailblazer in preparing the modern military for the role of women as combatants. Human rights advocate and Nobel Peace Prize-winner Rigoberta Menchu has achieved major strides in Guatemala. Elizabeth Dole has been ingenious in the development of the Red Cross as a relief organization. Linda Wachner, CEO of Warnaco, relaunched Warnaco as a public company, and its shares climbed more than 70 percent in just fourteen months. Carla Hills masterminded NAFTA.

The emergence of "soft power"—which I define as a positive power used for moral ends and wielded in a humanistic way—is not just a phenomenon that is proprietary to women. It also is impacted by a sense of the family of humanity. Beginning with the landmark Rio de Janeiro earth conference in 1992, governments across the world are actually taking ecological issues seriously, and so are firms. The humanists join forces with those who believe in the much larger family of life. A recent Florida condominium project was blocked by concern for endangered eagles' nests, and birdnests in the "Pan-Am" sign atop that New York City building set the timetable for its transition to the MetLife Building. Dolphins have forced revamping world commercial fishing behavior, and owls are proving a fiercer adversary for the lumber industry than competing metal or plastic furniture could ever be.[1]

A "soft power" world without grand-scale hostilities is certainly no easier to govern, nor necessarily less brutal in a micro sense than the era that we have just left behind. In fact, it is much tougher to exert power in peace than in war. That is one reason that heads of organizations are always using the language of warfare to dramatize problems or to justify their operating style. It implies an emergency situation. Machiavelli thought the only skill that a prince should or need prepare for was the conduct of war. War is, in fact, much simpler to govern than peace. *The Economist* put it quite eloquently: "It is simply harder to satisfy a nation's peacetime aspirations, both because those aspirations are more confused than in wartime, and because government's peacetime powers are so limited."

The Blue Helmets of the United Nations demonstrate how hard it is to manage a condition of relative peace where no conflicting superpowers have the justification to control regional hostilities for the sake of the bigger picture. Boutros Boutros-Ghali is having to decide just how to allocate the UN's scarce resources. We are in transition to an age where creating and sustaining peace is an active and expensive business. In order to afford to make peace in the former Yugoslavia, the UN will have to withdraw its presence

---

1. There are also implicit threats if such thinking is carried to the extreme. The creative minds in Hollywood today say that the Rambos and James Bonds of the future will be fighting new foes after the fall of the Evil Empire, enemies like environmental polluters and corporate exploiters of the Third World. That means that businesses and governments (in their domestic role) are in for much more heat and a far higher expectation of the extent to which conscience and values should govern their behavior. That heat is already being felt: the Michael Crichton novel-turned-Steven Spielberg movie *Jurassic Park* evidences the trend. Scientists in Britain have already publicly protested that science is being ill-treated in comic books as environmentally hostile, and that this is giving science a bad name. (*Economist*, January 18, 1992). That threat, and others like it, are more profound and ingrained in shaping opinion than one might initially think.

from countries like Cyprus. The demands of global governance will expand the role of "soft power" in making those decisions wisely.

Power's Appeal to Conscience

An important paradigm shift in the good use of power is taking place right now in religion. Powerful religious leaders today are often less likely to be preachers and more likely to be mediators between diverse and antagonistic groups. They are the best current role models for exerting power in entrenched antagonistic situations. The power base of religion is shifting from miracles to mechanics. When an American faith-healer and television minister came to London to hold a series of revival meetings in June 1992, some special interests representing the handicapped said he was just exploiting disabled people and their dreams. Today's watchdogs demand religion be derived from a different power base.

But what should that base be? Two years ago, at the World Economic Forum in Davos, Switzerland, Catholic Theologian Hans Küng questioned, "Why can't the world religions come together in the struggle against universal sins and in the promotion of universal virtues?" Dr. Küng thinks "real humanity constitutes convergence of the major religions," and why shouldn't it? But in Ireland, the Middle East, India, the former Yugoslavia, and countless other places, religion drives war. And the trend only promises to worsen.

Thinking of religion as some tender-touch plea for human understanding won't help us understand its workings. Mark Twain once said his mother was so loving that she even prayed for Satan, but Mrs. Clemens was an exception. The first cornerstone of religious power is knowing just who the villain is. *Who* is today's Satan? Now that Lenin has been knocked off his pedestal, the Evil Empire is no longer the serviceable villain it was for the West. Hordes of ideologues have raced to paint capitalism as the next worst thing to communism and to cast it as the new villain. I don't buy it, and neither does most of the world.

Still, people demand a world-class villain, such as Saddam Hussein, General Manuel Noriega, or Abimael Guzman of the Shining Path. Polluters, slum lords, and child abusers are clear villains, but they hardly pretend to be threats on a national or international scale. The day of the Big-Time Villain is over. The world's new villains will be fragmented, pluralistic, and relative. Said simply, they will be *other* people's beliefs—a disturbing idea and one that will cause respected religious leaders themselves to be targeted as villains. For example, *The Economist* states, "The death of communism has reanimated the centuries-old feud between Catholicism and Orthodoxy." On the "front-line" of a post-Soviet Ukraine, "The Polish pope in the Vatican and the Russian patriarch in the Kremlin are the generals. . . . Hostilities are so fierce that Pope John Paul II has been advised by the Kremlin not to make a visit to the former Soviet Union."

With the ideological war over between East and West, religious disputes that have smoldered below the surface for decades are erupting. The historical context for Armenian-Azerbaijani conflict is a religious one. The rivalry between many Orthodox Serbs and Catholic Croatians stands deep in history, as does the duel between Catholics and Protestants in Northern Ireland. The Arab-Israeli conflict is, of course, a religious war in many respects; and, even the nonaligned can get caught up in it. Consider the Archbishop of Canterbury's emissary Terry Waite's lengthy abduction.

The collapse of the big global blocs has multiplied the number of potential conflicts and is likely to insert religion as a negative issue in a host of new situations. Furthermore, modern marketing tools are stoking the fire—the niche marketing that has been so popular and successful in business strategy in the last decade. I now see its use as a weapon in emerging religious conflicts as more effective than its waning utility in selling soap. Perhaps we should call it "niche villainy." A crafty publicist with a grudge, gruesome video footage, and a smattering of slurs can create a new media villain overnight. Religious figures will also be prime targets. Religious figures will direct fire at their opponents more and more often. This rapid pluralization of the world has two other impacts on human behavior. First, it increases political instability, which leads to economic instability, and that means a bigger focus on self-interest and greed. Second, political and economic instability create attitudinal insularity—for both people and nations. It is much harder to meld big religions together and to go after universal values. The media and local religious constituencies will sift every comment by a national or international religious leader for its local or parochial impact, what it means to the diocese or synod back home. That demand for relevance is more than a little selfish and announces that the "me generation" has come to goodness. We are finding that religion may be as local as politics.

Locally, human problems raise money, and communities cocoon inside their own problems and neighborhood boundaries. At the same time, the money is sucked away from national agendas and priorities. Certain poor districts in the nation and in the world are less likely than ever to get needed support from outside their communities. One sure outcome is less money for breaking down the "big picture" barriers between religious groups. It is tougher and tougher to raise funds to advance a meeting of the minds on the big issues of religion. And the risks to attitudes and ethics if we don't agree grow steadily greater.

One of the most courageous mobilizations of opinion power in history (and perhaps one of the first in the modern sense) was the French novelist Emile Zola's campaign to win the release of the Jewish officer Alfred Dreyfus from Devil's Island in 1898, after Dreyfus had been imprisoned on treason charges. His accusers were, history now judges, driven by anti-Semitic motives. For his wisdom, his courage, and his tenacious ability and dedication to put power to good ends, Rabbi Arthur Schneier, the head of the Appeal for Conscience Foundation in New York City, has always reminded me of Zola.[2] From orchestrating relief for a number of disaster campaigns to organizing recognition of then German

2. The one trait in which Arthur Schneier and Emile Zola certainly part company is regarding religious tolerance. While Zola was a committed social reformer and champion of the underdog, he was also a fervent anti-Catholic. In terms of religious and social tolerance, I have never known Arthur Schneier to stand against any reasonable system of beliefs.

Foreign Minister Hans-Dietrich Genscher's contributions to world diplomacy, Rabbi Schneier always seems to be a step ahead of issues and to operate on a moral level above many other world leaders, including religious ones. Mostly, the Rabbi knows how to stay in touch with reality.

Rabbi Schneier once said to me, "There are not many great preachers in this era, and a great religious leader cannot just be a pulpiteer today. There are too many intense changes going on." What a different vision! Throughout history, religious leaders have been among the most powerful communicators, but they have also been preachers in the main—speaking segmented messages mostly to their own flocks. In the television age, this kind of narrowcast communication is risky. Everybody's listening and looking to learn what's good and what (and who) is bad. But Rabbi Schneier knows that the power of good, just like any other sort of power today, is transactional. The emerging role of the religious leader is as mediator and disinterested advocate. Today's multiplying regional and national conflicts are really an extension of the fights we are seeing within and between neighborhoods. Religious leaders today must be more outwardly directed than in the past, ambassadors for a particular religious congregation within the broader community—proving understanding, receiving and interpreting messages, reconciling viewpoints, and determining workable courses of action. I have personally witnessed Rabbi Schneier's shuttle diplomacy between the gospel churches of Harlem, the synagogues of Washington Heights, and the quiet congregations of White Plains. There is little difference in the *operating style* of a modern religious leader and that of an effective Washington lobbyist or a special-interest head. The motivations and the moral values may differ, but the basic behaviors do not. However, religious leaders best prove their mettle to the broader community in advocating a cause that is clearly removed from their specific own interests, as Rabbi Schneier did in organizing Armenian earthquake relief (just as Jesse Jackson gained a whole new status in mediating issues that were not fundamentally racial). However, helping Armenians *did* give Rabbi Schneier a great edge in Moscow in easing barriers against the immigration of Jews from the then Soviet Union.

Religious leaders face a heightened challenge to be more relevant. "The Bible," Rabbi Schneier points out, "is a best seller
because it deals with real life." Back in the sixties and seventies,
the "relevant" religious leader was automatically equated with the
"socially involved religious leader." I'm not at all sure that is the
case today. In fact, cultivating the religious attitudes and values of
the powerful may be far more important because those are the
values that "trickle down" in practice. While Rabbi Schneier has
a deep personal commitment to the issues of the poor and the less
fortunate, he also has a remarkable knack in reaching the ethical
marrow of international and national opinion leaders. To me, that
is the most insightful form of relevance. Although it's hardly on
the top of his agenda, Rabbi Schneier's institution and congregation are never attacked for being out of touch. What works for
churches works well for any other community institution, particularly those with a mission of benevolence or healing. It all relates
back to knowledge and competence. Religious leaders must provide premium advice: We live in a secular world. Religious leaders
may not like that reality and may not like to acknowledge it, but it
is true. Again, I point to Rabbi Schneier as a model because he is
such an effective sounding-board for influential people. However,
he only enjoys that role because he gives premium advice to secular leaders—perceptive and unbiased. In Rabbi Schneier's own
words, "The way you win trust is through clarity."

Religious leaders will be measured on their application, *not
their devotion*. To quote Rabbi Schneier once more, "You must
apply faith." Religious power is increasingly like every other exer-
tion of power in this respect: Power is essentially the art of getting
things done—in this case, with the accent on getting them done
morally. Religious institutions will absorb more and more of the
brunt of social problems and turmoil. The religious agenda is also
increasingly intersected by an array of "life issues" such as abortion, animal rights (and the new pantheism), the environment,
euthanasia, AIDS, and organ transplants. The religious community has recognized that it must link up more firmly with the business community. The vicars of the world are in hot pursuit of the

powerful. While the arts created dialogue in the eighties, religion will be more important in the nineties because values have a new-found importance. Why? One world, more or less compelled to full disclosure, has replaced two big ideological camps competing and squirreling away their assets as they try to divide up the pie. Haggling in the new global marketplace, religion will be at the center of more controversy.

As this book is being written, the bloody war in the post-Yugoslavian states of Bosnia, Herzogevinia, and Croatia continues to rage. During the Thanksgiving weekend of 1992, the Swiss government asked Rabbi Schneier to convene an "Appeal of Conscience" initiative and invited the ranking religious leaders of the region's Orthodox, Roman Catholic, and Moslem churches to meet in Switzerland's Wolfsburg Center. At that meeting, Schneier used certain techniques that constitute a textbook for the shrewd use of power for good ends. First, he invoked a carefully planned sequence of symbolic occasions and communications to reinforce a global mandate during the two-day meeting. These included reading aloud letters from President Bush and UN Secretary General Boutros Boutros-Ghali and a visit to Bern for a meeting with the president of Switzerland. He got the three religious chiefs to sign a hard-won agreement placing humanitarian ends above ethnic ones and issues of creed. Most importantly, he lifted these powerful regional figures to a new plateau of accountability—an accountability, not to their adherents back home, but to the most important forces in the international community. The Thanksgiving weekend retreat was in no sense a final solution, but it was certainly the beginning of a very constructive use of power that may gradually bring a vital moral force to bear on this crisis.

Summing up, there are two points I want to repeat in the current context of power's relationship to values. First, as Drucker has put it, power is a burden; and second, some of the greatest wisdom about power is to be found in unexpected places like the *"Pig Book," Tightwad Gazette*, or Milton's *Paradise Lost*. In his 1989 commencement address at Middlebury College, Senator Bill

Bradley showed that he too rummages for his power information down eclectic back roads: "Erma Bombeck tells the story of a successful career woman who decides she's had enough of making money and wants to give something back. She asks How? Who? Where? And in her puzzling, she writes Mother Teresa in Calcutta and offers to volunteer and seeks her advice. Weeks pass—finally a letter. She opens it and Mother Teresa has a one sentence reply. 'Thank you for your offer, but find your own Calcutta.'" Doing that may not be simple, but what must be done is certainly clear: The powerful person, who appreciates that power is a burden and who is still determined to make power serve the good agenda, should hop to it and get busy finding and fixing their own Calcutta. In a message to powerful people, Bishop Desmond Tutu once reminded them of the source from which their power was derived: "Your decisions affect people—people who are of infinite worth because they are created in the image of God," Tutu wrote. "God depends on you."

THE HIGHER USES

To be a positive force, power must be focused, systematic, and caring. The initiative is with those publics that assent to power and not with the powerful themselves. In the pursuit of positive ends, the powerful must be content to find themselves "caught doing something good."

APPENDIX

Power Resurges

There could be no honor in a sure success, but much might be wrested from a sure defeat.

—T. E. LAWRENCE

Out of the wreck I rise.

—ROBERT BROWNING, IXION

How is power sustained long term? Is an uninterrupted reign of power probable?

This appendix does not deal with the fleeting setbacks of power—setbacks that are prone to be either political or psychological and are usually temporary. Rather, this is power when it is down for the count and anxious to reassert. The rules of resurgence have changed because the rules of advancement have changed, too. The roads to the most powerful positions have become more varied and bending. Traditionally, one inherited power or rose to it in a steady linear progression. Now, especially because so many of the problems in large organizations appear intractable and seem to exist because of the managerial inadequacies of those presently in charge, more and more organizations are turning to outside sources for leadership to solve their problems. Outsiders have acquired a certain ineluctable mystique—especially those coming from comparably sized organizations in wholly different industries—or directors or retired managers brought in to place an organization back on track. This mystique of the outsider often paradoxically creates two kinds of resurgence situations: 1) the need for an ousted or fallen leader to deal with defeat and to find a way back to power, 2) but, equally, the need for the incoming powerful person to succeed in the new role, since one can generally assume that they too are resurging. After all, would they leave *their* present organization to join a new one if their present post was adequate for their power needs and/or if they fit their organization's current agenda? Why do they need or want a new home?

No discussion of resurgence can emphasize one particular point too much. *To lose a powerful position is not necessarily to lose one's power.* In fact, the ability to withstand the loss of a position—despite the inconvenience of instantly giving up status, compensation, and perquisites—and still to retain one's power is a triumph. The wisest powerful people recognize that *losing a position is merely losing a platform.* For the powerful who steer significant organizations, where dangerous risks must be addressed daily, the loss of the platform is an ever-present danger and must simply be accepted as something that could happen at any time. That's why I assign such importance to the personal board of directors and the informal power structure described in Chapter 4. And, while I use the term "out of power" throughout this Appendix, the truer description is really "out of platform." As will be seen, there are creative ways to retain and regain power even when a particular position (or platform) is lost.

Fallen Angels

Failure is no shame. At some point in their careers, an increasing number of powerful people were defeated or failed at exactly what they are now doing successfully. This is true for three simple reasons. First, we are living longer and engaging in extended career lives in a more complex world that gives us many more opportunities to make career-threatening mistakes. Second, the power world is more competitive, causing more people to want to take advantage of the mistakes of others. Third, and on the brighter side, because the causes of defeat are likelier to be more specific, they are generally more correctable. Also, a realization may be emerging in our consciousness: One of the most important enabling experiences in the exercise of power is having tasted defeat. Defeat teaches realism, perspective, ingenuity, and humility, among other valuable traits. When one resurges from defeat (or even severe trials) once, it is possible to do so again. Elsewhere, I have written about the difficulties of second comings, but the truth is now that second comings are becoming far more common. Third comings are truer indications of genuine stamina. Chrysler Corporation and Germany are clear evidence that power can resurge more than once or even twice. While warriors once rallied around chiefs they thought invincible, greater loyalty today is likely to be accorded someone who has known and overcome defeat. That's because the statistics are too overwhelming. Defeat is a routine rather than an exceptional experience, in the power resumé, and it is background adherents should expect the powerful to have. While second and third resurgences may be more frequent, there is still a large and substantial segment of powerful people who never recover from a first major defeat. Prudent adherents avoid them at all costs. There is now a protocol for defeat. Gifted defeat prescribes the messages, the gait, and the mood with which one leaves the ring.

An intimate knowledge of defeat is especially important for politicians. Joe Napolitan is a savvy campaign strategist who has managed major-league contests for the likes of Hubert Humphrey and Valery Giscard d'Estaing. Napolitan once wrote, "When I started my career as a political consultant I think I won the first thirteen elections I was involved in. Then I lost a gubernatorial primary, so I figured, 'Well, I might lose to another Democrat but I've never lost to a Republican.' Then I lost to a Republican and that theory was shot to hell."

Napolitan once compared notes with another Washington king-maker, Matt Reese. They were chatting about a young campaign consultant who had won a couple of elections and was making a name for himself. Napolitan wanted to know how sharp the kid really was. "'He's pretty good,' Matt said, 'but he'll be a lot better after he loses a couple of elections.'" It's risky business to entrust a major campaign of any sort (political, commercial, financial, organizational, spiritual, or any other) to anyone who has *not* experienced a significant defeat and who cannot explain how they overcame it in achieving their next mission. The issue is not solely one of recovery. The defeated also recognize the authentic signals of oncoming disaster—signals to which the untested are often oblivious—and the very inkling of which can help avert disaster from occurring again.

There are distinct traits and reasons that lead to any fall from power, and they must be identified. People, organizations, or regions do not all fall from power for the same reasons. Each fall has its own dynamics. In taking inventory, one must be careful not to reject one's strengths or stronger tendencies as weaknesses . . . or to blame the wrong behaviors for failure. Some powerful people who have run aground, for example, contend that what caused their fall was being too trusting or too collegial. In fact, they may not have been *trusting enough* or were too self-conscious or timid in the way that they trusted. Nor is an apparently fruitless agenda to be automatically discarded. One should never write off a seemingly dead agenda. When the exceptionally well managed American Airlines recognized that it didn't have the capital to acquire global partners and couldn't compete solely as a classical airline, it went into the additional business of managing air travel for other carriers. When dentists ran out of decay, they turned their business toward prevention. When the BBC faced cutbacks in its core network budget, it found ways to sell programs and services to other broadcasters—creating, in effect, a production strategy as a viable organizational offshoot. With the demise of communism, Deng Xiaopeng and his cronies would have been languishing in senior-citizen homes in the South Pacific using volumes of Marx and Mao as doorstops and footrests. Instead, this supposedly dottering Chinese leadership revitalized the world's largest economy.[1]

Successfully Out of Power

There is an art and science to being *successfully* out of power. Few people or organizations ever return to power if they are not accomplished at being out of power, and few people appreciate that being successfully out of power is a skill. In the United States, we tend to look at a defeat—especially a big one—as a terminal condition. The Chapter 4 discussion of risk tries to show how misleading and destructive that viewpoint really is. Consider Japanese politicians. They are tumbling out of power all the time, and then bouncing back into it. We tend to think that when the Japanese lose power all that's left is ceremonial disembowelment. Mostly, that's because we Westerners do a miserable job of distinguishing between *losing face*—which is a serious issue with the Japanese—and *losing power* (platform)—which is more or less a cyclical condition of one's career.

Anyone who is astutely out of power must plan for the inevitable resurgence of counter-trends and values. What enabled Richard Nixon to stage a comeback was the dramatically renewed importance of those foreign policy issues that had been the backbone of the Cold War—Nixon's area of acknowledged expertise. His return was highly likely, if also not unpredictable. Had the highly unlikely happened and the United States had submerged itself in

1. In Beijing receiving lines, visitors would create a veritable procession past Deng Xiaopeng as he sat in a great chair decorated with fine linen, and he would receive each of them in an audience of two to three minutes. When I once made the ritual filing past Deng, I tried to think of the simplest, most basic question I could ask: "What, sir, are your plans for China?" He smiled at me and said that he intended to ask each Chinese to plant one tree a year for the next eight years. Reflecting on the visit, my first reaction was that my question was a miserable gaffe. But, thinking about it further, it may not have been. Indeed, Deng's answer too might sound superficial . . . and, it *is* in a superbly intelligent way. Human capital thrown into a campaign for eight billion trees is a rather dramatic commitment—consistent with a similar pledge that Mao Tse-tung had made, but far beyond Mao's in sheer productivity.

solely isolationist concerns, Nixon's new limelight could not have been lit. Likewise, had the Soviet Union (and its disintegration) not become a center-stage phenomenon over the last several years, Zbigniew Brzezhinski could not have staged such a resurgence in his media presence.

To maintain access to the sources of power and to the flow of transactions in the stream of power, almost all experts recommend that the out-of-power position themselves as lobbyists. Certainly, it's one reliable way to sustain access. It's commonly believed that lobbyists exist only in the political arena, but they operate in finance and commerce as well: A displaced executive will often chair an important industry council or become an adviser on a particular project to a prestigious consulting group. At the very least, this is marketing, and often it is genuine lobbying, because the person is deployed for contacts more than competence and frequently asked to block a new initiative from happening. "A lobbyist's worth often is measured by 'what doesn't happen as much as what does,'" A *Cleveland Plain Dealer* article said about power in Washington. Perhaps the reason why is that people in power are expected to make things happen, while people out of power are often tapped to make sure things don't. In this sense, negative lobbyists of all sorts resemble a Congress in opposition to the executive branch of the opposing party. Sam Rayburn, House Speaker during most of the Eisenhower years and the cornerstone of the Democratic opposition, was fond of saying that he liked to "make running water walk." While this may certify one as a formidable choke point, such behavior is also a dangerous muscle-flexing addiction to develop for people who want to get things done. One must ultimately show a constructive side—one richer than being the biggest, meanest brick wall on the block. To put wind back in the sails and to find a platform, the message must ultimately be the positive one: "There are things to be done and *I* am the person who can do them."

Being out of power should be a time of constructive self assessment, including a review of the personal infrastructure. One reason that investors avoid aging cities, or the reason why some newer cities are viewed skeptically, is that there are serious doubts about their infrastructure—roads, schools, hospitals, and phone systems. Analogous concerns can be directed toward people, and I don't mean such obvious problems as those of health or aging. Are the thought processes fresh and reflective of current trends in leadership thinking? Has a person's network of contacts been continually updated to include important new players while individuals whose power is eclipsed are weeded out? Is the individual comfortable working in modern, more elastic organization structures? These issues and a number of others suggested by the overall theory of power outlined in this book need thorough and forthright answers.

There are also practical considerations. Any dislodged powerful person causes a squad of adherents to be out of "pork"—reformed or otherwise. In the discussion of formal boards in Chapter 4, I said that candidates for a directorship should always be evaluated in terms of the board contacts that they bring with them. Similarly, as soon as one believes that their power platform (that is, their official organizational role or job) is in jeopardy, they should analyze which supporters will also lose out if the powerful person is unseated. A powerful person is obliged to mobilize these networks of support that will suffer from a person being jostled from position.[2] There are often vast elements of support that suffer from a particular person's being out of power, and many may be geographically distant or scarcely identifiable on first consideration.

When one is out of power, one must also prove that they remain fresh in the transactional flow of issues. Until Bill Clinton's election, this was a real problem for the Democratic party in the United States. The Democrats had held no significant foreign policy posts for more than a decade. But, by mid-1991, the Democrats began to act on this problem. After twelve years out of power

---

2. I am consciously avoiding the tactics of using the potential unhappiness of *threatened* resources to avert being thrown out of power in the first place, because these tactics verge again on the exercise of political maneuvering and not true power.

in foreign relations—and, either as a compromise with the
Republicans or because they were able to forward the best quali-
fied people for the jobs—the Democrats filled pivotal openings:
Cyrus Vance as former secretary of state became the central U.S.
negotiator in the post-Yugoslavian political crisis and Robert
Strauss was named Ambassador to Russia.

A Tactical Plan for Resurgence

The theaters of power shift continually, which means that launch-
ing platforms to power are constantly changing. In the eighties,
the centers of business power fled from the Fortune 500 companies to smaller, entrepreneurial businesses. Now, the very same
small companies are in desolate shape and economic power is
returning to large corporations and government-business coalitions. One could almost say that the creative consciousness of
business retreated to the world of the small company to hobble
together the methods to reform large-scale business, just as
Martin Luther and other one-time Catholic clergy retreated from
their posts in the Roman Catholic church to castle hideouts and
community workshops in order to devise a concept of reformed
Christianity. Subsequently, Counter-Reformationists used the era
of reformist dominance to map out their own offensive.

When reversing a setback, it is essential to decide on what
exactly to repair and at what pace. There is almost always an
advantage in dealing with discrete blemishes than attacking gener-
alities. As I've contended, everything does not go wrong all at
once, nor will it all be restored at the same time. Organizations
and individuals in setback must distinguish between life support
and long-term rehabilitation as they control the timing and pace
of a comeback. Short-term, one must focus on how to keep contacts current. Simultaneous long-term thinking may demand an
entirely new set of goals and positioning, but these are unlikely to
take shape overnight. A *Wall Street Journal* article once reported
that "to get employees thinking long-term," the management of
Caroline Rose Hunt's hotel firm Rosewood in Dallas sometimes

asks them "to write their own imaginary obituaries as part of training." There are other ways to clarify long-term ambitions, but a thoughtful focus on one's epitaph is a sobering way to leave revenge and bitterness behind when planning the long-term future.

When the plan and goals are clear, the next step is to motivate support. To inspire potential adherents to return the individual to a formal position of power demands the creation of a focused need. Former Texas governor Bill Clements, a Republican, succeeded in getting reelected after a break in his terms of office. Like Ross Perot, Bill Clements was an outsider, not a professional politician. He started out as an oil driller and then managed business affairs for the Department of Defense. At his first press conference as Republican nominee for governor, the very first question, Clements once told me, nearly decked him. "It was: 'Did you vote for Lyndon Johnson in 1964?'" Clements said he thought to himself: "'What have you gotten yourself into?' But, then the answer came out as clear as a bell: 'Yes, and I'll tell you why. I'm a Texan and I want a Texan in the White House. I guess I'm a Texas ticket-splitter.' God must have put those words in my mouth," Clements declared. Regaining the governorship in Texas had been done only once before, in the twenties. In retaking the gubernatorial mansion in Austin, Clements did it through focus. His people concentrated the issue of *confidence* into a single memorable slogan: "A bumper sticker really did it for us," he told me. "It read: Gee, I miss Governor Clements." But, a bumper sticker, a rallying cry, or a single TV spot can't actually achieve a comeback in itself. It can only create a focal point that attempts to embrace a complex set of issues.

The renewed endorsement of authorities is fundamental to resurgence. Confidence in weak regions, economic sectors, and companies is always best restored when they earn the genuine endorsement of a handful of leading economists, analysts, and business institutions. This is far more important than anything that any power source can say about itself. For executives, fellow directors can be very important to the resurgence of the rebounding powerful. William Agee's board membership at Morrison Knudsen and that board's confidence in his mettle as an executive were essential to his being appointed CEO of that company. But, relying solely on fellow directors is often made difficult. For most large organizations, an individual only serves on an outside board as long as they are in their present principal position and must resign the board if they leave their primary post. A stellar exception to this reality has been Thomas Wyman, former CEO of Green Giant and then of CBS. Wyman's sheer competence and the esteem with which he was regarded by the investment banking community enabled him to sit on the boards of AT&T, S. G. Warburg, General Motors, ICI, and the Ford Foundation without holding a high visibility corporate top job in his own right. And Wyman's board presence helped lead to his appointment as Chairman of S. G. Warburg in the United States.

Outsiders and Innovation

One of the potent new threats to power is one's own incumbency. Because not enough seems to be done quickly enough, boards are ever ready to sift and churn top managers. If you've been around a while, and particularly if you haven't done anything striking, you're vulnerable. In the last U.S. presidential election, political incumbents were wearing big, red *I*'s on their chests. Political consultants across the nation censored the word "reelect" from campaign posters, lapel buttons, and all the other electioneering paraphernalia. Not long ago, incumbency was synonymous with power but, no longer. The same thing has happened in business.

In a decisive anti-insider strategy, Coca-Cola called upon Michael Ovitz to reform its marketing strategy and to inject it with creativity. PepsiCo's marketing success drove competitor Coke to Ovitz. PepsiCo has made their creative appeals a virtual extension of what is happening in the world of entertainment and music and truly forced Coke's hand. In Ovitz (Ovitz and Disney chairman Michael Eisner are considered to be the two most powerful people in Hollywood), Coke teamed up with Creative Artists Agency—the most successful talent brokerage in the entertainment business. Ovitz was hired because of his astute grasp of mass-market taste and how it is rendered in the images of the entertainment industry as well as for his contacts. A first Ovitz step was to retain directors like Oscar-winning director Francis Ford Coppola to create Coke spots. The reactive innovation at Coke is not just what was added to the power structure (Ovitz). What was subtracted was equally important, and that was the dominance of advertising agencies in creative matters. PepsiCo's Roger Enrico described the new world of merchandising this way: "On the marketing side . . . I can't see what the agency brings to the party. Why should great marketing minds go to work for an advertising agency?" Indeed, the conventional ad agency brings a huge bundling of expenses that have little to do with the creative processes. Today, most ad agencies are languishing, and they are increasingly being excluded from the power decisions of marketing. The Ovitz solution should also suggest to the out-of-power that there are opportunities to create new forms of power in organizations, and these possibilities should be identified and exploited when plotting a resurgence. Another agent, Clive Davis, is being similarly innovative in serving client needs, and what he brings to the table is the same intellectual capital of creativity.

A fresh industry vantage point can occasionally be an avenue to power even in very significant undertakings. Financier Sir James Goldsmith picked Dayton Hudson's Floyd Hall to lead the Grand Union supermarket chain not only because Hall was an accomplished merchandizer and operator but also because he had no background in supermarket retailing. He would not bring with him preconceptions about what could and could not be done in the running of a grocery store chain, and Goldsmith's selection of Hall proved extremely successful. Producers Simpson and Bruckheimer—who are responsible for the blockbuster movies *Flashdance*, *Top Gun*, and *Beverly Hills Cop*—have a record of choosing novice directors to guarantee that the final product would have "a positive emotional excess." This latter term is cited in a *Business Week* review of the book *Circus of Ambition* by John Taylor and represents an important ingredient that a more seasoned professional might restrain.

The Goldsmith solution has become a pronounced trend. The present tendency is to recruit outsiders for top management posts, for example, Stanley Gault at Goodyear, Robert Eaton at Chrysler, Michael Armstrong at Hughes Aircraft, and William Ruckelshaus at Browning-Ferris. As Stanley Gault himself says, "If you come from outside the industry, you come with a pretty clear vision. There are people who move within an industry without carrying a bias, but it's very, very difficult." Reform capability—especially in addressing problems of similar scale and character—has become an entrance ramp to power. The question is not: Can the candidate specifically run a furniture maker, an opera company, or a city council, but, have they overcome like challenges on a comparable scale? Examine the *provenance* of the Postmaster General Marvin Runyon. He served as president of Nissan USA for eight years, and then revitalized the Tennessee Valley Authority. Runyon demonstrated that he knows how to penetrate entrenched organizations and promote change, and he was picked for those powerful skills— not for his knowledge of mailboxes and postage meters.

Sword and Suitcase

Portability is absolutely central to the issue of resurging power. Power must be able to move, and, in our time, it must move nimbly. When the Russian Czar Peter the Great traveled to the Netherlands and England in 1698, he brought with him a "traveling embassy" that included dwarfs for entertainment and priests for religious discipline. During the "Organization Man" age of the 1950s and 1960s, an American executive who came in to run a company from the outside could often draw an entourage of hundreds or more of his former managers with him and often did so to buy loyalty and annihilate the invaded company's culture. Today, that doesn't happen—except in transitions of big city mayoralties, state houses, or the White House where the executive branch is a purely partisan affair. It's the exception certainly in commerce, where even in very large companies the landing force rarely exceeds five or ten from the CEO's past team, and this new trend exists for very good reasons.

First, today's revitalizing executive is morally obliged to travel light for the sake of example. The relocation of hundreds of high-priced executives doesn't set the right tone. Second, the problems of individual organizations are considered to be less standardized than in the past. No longer is it simply a question of getting "better" management, but getting a management more exactly qualified and experienced to cope with the specific problems at hand (as in the case of Postmaster General Runyon). Third, with many companies already cutting staff because of economic pressures, there is tremendous resistance to reforming a company through replacement as opposed to rejuvenation of the existing players.

There are many implications in this leaner, more specialized trend in the relocation of power. It may make the transplantation of power at the very top or at the head of highly specialized pyramids even easier than in the past. But, it also complicates the question of loyalty to a "sponsor" for millions of other executives. To whom should *they* be loyal? With competition fierce for the top spots, attrition high among those contestants, and only limited opportunities of moving with an executive sponsor (as against depressing odds that one's own job might be eliminated), many adherents are now more loyal to their profession or their specialization than to their leaders. The powerful can combat this, but usually only on a limited scale. And, if they try to advance the traditional arguments for loyalty and self-sacrifice, they are not likely to win hearts and may cripple their own agenda, because they will not be seen as credible.

Renewal and Resurgence

With longer lifespans and better levels of health, there is an expanding group of people between fifty-five and seventy-five who are ready to launch new roles—and roles with more impact than serving the special interests of AARP or the Gray Berets. Powerful retirees are changing their self-perception. What was once the elder statesman is now the better statesman, and there is great emphasis on revitalizing organizations through experience. John Swearingen at Amoco, Stanley Gault at Goodyear, and John Smale at General Motors were all hauled back into the fray out of retirement. What this also says is that a person who doesn't lust for a retirement of golf games and cruises should diagram their power aspirations for the fifteen to twenty years of their active "retirement" as carefully as they do the supposed halcyon last two decades of their "official" career.

The most exciting new form of resurgence taking hold is renewal. The most impressive demonstration of such resurgence is when a powerful figure is able to transcend the organization that he or she has shaped as a guiding force and to begin again, while the first institution continues. Obviously, this requires a unique combination of confidence and competence. The Rubbermaid that Stanley Gault made such a success story is still branded with Gault's GE-bred management style, even though Gault himself retired from it and then went on to initiate major breakthroughs at Goodyear. When Seymour Cray decided to leave the 5,000-strong Cray Research he founded, it wasn't long before he established Cray Computer in 1989, when he was over sixty, partly because he couldn't resist the temptation of making a computer out of gallium arsenide circuitry and partly because he hungered to work in an organization of limited size. (Cray Computer has fewer than three hundred people on staff.) At the age of eighty-six, architect Philip Johnson ended his legendary collaboration with colleague John Burgee, putting aside that achievement and the large organization that had been built and beginning again. Says Johnson, "It's like rebirth. . . . It's just that great thing of starting out and I get a second time, another chance, long after I'm supposed to." And, if power can shed its success and search out new burdens and challenges, that must be further proof that the energy to get things done is an inexorable force in the best of human nature.

RESURGENCE

Because power is more fragile and the conditions that exist for holding it shift constantly, the powerful are less likely to have a continuous long reign of power and are far likelier to have "interludes of power." That requires both a fundamental change in expectation, behavior, and conscious planning if living a full life with power is the goal.

NOTES

Introduction

p. 4
Bob Kerrey: "Bob Kerrey Feels His Way to the White House," *The Economist*, October 5, 1991.

p. 4
"The Emperor Charles V . . . ": Kenneth Clark, *Civilization* (New York: Harper & Row Publishers, Inc., 1969), p. 111.

p. 6
" . . . British census of 1910 . . . ": Peter Drucker, *Managing for the Future: The 1990s and Beyond* (New York: Truman Talley Books/Dutton, 1992), p. 331.

1. The Foundation of Power: Building from Drucker

p. 9
"We now know that . . . ": Peter F. Drucker, *Managing for the Future: The 1990s and Beyond* (New York: Truman Talley Books/Dutton, 1992), p. 26.

p. 10
All the members: "Being One of Us," *Economist*, December 26, 1992.

p. 10
Umberto Bossi: Lisa Bannon, "Lombard League Acts to Shake Up Politics in Hard-Pressed Italy," *Wall Street Journal Europe*, December 15, 1992.

p. 11
Tim McFeeley: "Toter Mann," *Der Spiegel*, November 30, 1992.

p. 11
Haruki Murakami: Daniel Max, "Japan's Invisible Pop Icon," *INK*, September, 1991.

p. 11

Pablo Escobar: James Brooke, "How Escobar, a Rare Jailbird, Lined His Nest," *New York Times*, August 5, 1992.

p. 11

Superbarrio: "Rächer der Entrechteten," *Der Spiegel*, April 27, 1992.

p. 12

Dr. Jacob Bronowski: J. Bronowski, *The Ascent of Man* (Boston: Little, Brown and Company, 1973), pp. 280–81.

p. 13

William Howard Taft: Ronald Brownstein, *The Power and The Glitter: The Hollywood-Washington Connection* (New York: Vintage Books, 1990), pp. 13–14.

p. 13

"pet rocks": George Melloan, "On Global Issues, Perot Sounds Texas League," *Wall Street Journal Europe*, July 7, 1992.

p. 13

Chung Ju Yung: "Korean Executive Is Leaving Politics," *New York Times*, February 10, 1993.

p. 14

General Motors: Peter F. Drucker, *Managing for the Future: The 1990s and Beyond* (New York: Truman Talley Books/Dutton, 1992), p. 187.

p. 14

Michael Korda: Michael Korda, *Power! How to Get It, How to Use It* (New York: Ballantine, 1975), pp. 4, 6, 7, 10, 14, 36, 302.

p. 15

Bruce D. Henderson: Bruce D. Henderson, "The Origin of Strategy," *Harvard Business Review*, November/December 1989.

p. 16

Harold Flammia: William P. Barrett, "The .44-caliber Mouthpiece," *Forbes*, September 18, 1989.

p. 16

collaborate rather than compete: "IBM, Microsoft Agree to Share Patents on Operating Systems," *Los Angeles Times*, June 29, 1992.

p. 16

" . . . smart in spots . . . ": "Two men screaming," book review of *Father Son & Co.: My Life at IBM and Beyond Economist*, July 21, 1990.

p. 18

Thomas J. Watson: Thomas J. Watson, Jr. and Peter Petre, *Father,*

Son & Co.: My Life at IBM and Beyond (New York: Bantam Books, 1991), p. 101.

p. 19

quality product: "America's Best Plants: IW's Third Annual Salute," *Industry Week*, October 19, 1992.

p. 20

Bausch & Lomb: James S. Hirsch, "Corporate Focus: Bausch & Lomb Shifts Focus from Eyes," *Wall Street Journal*, February 27, 1990.

p. 20

alcohol-free mouthwash: Dave Kansas, "Mouthwash Makers See Sales Evaporate," *Wall Street Journal*, December 1, 1992.

p. 20

Cray Research: "Supercomputers: Megaflopolis," *The Economist*, November 28, 1992.

p. 22

Knowledge and innovation: Peter F. Drucker, *Managing for the Future: The 1990s and Beyond* (New York: Truman Talley Books/Dutton, 1992), p. 26.

p. 22

definition of property: Peter F. Drucker, *Managing for the Future: The 1990s and Beyond* (New York: Truman Talley Books/Dutton, 1992), p. 4.

p. 23

Cygnus: "Freeware," *The Economist*, August 22, 1992.

p. 24

Michael Porter: Michael Porter, "Don't Collaborate, Compete," *The Economist*, June 9, 1990.

p. 24

Italy—footwear and handbags: Michael E. Porter, *The Com-petitive Advantage of Nations* (New York: The Free Press, 1990), p. 422.

p. 25

British Petroleum: "BP after Horton," *The Economist*, July 4, 1992.

p. 25

Iberia: Brian Coleman and Carlta Vitzthum, "Pain in Spain: Problems at Iberia Seem to Overshadow Clearing of Big Hurdle," *Wall Street Journal Europe*, July 23, 1992.

p. 26

Ciba-Geigy: Stephen D. Moore, "Medicinal Value: Ciba-Geigy Pioneers Marketing Approach for Pharmaceuticals," *Wall Street Journal Europe*, July 7, 1992.

p. 27
Bond market: Douglas R. Sease and Constance Mitchell, "The Vigilantes: World's Bond Buyers Gain Huge Influence Over U.S. Fiscal Plans," *Wall Street Journal*, November 6, 1992.

p. 27
" . . . crown powers . . . ": Martha Duffy, "Separate Lives," *Time*, November 30, 1992.

p. 28
"Europe of Fatherlands": Peter F. Drucker, *Managing for the Future: The 1990s and Beyond* (New York: Truman Talley Books/Dutton, 1992), p. 59.

p. 29
" . . . future lasts . . . ": Angelo Codevilla, *Informing Statecraft: Intelligence for a New Century* (New York: The Free Press, 1992), p. 48.

p. 29
Fernando Collor: Thomas Kamm, "Brazil's Collor Quits Abruptly in End to Impeachment Trial," *Wall Street Journal Europe*, December 30, 1992.

p. 30
" . . . function of news . . . ": Walter Lippmann, *Public Opinion* (New York: The Free Press, 1922), p. 226.

p. 31
Cresson—Japanese: "Couldn't we all do a little bit worse?," *The Economist*, April 4, 1992.

p. 31
Cresson—British: Alan Riding, "Gallic Dart Distresses British Men," *New York Times*, June 20, 1991.

p. 32
Suchocka—counter-strategies: "Hanna Suchocka soll Polens Regierungschefin werden: Solidaritäts-Parteien einigen sich," *Fränkischer Tag*, July 6, 1992.

p. 32
Suchocka—probation: "Iron Lady puts team on notice," *European*, July 16–19, 1992.

p. 32
Public standards: "Why a Scandal Does Not Scandalise Us Any More," *European*, July 16–19, 1992.

p. 32
Nicholas Lemann: Nicholas Lemann, "Confidence Games," *New Republic*, November 5, 1990.

2. The Mechanism of Power: The Wizard Fallacy, the Awe Factor, and More . . .

p. 34

" . . . power and its outward trappings": Kenneth Clark, *Civilisation* (New York: Harper & Row, 1969), p. 106.

p. 35

" . . . media events . . . ": Peter F. Drucker, *Managing for the Future: The 1990s and Beyond* (New York: Truman Talley Books/Dutton, 1992), p. 1.

p. 37

hypnotized by an event: Heinz Goldmann, "Crisis Management and Crisis Communication—What to Do and Say 'When Things Go Wrong,'" February 3, 1992, World Economic Forum, Davos, Switzerland.

p. 38

George Bush—supermarket demonstration: Rudolph A. Pyatt, Jr., "Checking Out the Significance of Bush's Supermarket Education," *The Washington Post*, February 13, 1992.

p. 41

" . . . new Sweden": "The Accidental Revolutionary," book review of *What Went Wrong with Perestroika*, by Marshall Goldman, *The Economist*, March 21, 1992.

p. 41

" . . . paralyzed by his own pragmatism": Paul A. Gigot, "Potomac Watch: Without Beliefs, Bush Stumbles into Carterism," *Wall Street Journal*, November 22, 1991.

p. 43

plasticized vision statements: David Johnson, "Leaders of Corporate Change," *Fortune*, December 14, 1992.

p. 43

plastered with signs: James C. Shaffer, "Quality Where It Doesn't Count," *Across the Board*, October 1992.

p. 43

single best-selling item: Sam Walton with John Huey, *Sam Walton, Made in America: My Story* (New York: Doubleday, 1992), p. 163.

p. 46

" . . . interactive video . . . ": George Stalk, Philip Evans, and Lawrence E. Shulman, "Competing on Capabilities: The New Rules of Corporate Strategy," *Harvard Business Review*, March–April 1992.

p. 49
Big Six: Robert K. Elliott, "U.S. Accounting: A National Emergency," *Financier*, August 1991.

p. 50
"large pedestals ... ": Peter Carlson, "The Image Makers," *Washington Post Magazine*, February 11, 1990.

p. 50
Warren Buffett: Patrick Harverson, "New Salomon Chief Alleges Cover-up," *Financial Times*, August 20, 1991.

p. 51
Dagmar Bottenbruch: Timothy Aeppel, "Surprise Performer: With Sudden Rebirth, Renault Is Proving It Can Make a Profit," *Wall Street Journal Europe*, March 20–21, 1992.

p. 54
"their souls": "Style wars: Fashion War Breaks Out," *European*, July 16–19, 1992.

p. 55
" . . . power and its outward trappings": Kenneth Clark *Civilisation* (New York: Harper & Row, 1969), p. 106.

3. The Mastery of Power: Beyond Ever-Pending Disaster

p. 57
Inspection Générale: "The Good Network Guide: Being One of Us," *Economist*, December 26, 1992.

p. 58
Ferdinand Piëch: "Eine aggressive Modellpolitik ist jetzt das Allerwichtigste," *Die Welt*, 126, June 1, 1992.

p. 60
Walter Lippmann—public opinion: Walter Lippmann, *Public Opinion* (New York: The Free Press, 1965), p. 228–29.

p. 61
Indonesia—GNP: "Poor Countries Rich in Wealthy People," *The Economist*, August 15, 1991.

p. 61
Indonesia—largest business organizations: "The Overseas Chinese: A Driving Force," *The Economist*, July 18, 1992.

p. 62
India—razor blades: Lawrence Ingrassia, "Keeping Sharp: Gillette Holds Its Edge by Endlessly Searching for a Better Shave," *Wall Street Journal Europe*, December 14, 1992. For more information on Gillette's marketing, see also Subrata N. Chakravarty,

"We Had to Change the Playing Fields," *Forbes*, February 4, 1991.

p. 62

Churchill—India: "The Fever in India," *The Economist*, December 12, 1992.

p. 62

Chinese—overseas: "The Overseas Chinese: A Driving Force," *The Economist*, July 18, 1992.

p. 63

Pao empire: Jonathan Friedland, "World Is His Oyster: Peter Woo Sets Pao-family Empire on New Course," *Far Eastern Economic Review*, April 16, 1992.

p. 64

Gulf War: "The Media at War: The Press and the Persian Gulf Conflict," a Report of the Gannett Foundation, New York City, June 1991.

p. 65

Leo Burnett: "Consumer Behaviour: Strategic Shopping," *The Economist*, September 26, 1992.

p. 66

optical scanning: Alvin Toffler, *Powershift: Knowledge, Wealth, and Violence at the Edge of the 21st Century* (New York: Bantam Books, 1990), p. 102.

p. 66

telephone solicitors: "It's Consumers vs. Callers," *New York Times*, June 20, 1991.

p. 66

Tightwad Gazette: Laurie Petersen, "The Voice of a New Anti-Brand Generation," *Adweek's Marketing Week*, February 17, 1992.

p. 66

New Hampshire primary: "The Other Big Loser in New Hampshire," *Business Week*, March 2, 1992.

p. 67

Americans—watching TV: "Roundup: Time Is Media," *Quill*, November/December, 1992.

p. 68

Lithuanians: "Falsche Strafe," *Der Spiegel*, 45/1992.

p. 68

Poland—parties: "How Many Polish Parties Does It Take to Make a Cabinet?," *The Economist*, November 2, 1991.

p. 69

"Choice erodes commitment": Steven Waldman, "The Tyranny of Choice," *New Republic*, January 27, 1992.

p. 70
Lever 2000: Valerie Reitman, "Marketing: Buoyant Sales of Lever 2000 Soap Bring Sinking Sensation to Procter & Gamble," *Wall Street Journal*, March 19, 1992.

p. 70
"'de-proliferate' . . . ": Getting General Motors Going Again," *The Economist*, May 2, 1992.

p. 71
" . . . industrial espionage . . . ": William M. Carley, "Prying Eyes: Concern Grows in U.S. As Some Nations' Spies Seek Industrial Secrets," *Wall Street Journal Europe*, June 17, 1991.

p. 71
Codevilla: Angelo Codevilla, *Informing Statecraft: Intelligence for a New Century* (New York: The Free Press, 1992), p. 49.

p. 72
John Bryan: "Sara Lee: Designs on Europe's Knickers," *The Economist*, November 14, 1992.

p. 72
Operational crises (vs. managerial crises): "Crises Caused by Executive Miscues on Rise," *Public Relations Journal*, October 1992.

p. 73
Latin American debt: William R. Rhodes, "The Disaster that Didn't Happen," *The Economist*, September 12, 1992.

p. 73
Abimael Guzman: "The Cell at the End of the Path," The *Economist*, September 19, 1992.

p. 73
Dillard's and Wal-Mart (Mexico): "Opportunities for International Retailing," *Loeb Retail Letter*, April 30, 1992.

p. 73
999 A.D.: Richard Erdoes, *AD 1000: Living on the Brink of Apocalypse* (New York: Harper & Row, 1988) as excerpted in the *Utne Reader*, March/April 1990.

p. 75
Honda, Gorbachev, etc.: Steven Schlossstein, "Looking Back at the 1990s," *Across the Board*, April 1990.

p. 76
Nestlé research: Guy de Jonquiéres, "Research Comes Back to the Nest," *Financial Times*, July 14, 1992.

p. 79
Zino Davidoff: Sabine Christiansen, "Nobler Rauch aus der Karibik," à *la Card Journal*, 1993.

p. 79

Akatsuki Maru: Edward W. Desmond, "Japan's Plutonium Gamble: Behind the Voyage of the *Akatsuki Maru* Lies a Controversial Nuclear Energy Program," *Time*, November 30, 1992.

p. 81

Walton and Barnard: Sam Walton with John Huey, *Sam Walton, Made in America: My Story* (New York: Doubleday, 1992), p. 82.

p. 81

Walton—intelligence gathering: Sam Walton with John Huey, *Sam Walton, Made in America: My Story* (New York: Doubleday, 1992), p. 71.

p. 81

Sertorius: Angelo Codevilla, *Informing Statecraft: Intelligence for a New Century* (New York: The Free Press, 1992), pp. 301–02.

pp. 83–84

Robert K. Elliott: Robert K. Elliott, "U.S. Accounting: A National Emergency," *Financier*, August 1991.

pp. 83–84

Robert Kuttner: Robert Kuttner, "Controlling the Climate that Let BCCI Bloom," *Business Week*, July 29, 1991.

pp. 87–88

Ueberroth—Olympics: Robert Ajemian, "Master of the Games," *Time*, January 7, 1985.

pp. 87–88

Ueberroth—Los Angeles: Richard W. Stevenson, "Patching Up L.A.—A Corporate Blueprint," *New York Times*, August 9, 1992.

4. The Organization of Power: Stoking the Structure

pp. 89

" . . . channel the creative forces . . . ": Nicholas Kent, *Naked Hollywood: Money and Power in the Movies Today* (New York: St. Martin's Press, 1991), p. 135.

p. 91

" . . . partly deterministic": Alvin Toffler, *Powershift: Knowledge, Wealth, and Violence at the Edge of the 21st Century* (New York: Bantam Books, 1990), p. 203.

p. 92

" . . . a thousand interns": Maureen Dowd, "White House Isolation: An Image of Bush as a Captive of Top Aides Who Make Their Own Sweeping Decisions," *New York Times*, November 22, 1991.

p. 93

General Electric—Bayamón: Thomas A. Steward, "Are You Flat, Lean, and Ready for a Bold New Look? Try High-performance Teams, Redesigned Work, and Unbridled Information," *Fortune*, May 18, 1992.

pp. 94–95

" . . . 'pursuing personal interests'. . . ": Joann S. Lublin, "Tense Times: More Chief Executives in the U.S. Are Being Forced Out by Boards," *Wall Street Journal Europe*, June 7–8, 1991.

p. 95

" . . . shaping the concept . . . ": Mike H. Walsh "A Crisis Helps" in "Leaders of Corporate Change," *Fortune*, December 14, 1992.

p. 99

Team Bandit: Alvin Toffler, *PowerShift* (New York: Bantam Books, 1990), p. 237.

p. 99

Pepsi to Apple: John Sculley with John A. Byrne, *Odyssey* (New York: Harper & Row, 1987), p. 133.

p. 100

" . . . the word 'win' . . . ": John Sculley with John A. Byrne, *Odyssey* (New York: Harper & Row, 1987), p. 133.

p. 100

"hot-potato" approach: Bennett Harrison, "How the Japanese Manage Risk," *Prism* (Arthur D. Little), Second Quarter 1990.

p. 100

"Tailhook Scandal": Fritz Wirth, "US-Minister stolpert über Party-Affäre," *Die Welt*, June 29, 1992.

p. 100

Special teams: "The dream teams," *The Economist*, September 5, 1992.

p. 101

Scott McNealy: "The Corporate Elite," *Business Week*, October 20, 1989.

p. 103

problems of survivorship: Brian S. Moskal, "Managing Survivors," *Industry Week*, August 3, 1992.

p. 103

Compaq: Jim Bartimo and Karen Blumenthal, "Surprise Casualty: Compaq Sacks Canion, Signaling Move to Be a Tougher Competitor," *Wall Street Journal Europe*, October 28, 1991.

p. 106

Davos or . . . Homestead: *The Wall Street Journal Book of Chief Executive Style* (New York: William Morrow, 1989), p. 276.

p. 106

Mitsubishi and Daimler-Benz: "Elefantenhochzeit zwischen

Daimler und Mitsubishi," *Wochenspiegel, zeitschrift für werbung und public relations,* July 6, 1992.

p. 110

Ted Turner: "Television Advertising: No Place to Hide," *The Economist,* July 13, 1991.

p. 112

Andre Agassi—Nike: Ian Hamilton, "Talent, Character, and Style: The Nike Athlete," *Harvard Business Review,* July–August 1992.

p. 113

Japanese television ads: "Foreign Celebrities Cash in on Japanese Commercials," *AP,* July 10, 1982.

p. 114

Alma Mahler: Susanne Keegan, *The Bride of the Wind: The Life of Alma Mahler* (New York: Penguin Books, 1991).

p. 114

" . . . a catalyst of incredible intensity": Susanne Keegan, *The Bride of the Wind: The Life of Alma Mahler* (New York: Penguin Books, 1991), p. xvi.

p. 115

Terkel and tape recorder: Robert E. Allen, "Competition in Telecommunications: An Unfinished Agenda," delivered to the Economic Club of Chicago, October 15, 1992.

p. 115

Bill Moyers: For a range of perspectives on Bill Moyers, see Andrew Ferguson, "The Power of Myth: Bill Moyers, Liberal Fraud," *The New Republic,* August 19 & 26, 1991.

p. 116

Richard von Weizsäcker: "Weizsäcker will Votum für Berlin," *Main Echo,* March 11, 1991.

p. 118

Pope's smallest sniffles: "The Pope's 'Fantastic' Recovery," *Newsweek,* July 27, 1992.

p. 118

Nixon's foreign policy memo: Richard Nixon, "The Challenge We Face in Russia," *Wall Street Journal,* March 11, 1992.

p. 119

Henry Schacht: "Kevin Kelly, "25 Executives to Watch," *The 1993 Business Week 1000,* 1993.

p. 120

"Night of the Long Knives": "Long Knives Buried in Brownshirt Backs," *Chronicle of the World* (New York: Prentice-Hall, 1990), p. 1105.

pp. 120–21

William Paley: Jeffrey Sonnenfeld, *The Hero's Farewell: What*

Happens When CEOs Retire (New York: Oxford University Press, 1988), pp. 138–41.

5. The Management of Power: A Guide to Heavy Lifting

p. 123
" . . . e-Mail votes . . . ": Stuart Mieher, "Young Turks: Baby Boomers Begin Taking the Top Jobs at Many Companies," *Wall Street Journal*, November 6, 1992.

p. 124
former IBM CEO: Thomas J. Watson, Jr. and Peter Petre, *Father, Son & Co.,: My Life at IBM and Beyond* (New York: Bantam Books, 1990), p. 156.

p. 125
Hong Kong: Jesse Wong, "Hutchison Whampoa Debates Strategy," *Wall Street Journal*, November 6, 1992.

p. 125
expatriate Chinese: "Hutchison Whampoa: The second generation," *The Economist*, November 28, 1992.

p. 126
understates its economic output: "China: The Titan Stirs," *The Economist*, November 28, 1992.

p. 126
League of Women Voters: Robert V. Pambianco, "Women Voters in Liberal League of Their Own," *Wall Street Journal*, October 1, 1992.

p. 127
IBM: Steve Lohr, "Company News; 2 Retired Officers to Return to I.B.M.," *New York Times*, December 22, 1992.

p. 127
"groupware": "Cure-all or Snake-oil?," *The Economist*, October 3, 1992.

pp. 128–29
Patents—Japan: "Intellectual Property: When Copying Gets Costly," *The Economist*, May 9, 1992.

p. 130
Napoleon: Paul Johnson, *The Birth of the Modern: World Society 1815–1830* (New York: HarperCollins Publishers, 1991), pp. 67–68.

p. 131
Pig Book: 1992 Congressional Pig Book Summary (Council for Citizens Against Government Waste, 1992).

p. 131

"power pork": "The Anatomy of Pork: A Reader's Guide to the Ways Lawmakers Bring Home the Bacon," *Newsweek*, April 13, 1992.

p. 132

Murray Weidenbaum: Murray Weidenbaum, "Robbing Peter to Bail Out Paul," *Reader's Digest*, September 1992. (Condensed from *Across the Board.*)

p. 134

psychology of joy: John S. McClenahen, "On the Job: Lean & Mean," *Industry Week*, November 2, 1992.

p. 135

" . . . Wilshire Boulevard . . . ": Nicholas Kent, *Naked Hollywood: Money and Power in the Movies Today* (New York: St. Martin's Press, 1991), p. 26.

p. 139

meter monitors: David Osborne and Ted Gaebler, *Reinventing Government: How the Entrepreneurial Spirit Is Transforming the Public Sector from Schoolhouse to Statehouse, City Hall to the Pentagon* (Reading, PA.: Addison-Wesley, 1992), pp. 261–62.

p. 140

John Wyclif: "English Lollards Challenge Papal Power," *Chronicle of the World* (New York: Prentice-Hall, 1990), p. 403.

p. 140

Saul Alinsky: M. W. Newman, "Power to the Leftouts," *Notre Dame magazine*, Autumn 1990, Volume 19, No. 3, pp. 29, 31.

p. 140

Jesse Jackson: "Jackson Asked to Mediate Daily News Strike," *Stars and Stripes*, November 4, 1990.

p. 141

Saddam Hussein: Wes Janz and Vickie Abrahamson, *War of the Words: The Gulf War Quote by Quote* (Minneapolis: Bobbleheads Press, Inc., 1991), p. 46.

p. 141

British Petroleum: "BP After Horton," *The Economist*, July 4, 1992; "BP Says 4th-Period Net Rose as Its Recovery Continued," *Wall Street Journal Europe*, February 12–13, 1993; "BP surpasses Forecast with £172m," *Financial Times*, November 6, 1992.

p. 142

"downsizing firms . . . ": Amanda Bennett, "Study Says Downsizing Firms May Not Bring Profitability," *Wall Street Journal Europe*, June 7–8, 1991.

p. 142

Berlin: John Rockwell, "United Arts: Berlin's Cultural Mediator," *International Herald Tribune*, July 18–19, 1992.

p. 143

Compaq: Jim Bartimo and Karen Blumenthal, "Surprise Casualty: Compaq Sacks Canion, Signaling Move to Be a Tougher Competitor," *Wall Street Journal Europe*, October 28, 1991.

p. 144

" . . . e-mail . . . ": Stuart Mieher, "Young Turks: Baby Boomers Begin Taking the Top Jobs at Many Companies," *Wall Street Journal*, November 6, 1992.

p. 147

Paul Johnson: Paul Johnson, *The Birth of the Modern: World Society 1815–1830* (New York: HarperCollins Publishers, 1991), p. 455.

p. 148

Sun Tzu: Sun Tzu, *The Art of War*, edited by James Clavell (New York: Delacorte Press, 1983), p. 37.

p. 149

snake collection: Walter K. Olson, *The Litigation Explosion: What Happened When America Unleashed the Lawsuit* (New York: Truman Talley Books, 1991), p. 231.

p. 149

Snake collection costs: Paul M. Barrett, "At the Zoo," *Wall Street Journal*, March 22, 1990.

p. 149

" . . . Potemkin Hospital": "North Korea's Potemkin hospital," *The Economist*, September 12, 1992.

p. 150

Colonel Gadhafi: Geraldine Brooks, "An Era of Tension and Change Forces Libyans to Adapt," *Wall Street Journal*, January 9, 1989.

p. 150

" . . . iron and blood": "Blood and Iron—the Ultimate Arbiters," *Chronicle of the World* (New York: Prentice-Hall, 1990), p. 938.

p. 152

"small luxuries": Claire Poole, "Pepsi's newest generation," *Forbes*, February 18, 1991.

p. 154

John von Neumann: Matt Ridley, "Mathematicians: Best of them All?," review of the book *John von Neumann* by Norman Macrae, *The Economist*, December 19, 1992.

6. The Communication of Power: Solidly Superficial

p. 156
" . . . mental models . . . ": Peter M. Senge, *The Fifth Discipline* (New York: A Currency Book, 1990), p. 175.
p. 157
FDR, JFK: Ronald Brownstein, *The Power and the Glitter: The Hollywood-Washington Connection* (New York: Vintage Books, 1992), pp. 75, 154.
p. 157
" . . . the outsider . . . ": Frederic Morton, "Chaplin, Hitler: Outsiders as Actors," *New York Times*, April 24, 1989.
p. 157
Iain Mangham: Iain L. Mangham, "Managing as a Performing Art," *British Journal of Management*, Vol. 1, (1990), 105–115.
p. 158
"THINK": Thomas J. Watson, Jr. and Peter Petre, *Father, Son & Co.: My Life at IBM and Beyond* (New York: Bantam Books, 1991), p. 71.
p. 158
Lord Nelson: "French Lose at Trafalgar," *Chronicle of the World* (New York: Prentice-Hall, 1990), p. 811.
p. 158
Fiorello La Guardia: Introduction by Keith Thomas, in Jan Bremmer and Herman Roodenburg, *A Cultural History of Gesture* (Ithaca: Cornell University Press, 1992), p. 6.
p. 158
Coco Chanel: "Frau ohne Gnade," *Der Spiegel*, November 2, 1992.
p. 159
Peter Ueberroth: Robert Ajemian, "Master of the Games," *Time*, January 7, 1985.
p. 160
mental models: Peter M. Senge, *The Fifth Discipline* (New York: A Currency Book), p. 175.
p. 160
Spike Lee: "Hollywood's Black Bard," *The Economist*, November 21, 1992.
p. 161
Shanghai: Deyan Sudjic, "Birth of the Brave New City," *The Guardian*, December 2, 1992.
p. 162
Republican conservatives: "GOP Botched 'Values' Issue—Wirth-

lin," *Jack O'Dwyer's Newsletter,* J. R. O'Dwyer Company, October 14, 1992.

p. 162

rap song: Carla Hall, "Time-Warner Takes Heat Over Rapper's 'Cop Killer' Song," *International Herald Tribune,* July 18–19, 1992.

p. 163

"political mantra": "GOP Botched 'Values' Issue—Wirthlin," *Jack O'Dwyer's Newsletter,* J. R. O'Dwyer Company, October 14, 1992.

p. 163

security transport vehicles: "The 1992 Campaign," *New York Times,* August 6, 1992, p. A20.

p. 164

United Way: Felicity Barringer, "United Way Head Is Forced Out in a Furor Over His Lavish Style," *New York Times,* February 28, 1992.

p. 165

Michael Mann: David Ansen, "Man in the Wilderness," *Newsweek,* December 7, 1992.

p. 166

Lee Atwater: "Critically-ill Atwater Apologizes to Dukakis," *Stars and Stripes,* January 14, 1991.

p. 167

Ellen Goodman: As quoted in *Leadership* by William Safire and Leonard Safir and as appearing in "Let Go and Go On," *Forbes,* December 7, 1992.

p. 168

IBM 702: Thomas J. Watson, Jr., and Peter Petre, *Father, Son & Co.: My Life at IBM and Beyond* (New York: Bantam, 1991), p. 277.

p. 170

" . . . Macintosh creators . . . ": John Sculley with John A. Byrne, *Odyssey: Pepsi to Apple . . .* (New York: Harper & Row, 1987), p. 164.

p. 170

nostalgia value: Elaine Underwood, "What's in a Smell?," *Adweek's Marketing Week,* November 11, 1991.

p. 171

Barbara Bush: "Talk-radio Meets Rock-TV," *The Economist,* September 5, 1992.

p. 171

Latin America: "Power Comes Out of the Tube," *The Economist,* December 8, 1990.

7. The Emotional Fabric of Power:
The Perils of Perfectionism

p. 175
Napoleon: Paul Kennedy, *The Rise and Fall of the Great Powers: Economic Change and Military Conflict from 1500 to 2000* (New York: Random House, 1987), p. 133.

p. 176
"CEO disease": "CEO Disease: Egotism Can Breed Corporate Disaster—And the Malady is Spreading," *Business Week*, April 1, 1991.

p. 176
Wayne Calloway: Brian S. Moskal, "Arrogance: The Executive Achilles' Heel," *Industry Week*, June 3, 1991.

p. 177
Gitano: "Is This Any Way to Run the Family Business?," *Business Week*, August 24, 1992.

p. 179
Frank Lloyd Wright: Meryle Secrest, *Frank Lloyd Wright*, a book review in "Architecture: Leaky Roofs," *The Economist*, November 28, 1992.

p. 179
Kurt Waldheim: William Echikson, "Ein Fürst im Dienst der CSFR," *Reader's Digest*, May 1992.

p. 180
Edward Teller: William J. Broad, *Teller's War: The Top-Secret Story Behind the Star Wars Deception* (New York: Simon & Schuster, 1992), p. 118.

p. 181
Walter Winchell: Nicholas Lemann, "Confidence Games," *New Republic*, November 5, 1990.

p. 183
Bill Smithburg: Lester Korn, *The Success Profile* (New York: Simon and Schuster, 1988), pp. 97–98.

p. 184
"Exorcist Plan": George Anders, *Merchants of Debt: KKR and the Mortgaging of American Business* (New York: BasicBooks, 1992), p. 174.

p. 186
"pharmacists": William J. Broad, *Teller's War: The Top-Secret Story Behind the StarWars Deception* (New York: Simon and Schuster, 1992), p. 206.

p. 186

" ... sugared water ... ": John Sculley with John A. Byrne, *Odyssey: Pepsi to Apple* ... (New York: Harper & Row, 1987), p. 90.

p. 187

" ... KKR partners ... ": George Anders, *Merchants of Debt: KKR and the Mortgaging of American Business* (New York: BasicBooks, 1992), pp. 161–162.

p. 187

Philippe de Montebello: "Culture Power: Philippe de Montebello Artful Persuader," *M. Inc.* September 1991.

p. 189

" ... big transaction ... ": Kurt Vonnegut, *God Bless You Mr. Rosewater* (New York: Dell, 1965), p. 9.

p. 190

" ... 'inappropriately directed laughter'. . . ": "From There to Intolerance," *The Economist*, July 20, 1991.

p. 190

" ... sexual harassment ... ": David Margolick, "Take It from Her, the Judge: Lighten Up on Men," *International Herald Tribune*, December 5–6, 1992.

p. 190

Reuven Frank: Speech, Princeton, New Jersey, June 21, 1991.

p. 191

" ... 'politically incorrect'. . . ": Irving Kristol, "America's Multiculturalism Tragedy", *Wall Street Journal*, August 1, 1991. Further information on the same issue can be found in an article entitled "Not Out of Africa" by Mary Lefkowitz in the *New Republic* of February 10, 1992.

p. 191

confrontation: "To: All Readers. Subject: Corner-Office Sound-Offs," *Business Week*, July 22, 1991.

p. 191

"Disagreements ... ": Bruce G. Posner, "Looking Out for Number 2", *Inc.*, July 1991.

p. 191

Bill Clinton: "The Bill Clinton Nobody Knows," *The Economist*, November 7, 1992.

p. 192

John Quincy Adams: Paul Johnson, *The Birth of the Modern: World Society 1815–1830* (New York: HarperCollins Publishers, 1991), p. 35.

p. 193
Von Clausewitz: Carl von Clausewitz, *On War* (New York: Penguin Books, 1982), p. 341.

8. *The Higher Uses of Power: The Art of Getting Caught*

p. 196
"Throwing Things Away": "Throwing Things Away," *The Economist*, October 5, 1991.

p. 197
Merck: Michael Waldholz, "Merck, in Unusual Gesture, Will Donate Drug to Fight Leading Cause of Blindness," *Wall Street Journal*, October 22, 1987.

p. 197
Lech Walesa: "Walesa will das Volk nicht hören," *Süddeutsche Zeitung*, November 28/29, 1992, and Victoria Pope, "Lech-Luster," *New Republic*, December 3, 1990.

p. 197
Aung San Suu Kyi: "Myanmar: A prison still," *The Economist*, May 2, 1992.

p. 198
Dietrich Bonhoeffer: Jane Pejsa, *Matriarch of Conspiracy* (Minneapolis: Kenwood Publishing, 1991), p. 255.

p. 200
"Top jobs . . .": *The Economist*, March 28, 1992.

p. 200
Gail Sheehy: Gail Sheehy, from *Passages* as quoted in *Bartlett's Familiar Quotations* (Boston: Little, Brown & Company, 1980), p. 914.

p. 200
Linda Wachner: Linda J. Wachner, "Do It Now," in "Leaders of Corporate Change," *Fortune*, December 14, 1992.

p. 201
Machiavelli: Niccolò Machiavelli, *The Prince*, translated by George Bull (England: Penguin Books, 1981), p. 87.

p. 201
" . . . peacetime aspirations . . .": "Presiding or Leading?," *The Economist*, April 21, 1990.

p. 202
faith-healer: Source 25 June 1992, 7:00 A.M. CET CNN International News.

p. 202
Dr. Hans Küng, "Towards a Universal Ethics for World

Religions," World Economic Forum, Davos, Switzerland, 1991.
p. 203
Ukraine: "Your Church or Mine?," *The Economist*, April 25,
1992.
p. 208
"Erma Bombeck . . . ": Bill Bradley, speech delivered May 28,
1989, Middlebury College Commencement.
p. 208
Bishop Desmond Tutu: Desmond Tutu, "Do More Than Win,"
Fortune, December 30, 1991.

Appendix: Power Resurges

p. 211
Joe Napolitan: Joseph Napolitan, "100 Things I Have Learned in
30 Years as a Political Consultant," paper presented at the nine-
teenth annual conference of the International Association of
Political Consultants, November 11–15, 1986. (Printed by Mass
Mutual Life Insurance Company, August, 1988.)
p. 212
American Airlines: "Managing the Future," *The Economist*,
December 19, 1992.
p. 214
Cleveland Plain Dealer: Tom Diemer and Rodney Ferguson,
"Top Agents of Influence," *Cleveland Plain Dealer*, April 14,
1991.
p. 216
Caroline Rose Hunt: "Dallas Dowager: For a Hunt, Caroline
Doesn't Gamble Much, But She's Sure Solvent," *Wall Street
Journal*, March 8, 1990.
p. 218
Thomas Wyman: James C. Hyatt, "Ex-CBS Chairman Is Appointed
to Head Warburg's U.S. Operations," *Wall Street Journal Europe*,
July 23, 1992.
pp. 218–19
Michael Ovitz: "Coppola Konzipiert Coke-Spots," *Horizont*, 40,
October 2, 1992.
p. 219
Roger Enrico: Martin Mayer, "Madison Avenue: At a Dead End?,"
Best of Business Quarterly, adapted from *Whatever Happened to
Madison Avenue? Advertising in the '90s* by Martin Mayer, Fall
1991.

p. 219
Simpson and Bruckheimer: Judith H. Dobrzynski, "Lifestyles of the Rich and Shameless," book review of *Circus of Ambition* by John Taylor, *Business Week*, November 13, 1989.
p. 220
Stanley Gault: Barnaby J. Feder, "When Outsiders Get the Top Job," *New York Times*, March 20, 1992.
p. 220
Marvin Runyon: Felicity Barringer, "A Samurai Manager Takes on the Postal Service," *New York Times*, August 8, 1992.
p. 220
Peter the Great: "Czar Goes to Work in English Shipyard," *Chronicle of the World* (New York: Prentice-Hall, 1990), p. 673.
p. 222
Seymour Cray: Michael Stroud, "Seymour Cray's New Firm Readies Its First Computer," *Investor's Daily*, May 29, 1991.
p. 222
Philip Johnson: Michael Z. Wise, "The Latest Incarnation of Philip Johnson," *International Herald Tribune*, December 5–6, 1992.

BIBLIOGRAPHY

Helpful readings on the subject of power can be as eclectic as the topic itself. As the endnotes for this book indicate, the most revealing studies of power are often found in the analysis of breaking news. However, a number of thoughtful books have, of course, been written on the subject, too. The following list suggests some selected readings, but it does not pretend to be inclusive. I have also picked works for their impact on my practical thinking rather than for their scholarly stature.

Perhaps books on power with military roots have the longest tradition. Some of the most notable are:

Clausewitz, Carl von. *On War*. New York: Penguin Books, 1982.
Codevilla, Angelo. *Informing Statecraft: Intelligence for a New Century*. New York: The Free Press, 1992.
Sun Tzu. *The Art of War*, edited by James Clavell. New York: Delacorte Press, 1983.

Other books contain a more general treatment of power. Among them:

Korda, Michael. *Power! How to Get It, How to Use It*. New York: Ballantine, 1975.
Lippmann, Walter. *Public Opinion*. New York: The Free Press, 1922.
Machiavelli, Niccolò. *The Prince*, translated by George Bull. England: Penguin Books, 1981.
Toffler, Alvin. *Powershift*. New York: Bantam Books, 1990.

Historical studies are obviously fertile ground for studying how power has been used. Two particularly good sources are:

Johnson, Paul. *The Birth of the Modern: World Society 1815–1830*. New York: HarperCollins Publishers, 1991.

Kennedy, Paul. *The Rise and Fall of the Great Powers: Economic Change and Military Conflict from 1500 to 2000.* New York: Random House, 1987.

Certainly, there are several important business and economic books that address power:

Drucker, Peter F. *Managing for the Future: The 1990s and Beyond.* New York: Truman Talley Books/Dutton, 1992.

Porter, Michael E. *The Competitive Advantage of Nations.* New York: The Free Press, 1990.

Sonnenfeld, Jeffrey. *The Hero's Farewell: What Happens When CEOs Retire.* New York: Oxford University Press, Inc., 1988.

Thurow, Lester. *Head to Head.* New York: William Morrow and Company, Inc., 1992.

My files are jammed with articles on power, but some of the most provocative ones for me have been:

"The Anatomy of Pork: A Reader's Guide to the Ways Lawmakers Bring Home the Bacon," *Newsweek,* April 13, 1992.

Mangham, Iain L. "Managing as a Performing Art," *British Journal of Management,* Vol. 1, (1990): 105–15.

Morton, Frederic. "Chaplin, Hitler: Outsiders as Actors," *New York Times,* April 24, 1989.

Waldman, Steven. "The Tyranny of Choice," *New Republic,* January 27, 1992.

This book itself is really part of a series on the use of power. For readers who want to explore my views on the topic further, I include these two entries:

Dilenschneider, Robert L. *Power and Influence.* New York: Prentice Hall Press, 1990.

Dilenschneider, Robert L. *A Briefing for Leaders.* New York: HarperCollins Publishers, Inc., 1992.

INDEX